TO NORTH VIETNAM AND BACK AGAIN

ED ENGLE

A Personal Account of Navy A-6 Intruder Operations in Vietnam

Copyright © 2019 by Ed Engle.

ISBN   Softcover   978-1-950580-27-9

All rights reserved. No part of this book may be reproduced or transmitted in any form or by any means, electronic or mechanical, including photocopying, recording, or by any information storage and retrieval system without express written permission from the author, except in the case of brief quotations embodied in critical reviews and certain other non-commercial uses permitted by copyright law.

Printed in the United States of America.

To order additional copies of this book, contact:
Bookwhip
1-855-339-3589
https://www.bookwhip.com

PREFACE

This is an autobiography of my experiences throughout the very different phases of my life. I was very fortunate to have two sets of parents who nurtured my growth and guided me into a life of achievement, which required many different kinds of courage. Both my parents and my maternal grandparents gave me the tools I needed to overcome the many obstacles which faced me throughout my life. While I was never able to achieve greatness and my name is neither a household word nor even a footnote in history books, personally, I know I was able to make a difference in everything I undertook.

My parents and grandparents, and for that matter all the adult relatives I knew as a child, had lived through the Great Depression and exhibited what today would be considered some strange behavior over basics, like food and finances. My paternal grandfather supported three families in his home with the job he had, working for the Baltimore and Ohio Railroad as a brakeman and, later, a fireman. He worked ten to twelve hours per day, seven days a week with one day off a year—the Fourth of July—until after the Depression. My maternal grandfather, with whom I lived, was a master machinist who had made artillery shell casings in World War I. He had a wonderful philosophy toward maintenance I will never forget: "It worked once. It'll work again." He was one of the first people in his neighborhood to own a car. It was a Model A Ford, which he pulled into his garage every winter, where he removed and rebuilt the engine. That was the first car I remember as a child. I rode in the rumble seat, which was located where the trunk is on modern cars. It pulled up and created an open-air bench seat—instant convertible!

The Engle side of my family was very lucky to have a genealogy prepared by a distant cousin and printed in the '30s which showed me that I came from excellent stock. The first Engle in the New World was Melchor who emigrated from the Palatinate (Heidelberg) in what is now Germany in the early eighteenth century and eventually bought a land grant from Lord Fairfax in the lower Shenandoah Valley of Virginia. He sired four sons who fought in the Revolution. Other descendants participated in the War for Southern Independence and World Wars I and II. Both uncles for whom I was named (Uncles Ed and Charles) had fought in World War II, and I knew them both well and reveled in the stories of their experiences in the war.

My early academic career was quite ordinary. I was a truly indifferent student. My future would have been quite different had I not had a desire to follow my best friend into a truly remarkable high school which taught me how to study. That resulted in my later success in college and graduate school as well as my career as an NFO (Naval Flight Officer).

So from being an engineer at Pratt & Whitney Aircraft to flying the Navy's A-6 Intruder aircraft from the decks of the USS *America* (CVA-66) and USS *Constellation* (CVA-64) in the Vietnamese War, where I was privileged to fly the first bombing mission into Haiphong, North Vietnam, on 16 April 1972, after President Johnson's bombing halt in 1967, to joining the US space program and helping win the Cold War, to bringing innovative satellite communications to Navy ships at sea, I have been able to make a difference in many different arenas.

I have purposely given more emphasis to my time with Naval Aviation because the plane I flew was truly remarkable and clearly was built before we had the technology to execute the concept reliably, but nonetheless, it worked well enough for the Intruder to make its mark in history, though most aviation historians ignore it. So I have attempted to right that oversight here. Besides, it is more exciting than most of the other things I've done in my life. I believe Winston Churchill once said about his experience in England's war with the Boers in South Africa: "There was never an event in a young man's life quite as exciting as being shot at and not hit."

ACKNOWLEDGMENTS

Dan Graham, the gentlemen with whom I flew into Haiphong that early morning in April 1972, had the forethought to rig a small tape recorder to his communications connection to the aircraft and consequently still has the timed details of that mission was of inestimable value to me in reconstructing those events and others of that cruise over four decades ago. Without his help, this book would lack much of the detail it currently has.

Hugh Replogle deserves my most sincere gratitude for his summary of the contributions to the war effort by the A-6Bs and their crews. It is a story which is even less understood than the story of the A-6 Intruder itself.

My wife Peggy's recollections of her time back on Whidbey Island with the other wives and the stress they endured when they read newspaper headlines of Navy aircraft shot down and couldn't know whether they would be getting an official visit to inform them that it might be their husband would not have been possible to relate here without her help. The stories of their off-the-line parties were unknown to us, until we got the bills for the damage they caused at the Club at Ault Field. Once again, her help was critical in saving those events for posterity. More than that, she has stood as a firm foundation to my life, with all its highs and lows, by my side to celebrate and just as closely to help me get over the most recent disaster. We have been together a very long time, and I hope we will be together for a lot more.

Thanks also are due to the Intruder Association's website for providing much of the background historical information on the squadrons and the priceless photographs they host there. Without that website's information, I would not have been able to reconstruct as clearly as I have the squadron histories and the names of the Intruder pioneers who helped introduce that unique aircraft to the Fleet and develop the tactics to use it as a weapon in the unforgiving air environment over Southeast Asia.

Jeffrey Ethell and Alfred Price's book *One Day in a Long War: May 10, 1972, Air War, North Vietnam* was a great help in sorting out Air Wing Nine's operations on that very important day. As a member of the operation, it is difficult to achieve the overview needed to put the memories into a meaningful and historically accurate context, and their book was extraordinarily helpful in that regard.

CONTENTS

Preface 3
Acknowledgments 5

Chapter 1: Early Life 9
Chapter 2: VA-128 38
Chapter 3: VA-165 VA-165 Boomers History 51
Chapter 4: Peggy Engle's View from the Home Front..............147
Chapter 5: The Operational Test and Evaluation Force..............151
Chapter 6: VA-52 165
Chapter 7: Graduate School 200
Chapter 8: The Navy Space Program Office..........................204
Chapter 9: Defense Support Program Office 208
Chapter 10: Life as a Contractor 210

Afterword..243

CHAPTER 1

EARLY LIFE

I was born in midwinter of 1944 into a lower middle-class family in Baltimore, Maryland. World War II was quickly evolving into a victory for the Allies in all theaters, and this year would pretty much decide the end of it all. I was named for each of two uncles who were fighting overseas: my Uncle Ed with McArthur in the Pacific, and my Uncle Charles, a member of the Armed Guard on a tanker running oil from the Caribbean to refineries on the upper East Coast through U-Boat Alley. My parents and grandparents had survived the Great Depression and were now coping with rationing, although my Father was not physically qualified to be drafted. If he had been, I would probably not be around to write this.

Engle Family Spring 44

My parents lived with my Mother's parents, so my Brother, Ron, and I had lots of supervision since our Mother did not work. My maternal grandfather retired, as a master machinist, when I was still quite young, so he and I spent a lot of time together. He very quickly became my mentor and would have a profound effect on my future. My maternal grandfather was Charles Coleman from Scotch-Irish ancestry, while my maternal grandmother was Emma Gutheil (pronounced *goot-hile*, although the family had changed that pronunciation during World War I to *guthel*), the daughter of a toy maker from the Black Forest in Germany who declared in 1917 when the US entered the war in Europe that the family was now American, and German would no longer be spoken. I regret his decision to this day.

My paternal grandfather, now retired, lived several neighborhoods away, so I had limited contact with him. He had survived two wives, though, and supported three families during the Great Depression, thanks to his job as a fireman with the Baltimore and Ohio Railroad.

At the time, my Father worked at the Crosse and Blackwell factory in East Baltimore, driving there and back each day, since gas rationing had been lifted. He had not attended school past the eighth grade. My Mother, however, at her parents' insistence, had graduated from High School—a major accomplishment for a girl at the time. I think about her now, and I see clearly that she was very smart, and I often wonder how far she might have gone had she not married my Father and raised a family with her whole heart and all her energy.

One of the greatest joys of my life was living at our summer place on Back River along the Chesapeake Bay. My grandfather taught me to love boats and fish and crab. I received my first rowboat when I was about eight years old, and I would set a trotline for crabs in the morning and have about a half bushel, which I would proudly hand to my grandmother to steam, by lunchtime. During the season, my parents ran a gill net for rock (stripers or striped bass, if you prefer). Life was good.

I remember that our family bought one of the first television sets in our neighborhood. It was made by Hallicrafters in Chicago and looked like an oscilloscope that one would use in a laboratory. But it fascinated my Brother and me to the point that when there was no programming available (which was the majority of the day), we would sit and watch the test pattern. I'll never forget that Indian Head! I certainly stared at it long enough.

Electric streetcars ran up and down our street, and I remember sitting in my grandmother's lap while she rocked me to sleep, as I looked out at them clattering their rhythmic beat into town and back out again. Of course, the motors made neither noise nor exhaust fumes. Somehow, we were all happy to see them go and be replaced by diesel engine noise and exhaust from the new buses which replaced them. How could we have been that stupid?

Starting in February of 1949, I attended PS34 (public school number 34), which was just three blocks down the street, so I walked there and back each day. My Mother was very active in the PTA, and both she and my Father worked at the school's major fund-raiser each year—the Spring Bazaar. I was not much more than an average student. I didn't know that we were as poor as we were because I never felt that way. My family's love and support overcame the lack of money.

We were lucky to live in a row house which looked on Carroll Park, named after Charles Carroll of Carrollton, a signer of the Declaration of Independence. I believe it was originally his estate since his mansion, Carrollton, was still there and maintained. The park gave me a great place to play sports (football, baseball, and tennis) as well as "Army" with my school friends—always boys, never any girls. Parents didn't worry about their kids going outside to play in those days. There didn't seem to be any of the predators about that we read about today. I believe I spent every moment outside that I could when I wasn't doing homework or helping with the housework (my Brother and I received a nominal allowance but had to do chores to get it).

My Brother joined the Boy Scouts, and I was jealous. He and our Father, a member of the troop committee, would go out on camping trips and do all kinds of fun things, while I twiddled my thumbs at home. Finally, I became eight years old and joined the Cub Scouts. My Mother volunteered to be the Den Mother, and her Father helped her make up crafts for us all to do. It was OK, but it wasn't camping. Finally, when I turned twelve years old, I joined the Boy Scout Troop. Of course, by now, my Brother had become an Eagle Scout and moved on to the Explorer Post. So in due course, I followed him there too. Now, I was camping all the time—even in the snow in winter—and learning new skills all the time. But I never made it past Star Scout, although I had lots of merit badges, but I was never interested in the Civics merit badge set, which were required to make Life and Eagle. Both my Brother and I were very active in the Order of the Arrow, each one in their turn becoming the chief of our lodge, Nantico #12. We each also became vigil honor members.

But time passed, and I passed out of PS34 after the sixth grade, still in February, since Baltimore allowed us winter-born kids to start and graduate from schools in that month as well as the more normal June. So now I had to move onto Junior High School. My Brother, who was then attending Southern High School, which had a Junior High School associate with it, absolutely insisted that I not attend either of them, so I chose to attend Gwynns' Falls Junior High School some miles west and north from our home. I now had to ride the bus to and from school since we no longer had electric streetcars. I expected to be in that school through the ninth grade because that was normal.

At Gwynns' Falls JHS, I continued to be an indifferent student and had to endure those embarrassing parent-teacher's conferences where both my teachers and my Mother tried to figure out why I didn't have better grades. However, my life changed fundamentally one day when I attended an assembly with my best friend Bob Walsh. He had I had been in every class together since Kindergarten and generally played together in Carroll Park. While I can't recall today what the assembly was about, I know it included some faculty from the Baltimore Polytechnic Institute, a public high school but with a very unique structure. Of course, it emphasized a technical education, but there were three different curricula offered: an A Course (Advanced College Preparatory), a B Course (College Preparatory), and a G Course (General Technical). A Course graduates could start as sophomores in most Colleges and Universities in the country. B Course graduates were accepted as freshmen. G Course graduates generally entered apprenticeships in the skilled trades. The concept fascinated me, but my friend, Bob, shocked me when he said he wanted to be an engineer and was going to leave JHS and start at Poly after the eighth grade because it was a full four-year high school. I couldn't believe we were going to be separated at long last, and I remember clearly asking him what an engineer was anyway. After he explained it, I declared that I was going to go with him, if I could get accepted. Suddenly, grades were very important to me.

The Baltimore Polytechnic Institute

So began my campaign to get accepted, not only at Poly, but also into the A Course. I had a meeting with my counselor who advised me to not enter the A Course but rather go into the B Course because, she said, high school was a time to play since college would be the time to buckle down and work hard for academic recognition. That advice no longer seems to hold true today. My impression is that most young people go to college to avoid working. Despite her urging, I insisted on entering the A Course and was able to get my grades up to the point that Poly accepted me at that level.

Unfortunately, my fraternal grandfather, John Starry Scott Engle, whose uncle, Brent Fletcher Engle, fought with the 12th Virginia Cavalry in the War for Southern Independence, died of heart disease during my junior high days. Toward the end of his life, we had become much closer, and his passing left me in a state of great sadness.

My Paternal Grandfather, John Starry Scott Engle

Bob and I started together in February 1958. There were two sections of us A Course freshmen: DX-1 and 2 (the D was for the first year, A for the senior year, etc., and the X was for February). While my parents did not have to pay for any tuition or books, they did have to buy me clothes because Poly had a dress code: coat and tie every day, except one which we'll talk about later. There were no girls in the school. So there were few distractions. My nightly study period was some three to four hours, and I usually came home with a pile of books that went all the way out to my elbow from my side. Backpacks were unknown in school, and if a student was bold enough to use one, he would probably have been laughed at by the rest of the student body. Later on in my Poly career, my class shrank to a single section, I think in my junior year, or BX-1. So by our senior year, there was only AX-1.

While I played freshman football (both my Father and Brother played when they were younger), I did not make the junior varsity team the next year, and my athletic career came to an end. I was very active in the rocket club, thanks to a cousin, Howard Galloway, who worked for NASA, and the model railroading club, thanks to my paternal grandfather of B&O fame. I spent a good deal of time after school working in the attic of our building on a huge HO gauge railroad layout that had been constructed there. I even joined the Baltimore Society of Model Engineers in downtown Baltimore who had extensive O and HO gauge layouts with multiple model trains running all the time. Unfortunately, we did not have much room in our basement at home, so we only had our trains up during Christmas time.

In the Fall of 1960, my high school teamed up with Southern High School to introduce students to colleges and universities. The idea was to take students to visit both a small and a large institution away from home. So I hitched a ride with a friend of mine, Frank Perry, and we joined the group at Juniata College in Huntingdon, Pennsylvania, on a Friday afternoon/evening, touring the campus and chatting with the faculty. No one from Southern was present, and we all thought that a little strange. The next morning, when we met in the parking lot of the motel, there were all the Southern High people—with girls! That's when I first saw Peggy Brown, and I wasn't interested. I really fell for her friend, Kay Baker. That Saturday, we visited the campus of Penn State, State College, Pennsylvania, and were invited to attend a football game at the conclusion of our visit. Frank and I sat with Peggy and Kay for the game and were able to gain their phone numbers. So our trip back to Baltimore was euphoric—that was just before Frank hit a male pheasant in the road. I got him to stop, and I picked up the bird and tossed him in the trunk. When he dropped me off, I presented my grandmother with that magnificent bird, which she prepared for us that night. Then, I really was euphoric! In fact, I had the head stuffed, and I still have that head in my home as a memento of my first meeting with Peggy. Yes, things with Kay never worked out, so I started dating Peggy, and we stayed together ever since. That was her senior year, 1961, and we've been together ever since.

Naval Reserve

During my early high school days, I became fascinated with two TV shows (no, we didn't have to watch the Indian in the test pattern any longer): *Men of Annapolis* and *Navy Log*. Since the family spent every summer at a piece of land that they rented on the Chesapeake Bay and my maternal grandfather had boats all his life and delighted in introducing me to them and their operation, these TV shows really lit a spark in me. So much so that I started hanging out at the Naval Reserve Center at Fort McHenry in Baltimore Harbor. While I was too young to join, I did get several of my older friends to sign up. But right after my seventeenth birthday in 1961, I raised my hand and took the oath. Most of the senior members of this unit had been in the Pacific during World War II and several had had at least one ship shot out from under them. Their influence on me was profound, and a young sailor had better watch his actions around them because they took no prisoners when it came to any sort of a breach of the rules. People in today's Navy would not recognize their service at that time. They were very tough guys, and they knew that they had utterly defeated the Imperial Japanese Navy—probably the best in the world at the start of the War. It was a very different Navy from the one I experienced later and so far from today's version, that one might think it had belonged to another country. Maybe it did because the United States in the late '60s through '80s was not at all the same one it was in the '40s.

I remember bringing home my first seabag, which I still have. My Mother didn't know whether to cry or be proud of me. But I was certainly proud. And yes, I was issued a regulation Navy flat hat, which I was told had to be worn within the confines of the Naval District of Boston, when on liberty, though I never found myself in those circumstances. That summer, after school, I went to the two-week boot camp set up for reservists at the Great Lakes Naval Training Center, just outside Chicago. It was my first ride in an airplane. I was feeling pretty good when I first mustered with my new Company Commander, Chief Aviation Machinist's Mate Ginsterblum, on the "grinder" adjacent to our barracks. It took him about two minutes to reduce me to a quivering bowl of Jell-O. All my pride and haughtiness dripped out of me right then and there, like blood pouring from my jugular vein onto that grinder. He was an expert at humbling us "boots." The Berlin Wall went up while I was at Great Lakes, and the rumors circulating had us being graduated early and heading out to sea to do something none of us quite understood. Like most "scuttlebutt," this turned out to have no truth to it.

Boot Camp Photo Summer 1961

Yes, Boot Camp was an experience, all right, and I think it helped me to grow up a lot more. By now, though, my scouting days were about over. The Navy was taking up most of my spare time. Not that I had much, considering all the studying I had to do. But I did manage to get awarded with a membership in the National Honor Society, another proud achievement in my life.

In order for the senior class to graduate, it was a school policy that they had to spend one day performing what was known as the Senior Boiler Test. The rest of the student body always knew when that day was because the seniors showed up in work clothes—the one and only day it was allowed. We started with measuring the amount of energy in the coal our power plant was using and measured everything else up to and including the energy in the waste stack gases. At the conclusion of the day, we produced an efficiency level for the high school's power plant. My senior homeroom just happened to be in the Heat Engines Laboratory in the basement of the building, so none of us had to move very far throughout the test to take the required measurements.

But High School ended for me in February 1962. Bob Walsh and I, still in the same class, now split up forever. Bob had gained an appointment to Webb Institute located at Glen Cove, New York, on Long Island Sound, to learn shipbuilding; and I had gained an appointment to the United States Naval Academy, which was good for my parents, because they could never afford to put either one of us through college. My Brother had already graduated from a local teachers' college, and he was employed teaching Baltimore County high school kids English and History. Yes, he worked and paid his own way through school and got a master of arts in education at Loyola College at night, again, on his own dime.

But I had probably made a bad choice because all the hard work I had done to graduate with high grades from the A Course at Poly did not matter when it came to the Naval Academy. I would start as a lowly Plebe just like everyone else. So I was actually behind when I started there in June of 1862, but at least, I would become a Man of Annapolis, just like in the TV show.

I had some months to kill while I was awaiting my reporting date and was able to get a job in Plant Engineering at the Bethlehem Steel Plant at Sparrows' Point, located just outside the Baltimore Outer Harbor on the Patapsco River. I was able to get hired onto a surveying crew because I had learned surveying at Poly. The plant was some sixteen miles around in perimeter—the largest tidewater steel mill in the world at the time I worked there. So I now found myself as a rodman in a surveying crew, tasked with checking our construction contractors' work in and around the steel side and coke ovens. It was an exciting job but very dangerous. My introduction to work was to hold the measuring rod for the man working the transit in order to lay out a new narrow-gauge railroad section in #4 Open Hearth. Of course, the new line would be on the floor of the open hearth which was a very busy place. At that one job, I had to watch out for super trucks, we called Euclids for their manufacturer, driving around the dirt floor, narrow-gauge trains running around on the same floor, and overhead cranes with million-pound ladles full of molten steel. Oh, and the best part, one had to watch where one stepped because the slag, a waste product of steelmaking, was lying around on the floor at random places. It looked gray and solid on the outside, but if one stepped on it, one had a good chance of breaking through the crust into the molten slag, just a bit cooler than the molten steel. That would eliminate as much of one's foot and leg that touched it.

I remember another job we were sent out on in the same open hearth. We were to check for settling of the pilings under the hearth itself while it was in full operation. I don't know how long that open hearth had operated since it was last rebuilt, but it had been quite a while because when we got under the hearth and got my ruler up to the first piling so our team lead could take a measurement with the level, I heard something plinking off my hard hat like small pieces of hail. Then I smelled cloth burning. Just about that time, our team leader yelled at us to get out from under the hearth immediately. When I turned to leave, I saw molten steel falling down through holes in the hearth. That's what had hit my hard hat and burned several holes in my jacket. Yes, indeed, there was never a dull moment "at the Point." I should mention that my Father had been working on the blast furnace side since my junior year in high school. He was now a labor foreman over there and had been burned so many times, he had lost his fear of fire. The man seemed to be impervious to pain. He amazed me!

Before long, my time was up with my surveying crew because I had to perform my two weeks' active duty for the Naval Reserve. I was best man at my Brother's wedding that June in Baltimore, but I had to take a bus that evening for Norfolk, where I was to report to my first ship: USS *Roberts* (DE-749). She was built in San Pedro, California, in 1943–44 and saw active service in the Pacific. At the time I was aboard in June 1962, she had been transferred to the duty of training reservists at the Naval Operating Base, Norfolk, Virginia.

We never left the pier the entire two weeks I was aboard, but we worked like demons. I was in the deck division with an ensign as a division officer, whom we only saw at quarters in the morning. I reported to the leading seaman and never even had an interaction with the bos'n (Navy contraction of "boatswain"), our senior petty officer, at all. This is very different from today's Navy, as anyone who has served in it will verify. Of course, I was full of all the scuttlebutt about not picking up the soap in the shower, so I was initially terrified of getting in there with my shipmates. After my first day of hard work aboard, I waited until everyone else had showered and then I quickly sprinted to the shower. I had it all to myself when all of a sudden, in came the bos'n. Now, the reader must understand that our boatswain (pronounced "bo-sun") was as salty as they came. He had hash marks for time in service all the way to his elbow, but they were red, not gold (indicating he had problems with authority). I was told, and still believe, that he was a chief petty officer (E-7) a couple of times but always managed to get himself busted in rate. When I knew him, he was a second class petty officer (E-5). So here I am with the saltiest petty officer in the crew alone in the shower. He said nothing to me, of course, and I tried to avoid looking at him, but I just had to sneak a peek. What did I see but a propeller tattooed to each butt cheek with the words "Twin Screws" tattooed across the small of his back. Oh yeah! "Boats" was a real destroyer man!

United States Naval Academy

Just a few days after I returned home from my two weeks' active duty, I had to report to the Naval Academy in Annapolis. My parents and grandparents were there to witness me take the oath of office, and I can only imagine how proud they were of me. That day turned out to be the beginning of the worst year of my life. In 1962, being a plebe was the most humiliating, frustrating, and depressing position a young man could have. That said, I seem to have attracted the ire of the upperclassmen in my company who decided that I was not fit material for a position as a navy officer. So they spent most of their extra energy focused on the goal of having me quit. Toward the end of the year when my classmates were all enjoying a more relaxed relationship with the upperclassmen, I was still enjoying their excesses. It didn't stop until June 1963 began, and I put on my third class stripes. They had given me so many "professional questions" to research that I found I had no time to study that year. I'm sure that was the plan: have me fail academically if I wouldn't quit. What they hadn't counted on, didn't understand, and never took the time to find out, was that I had, in fact, graduated from the Poly A Course and already had studied just about everything they tried to teach me that year, so I really didn't need a lot of study time to do well.

Midn 3C Ed Engle
June 1963

Finally, Plebe Year Is Over!

So about this time, I asked Peggy to marry me, and we became engaged. Time passed, and I was now excelling academically, taking extra courses to major in mechanical engineering, not just the standard naval science degree which the Naval Academy offered, and I was on the Superintendent's list most quarters.

On the twenty-second of November 1963 (during my "youngster" or third class year), I was returning to Bancroft Hall from classes, when I heard that President Kennedy had been shot in Dallas. By the time I got back to my room, the radio was already broadcasting news of his death. I remember thinking that the assassination had to be bad for the Navy because he was such a supporter, and I didn't think that now President Johnson would feel the same way toward us.

During the summer of my second class (junior) year, Peggy became pregnant (good Catholics didn't use birth control methods), and I agonized over not marrying her for most of the fall semester. One night, while studying in our room with my two roommates, Steve Arendt and Tom Reynolds (both would retire as Captains), they suggested that I just quit fretting about it and marry Peggy. So we were married secretly on the first day of my Christmas leave in 1964. Our first daughter, Jeannine, was born on 27 February 1965. The next day, the Varsity Pistol Team had a match with Army at home in Annapolis. I was so nervous, I shot the lowest score I ever shot, and we failed to beat them. A short time later, I took a weekend liberty and attended her christening. When I returned back to my parents' home, where my family was now living, I made the decision to turn myself in to my company officer first thing Monday morning because I could not deny that beautiful little girl for whom I was now responsible.

So I very quickly found myself out of the Naval Academy and out of work with a family to provide for in March of 1965. I immediately applied to the Johns Hopkins University but discovered I was too late for the fall semester, but due to my extraordinary circumstances, the Registrar made an exception, and not only accepted my application but gave me sufficient credits to begin as a senior, even after all the leadership, navigation, and ship-handling credits were deleted. However, in order to graduate from the college of engineering, the student had to successfully complete a rather large number of hours of graduate level work. Since I had not taken any at all, my senior year classes would consist of mostly graduate level courses. I was in for a really tough academic experience.

The Johns Hopkins University

But I still needed a job, and I looked at quite a few different positions around Baltimore but finally decided to try Bethlehem Steel again. Once again, I was hired into the Plant Engineering Department but this time as a detail and layout draftsman. I would be wearing a coat and tie and not be dodging threats in the open hearth any longer. So I worked and saved as much of my money as I could, thanks to my parents and grandparents. Peggy also was able to get a job as a third grade teacher with one of the Catholic Schools in Baltimore. So we could contribute to the family's income at least. All too soon, it was time to quit my job and head back to school.

I'll never forget my first day at the Johns Hopkins University. I wore a coat and tie. What else would one wear to school? Of course, no one in my class was dressed that way. Then, I asked the class if anyone was going to take a muster? I'm not sure to this day if anyone in the class even knew what a muster was, but I certainly received a lot of strange looks. I think half of them thought I was working for the FBI or some other clandestine organization and had come to spy on them. This was the beginning of the Vietnam War protests on college campuses across the country after all.

The second day, I dressed like everyone else, and things began to become more normal, except for the academics. My cousin, Howard Galloway, who worked for NASA, had warned me that Johns Hopkins engineering classes were being taught in form of mathematics known as tensor mathematics. I had never heard of it so I knew this would be an interesting year. When I attended my first class in solid mechanics, I discovered that I could not follow the professor's mathematics at all. I was totally lost. Then, I had similar experiences in other classes, so it was obvious I was going to have to learn this brand of mathematics on my own because the other students had already learned it and the professors were teaching at their level.

I bought a book on the subject, and when I wasn't in class, I was in the library studying tensor mathematics. Then, typically, I would pack up and head to Peggy's school where I would pick her up after work and drive us both back to our family in East Baltimore. My academic experience at Johns Hopkins was a shock because I had always thought the Naval Academy had fine academic credentials, but believe me, they didn't come close to matching what was going on at Johns Hopkins in the '60s.

While no one ever took any kind of an attendance in class, none of my classmates would miss a lecture unless they were hospitalized because everyone knew that if you weren't there, you would fall behind; and if you did, you would, in all probability, never catch up. The professors did not give quizzes either. The student's entire grade depended on the midterm and final examinations—talk about pressure! We did get help from graduate students once a week who went over our homework with us. I know I learned a lot from them, and I think my classmates would agree.

I had a professor from the Institute of Metals in Aachen, Germany, Herr Professor Mengelberg, who taught a full two-semester course in Metallography in the European style, which we were to discover in a very interesting way. We, just six of us in the class (which was another characteristic of Johns Hopkins at the time), had been attending his lectures routinely like we did in all our classes when one day, we noticed that Professor Mengelberg had called each student to the blackboard (yes, slate and chalk) to answer questions he posed. At the end of the recitation, he declared that we had all passed our midterm examination. At the mention of that phrase, we all went into overdrive but realized that it was over, and there was no longer any reason to fret about it. Our final exams with him were just as interesting. Two of us would schedule a time would schedule a time with him on final examination day. When we appeared at his office, he had a table prepared with two pads of paper with two pencils each and a blackboard with lots of chalk. Then he began a conversation with each of us in turn. We would respond with dialogue and diagrams. Then, he gave us our grades when it was all over. That was the first and only time I ever experienced that format in academia.

I had a professor for Fluid Mechanics (again, two full semesters), Professor Corrsin, who was famous for developing machines for medical applications (e.g., dialysis, intubation, etc.). He was always trying to get his students to go to medical school and move into his field—a remarkable man, and the world is a poorer place since his passing. Professor Stanley Corrsin[1] was most famous for his final examinations. They were take home, open book, open source.

---

1. Stanley Corrsin (3 April 1920–2 June 1986) was an American physicist, fluid dynamicist, and Theophilus Halley Smoot Professor of Engineering at the Johns Hopkins University. He was known for his contributions in the field of fluid dynamics in general and turbulence in particular. He was a recipient of Fluid Dynamics Prize in 1983. Corrsin died of cancer on 2 June 1986 at the age of sixty-six.

He would hand out ten questions from which we would have to answer seven, and those would be the ones we would be graded on. I averaged about a week on each of his exams. They were killers! And the word was around the college that he never asked the same question twice—remarkable. The only question I can remember today is one I actually chose to answer. It went something like this: *It has been postulated that the sperm cell propels itself up the uterine canal by spinning its helical tale. Assuming that this is true, derive the equation which describes the streamlines such motion would leave behind.* I believe I spent three hours staring at that question until I made the first mark on the page. After all, one had to decide what coordinate system to use, Eulerian or Cartesian, to make the mathematics more practical. OK, enough of the technical mumbo jumbo, but I hope the reader gets the idea. People ask me today if school wouldn't have been a lot easier with an engineering calculator instead of a slide rule. I hope the above exam question answers that fully.

Just as the spring semester was starting, Peggy announced that she was carrying our second child. Now, the pressure was really on. The consequences of failing to graduate were just too horrible to contemplate. I was already forced to take out a loan to cover my tuition and books for that semester, and I was currently unemployed. I didn't think it was possible, but I ramped up my studying even more. Consequently, my grades improved by such a degree that my Advanced Engineering Mathematics professor invited me to stay at Johns Hopkins on a fellowship with him. But all I could think of was my need to make a decent living and provide for my growing family. I found out later that that fellowship would result in a PhD at the end. I often wonder what life would have been like had I taken that road.

Beginning in February, the senior class began interviewing with recruiters from various companies, including the Federal Government. I managed to achieve a job offer from Pratt & Whitney Aircraft in East Harford, Connecticut, at the highest starting salary of anyone in my graduating class. So it looked like my goal of providing a decent living for my family was to be achieved. I now couldn't wait for graduation, but the pressure was on to do well in my final examinations, which I managed to do.

If I Look Happy, It's Because I Have a Great Job

Pratt and Whitney Aircraft

On graduation day, my parents drove my family to the airport where we got on a Super G Constellation (four piston-engined airliner) of Eastern Airlines and flew up to Connecticut. I started work the next morning in the smallest engineering group in the company: Structures Research and Technology, composed of just sixteen engineers out of the thousands who worked at the facility. I received every promotion and pay raise for which I was eligible and rose from a Junior Engineer to Technical Engineer while working on a Master of Science degree at the Windsor Locks Graduate Campus of Rensselaer Polytechnic Institute, Troy, New York. In those days, I had only one job: *Derive the equation which predicts the failure of a first stage turbine blade in a jet engine*—sounds a lot like the tasks my professors at Johns

Hopkins gave me, doesn't it? Well, I did develop an equation which tracked the loading (both thermal and mechanical) on those parts and predicted a failure point, but I could never get good correlation with laboratory tests of the kinds of materials Pratt & Whitney used in the hot sections of their jet engines. My seemingly identical samples would fail anywhere from 1,000 cycles to 10,000 cycles. While my equation lay right in the middle of the test data, no one would use it to design an engine to carry people. The lab results were simply too scattered and too unpredictable to be considered safe.

About this time, with gathering frustration over my inability to do better, the War in Vietnam was heating up. By now, I had not only received my honorable discharge from the Naval Reserve but was working in a war critical industry. I was clearly undraftable. One day, a colleague, who was against the war, was needling me over lunch about my attitude toward that war, saying I only was behind the war because I couldn't possibly be drafted to fight in it. That started me thinking—usually a bad sign.

Having an all-night discussion with my wife, Peggy, about the possibilities of my going back into the Navy, we decided that I should. But instead of the nuclear-powered submarine program I had intended to try for out of the Naval Academy, I had determined to try and get a seat flying bombers for the Navy. I knew I couldn't be a pilot because I had been wearing glasses since before I left the Naval Academy—too much studying in bad light, I suppose. When I looked at the aircraft the Navy flew at the time, I fell in love with the A-6A Intruder. I had read *Thirty Seconds Over Tokyo* in elementary school and had been fascinated with the bombing mission ever since. So I thought there would be no better job for a guy without 20-20 vision than bombardier/navigator in those aircraft.

Christmas time came, and I packed up the family for a trip back to Baltimore; but on the way, I stopped at Floyd Bennett Field in Brooklyn, New York, and took the entrance examinations for naval aviation. The recruiter, an Ensign, was ecstatic over my scores and couldn't wait to give me the oath of office. My class convening date in Naval Aviation Officers' Candidate School at NAS Pensacola,

Florida, was scheduled for mid-January 1968. So I left the family in Baltimore with my parents and grandparents, who were delighted, and drove back to Connecticut to pack up our house and put our furniture into storage in preparation for my move to Florida. My Father was furious with me at the time. I was making a lot more than he was at the time; we were driving a late model Chrysler and would be getting paid as an E-5 while I was in NAOC School—that was quite a pay cut from which we would not recover for years.

Naval Aviation Officers' Candidate School

Reporting into the NAOC School that first evening was a nightmare. New candidates were assigned to the Indoctrination Battalion and were issued old Marine utilities, which were lovingly known as poopy suits. Unlike the movie *Officer and Gentleman*, made much later, there were no females at the school, but it was run by Marine Drill Instructors, a real change from the Naval Academy, where the "enemy" was the upper class. However, on that first evening, the drill instructors were all home, and we were introduced to the candidate officers responsible for the battalion. They ran us around the building, screaming at us constantly. Then they screamed in our faces while we were braced up against a bulkhead (wall to you, non-Navy types) telling us how worthless we were and encouraging us to DOR (drop on request). Of course, if one did that, one went right to the fleet as an enlisted man, and the reader must understand that all the candidates were already college graduates. But most, including the candidate officers, had come right to NAOC after graduation with almost no work experience.

So I found myself braced up against a bulkhead after thirty-three months of the Naval Academy and my reserve experience being screamed at by a guy who was hardly old enough to shave and had no military experience at all telling me how screwed up I was without even knowing anything about me. I will admit that my boss's last words at Pratt & Whitney Aircraft were very much in the forefront of my mind: "If things don't go the way you think they should, don't hesitate to come back here. I'd love to have you back." I will freely admit that I was sorely tempted. We did get a phone call to tell our families we had arrived safely, so I called Peggy and told her I wasn't at all sure that I hadn't made a huge mistake. She was very supportive of having me return to her and go back to my old job, but I told her I'd stick it out for a bit and see what happened. After all, unlike my year as a plebe at the Naval Academy, this school was just sixteen weeks. I'm glad I decided to stick it out.

The next morning, we met our drill instructors, and they proved to be everything I had heard them to be—very professional and very severe. They would brook no nonsense from anyone. Our class's

DORs started very soon after that. It was a tough sixteen weeks, but I came to admire our drill instructor, SSgt Borcie, seen in the photograph below. But I will admit when I heard his voice anywhere in the barracks, my knees would shake.

At the end of a 31 March speech, President Lyndon Baines Johnson shocked the nation when he announced he would not run for reelection by concluding with the line: "I shall not seek, and I will not accept, the nomination of my party for another term as your President." The next day, his approval ratings increased from 36 percent to 49 percent. Little did I know then, as I struggled to graduate from the NAOC School, that the next President, Richard Nixon, would eventually remove the restrictions which plagued our predecessors in the Vietnamese War and allow us to operate at our full potential.

Within two weeks of that speech, my class graduated.

My NAOC Graduating Class at NAS Pensacola, Florida.
My head is circled, and SSgt Borcie is to the right.

Naval Aviation Training Command

Graduation finally did arrive, and we were all made new ensigns in the Naval Reserve and sent off to start preflight training in either the Pilot or NFO (Naval Flight Officer) pipelines. Peggy and the kids, Jeannine and Steven, joined me in Pensacola, where I was assigned to VT-10, after survival school at Eglin AFB, which was nearby. VT-10 was primary flight training for all NFOs. Believe it or not, our main aircraft was the UC-45J, or "Bugsmasher," which the Navy had purchased in the '30s as a "high speed" transport. It was already obsolete when World War II started, but it had two engines, even though it would not fly on just one, and carried a pilot, an NFO instructor, who usually flew as copilot, and three students in the back. Each student would rotate into the copilot's seat for his part of the flight, navigating us around the Florida panhandle and Alabama.

Of course, in addition to the flights, we had ground school, where we learned Morse code, radio procedures, electronic and visual navigation techniques, and general safety of flight principles. Many of our instructors had already had a combat tour of duty in Vietnam and knew what was important. I had one instructor who always drummed into our heads that "What belongs to the pilot, belongs to the pilot, but it all belongs to me," meaning, the NFO must take responsibility for safety of flight items just like the pilot, even though he doesn't actually "sign" for the airplane. That principle helped me a great deal in my future A-6 career.

Toward the end of our time at VT-10, each student had to submit a wish list of aircraft which he wanted to fly in the fleet. Only the top graduate of each class was guaranteed the seat of his choice. Everyone else's choices were subject to "the needs of the Service." While I had a very high class standing, I was certainly not #1, and that guy wanted A-6s on any coast (since the aircraft was located at NAS Ocean, Virginia, and NAS Whidbey Island, Washington). When it was time to actually make our selections, the instructors told us not to select A-6s because there were simply no seats available, anywhere. Well, being a stubborn German, I selected A-6s[2] East Coast and West Coast for my first and second choices, anyway, to the consternation of my instructors. As it turned out, a few seats did come open just before assignments were made, and I got one, West Coast, while others who had switched their choices to F4s, as urged by the instructors, didn't. They were a bit upset, but I was off to BJN (Basic Jet Navigator) School at NAS Glynco, Georgia, just north of the town of Brunswick. Since I would be there only a short time, I packed Peggy and the kids up and moved them back to my folks in Baltimore. We were homeless vagabonds once again.

BJN School was taught at the same field and with the same aircraft that our future F-4 NFOs were trained to perform intercepts of other aircraft. We used a small business jet which, like the Bugsmashers in VT-10, had a pilot an NFO instructor and three or four students in the back, who would rotate to the copilot's seat for visual navigation flights. When we did our radio navigation flights, we stayed in the back and used the instruments and maintained our plots and logs. SOP (Standard Operating Procedure) was to carry three plots: DR (ded, for "deduced," reckoning), no wind, and true track. At 420 knots (nautical miles per hour), or 7 NM every minute, one had to really work to keep it all going. Of course, we also had classroom instruction in electronic and visual navigation techniques and more radio procedures.

About halfway through our syllabus in September 1968, we had to execute a hurricane evacuation from our field, NAS Glynco, Georgia, to NAS Olathe, Kansas, just west of Kansas City. We packed up everything and flew away in our business jets and continued our training in Kansas while Georgia got clobbered by the storm. Flying low-level visual or contact navigation flights over the prairies of

---

2. The Grumman A-6 Intruder was a twin-engine, mid-wing, attack aircraft built by Grumman Aerospace Corp. in Bethpage, New York, on Long Island. In service with the US Navy and US Marine Corps between 1963 and 1997, the Intruder was designed as an all-weather medium attack aircraft to replace the piston-engined, single-seat Douglas A-1 Skyraider.

Kansas was almost as bad as our flights over the Okefenokee Swamp had been.

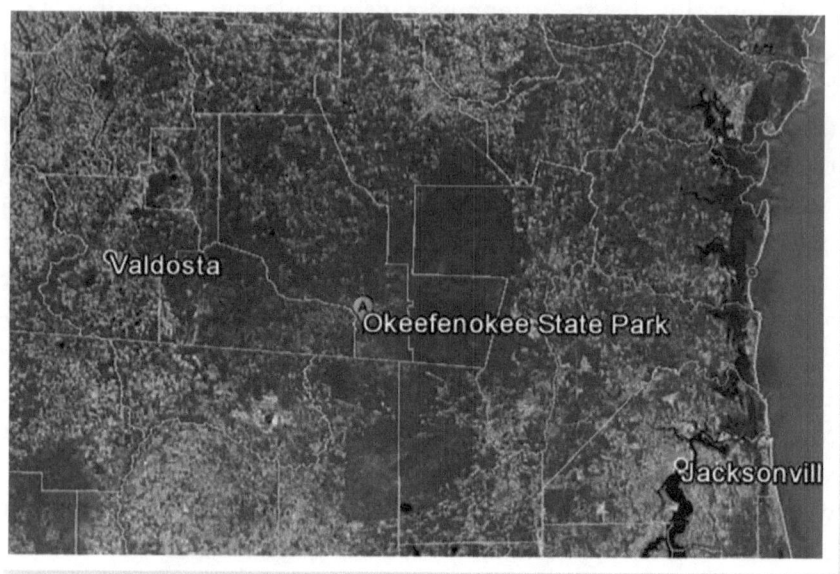

There just aren't that many landmarks you
can use to figure out your position.

The hurricane blew itself out eventually, and we returned to NAS Glynco, completing our training in early October 1968, with a graduation cross country flight to San Francisco, California. That might sound like fun, but navigating a third (there were three of us students) of the way across the US in the jet route structure sitting in the back of the plane, keeping three plots and accompanying logs, and not having access to radio aids to navigation unless we made a request to the pilot for a fix, it was not a lot of fun. But we all did well and received our NFO wings back at NAS Glynco. I was now off to the A-6 fleet replacement squadron on the West Coast, VA-128, at NAS Whidbey Island, located north of Seattle at the end of the Strait of Juan de Fuca. Of course, I had to get a few maps to figure all that out. Neither Peggy nor I had any idea where it was.

I drove back to Baltimore and picked up the family—Peggy was now carrying our third child—in our Volkswagen Squareback and headed West, with our now three-year-old daughter, Jeannine, and our two-year-old son, Steven. I had to report to VA-128 no later than 6 November. When we got up at the motel somewhere in Montana to have breakfast, I'll never forget Steven looking at all the stockmen in the café with wide eyes, asking me if they were real cowboys. I told him that they certainly were, and his eyes got even bigger, though I didn't think it possible.

CHAPTER 2

VA-128

A trip across the northern US in November is bound to result in some driving in the snow, and this trip was no exception. We hit quite a bit of snow in Montana, but we really got it in Idaho. The drive through the hills around Coeur d'Alene was truly exciting! But one way or another, we were able to keep the car on the road and everyone alive and finally pulled into Oak Harbor, Washington, the town adjacent to NAS Whidbey Island. At that time, the population was 5,800 souls; it's gotten a lot bigger since. We moved into another motel while we applied for base housing. Unfortunately, there was a long waiting list, and as a new Ensign, I wasn't very high on it.

We couldn't afford to keep staying in the motel because it was simply too expensive, so we investigated a rental property. The only thing we found in our price range was an old trailer which had seen better days, jalousie windows, books holding up one leg of the master bed, etc. But we would all fit, and we would be able to cook and not have to eat all our meals out. Unfortunately, we had arrived just in time for a record-setting winter in Island County, Washington.

It snowed hard just about every week, and the air station was not equipped to deal with it since, as we were told over and over again, "it doesn't snow here." Well, it certainly did in the winter of '68–'69! Again, we were told by the locals that it was their worst winter in sixty years. Weren't we the lucky ones! Those jalousie windows leaked badly from the cold wind, the kids were sick all the time, and we found an abandoned puppy under the trailer. There was no way we could leave it out in that weather, so we now had a black Labrador puppy named Heidi to go along with everything else we were dealing with. I believe Peggy qualified for sainthood that winter.

VA-128 Golden Intruders History

The squadron patch depicts a bird with outstretched wings. This bird is a phoenix who, in ancient mythology, was consumed by fire and resurrected from its own ashes. As VA-128 was created from VAH-123, in 1967, the new A-6A Intruder replaced the A-3B Skywarrior as the Navy's all-weather attack bomber.

The body of the phoenix in the patch is the number 1 which symbolizes the first west coast A-6 Intruder operational unit. The color gold is representative of the squadron's nickname, "The Golden Intruders." It was derived from the color which most aptly describes the mythological phoenix and for the geographical area in which our squadron aircraft operate, "The Golden West." The color also represents the squadron's product, i.e., the replacement flight crews and maintenance personnel, which were literally "worth their weight in gold" to the US Navy's aerial offensive striking arm, in peacetime or at war.

When VA-128 disestablished in 1995, the squadron patch was transferred to the Wing commander. In 1997, it was given to a newly formed EA-6B Electronic Warfare Squadron, VAQ-128.

Originating as a maintenance detachment from Heavy Attack Squadron One Two Three (VAH-123), the Golden Intruders had a humble beginning. In June 1965, 100 members from VAH-123 went to NAS Oceana, Virginia, for A-6A ground maintenance training. The following January, six flight crews from VAH-123 went to NAS Oceana to begin their flight training in the Intruder. The Squadron Plankowners are LT Hugh Brainard, LT Lyle Bull, LT Don Cotter, LT Robert Eichner, LCDR Buzz Eidsmoe, LT Fred Holmes, LCDR Charles Hunter, LCDR Don King, CDR Jerry Patterson, LT John Smith, LT Jim Vester, and LCDR Carl Wiechert.

In June 1966, the original maintenance detachment returned to Whidbey Island to form the nucleus of the West Coast A-6 training squadron. The first Whidbey Island Intruders arrived in August 1966, whereupon VAH-123 began A-6 flight training in earnest, drawing on their core of trained A-6 pilots and bombardier/navigators. The addition of combat-seasoned flight crews further enhanced their experience and training capabilities, and in November 1966, VAH-123 began to transition training Attack Squadron One Six Five (VA-165) in the Intruder aircraft. By June 1967, VA-165 had become the first West Coast fleet squadron to fully transition to the A-6.

On 1 September 1967, VA-128 was commissioned as the Navy's West Coast A-6 Intruder training squadron, finally severing the link to VAH-123. In the years that followed, VA-128 transitioned Attack Squadrons 52, 95, 115, 145, and 196 to the A-6 Intruder. Attack Squadrons 155 and 185 were also commissioned later.

Duty with VA-128

At VA-128, I was in ground school initially to learn all the A-6 systems in preparation for actually flying it for the first time. I was very impressed with the incredible innovation incorporated into the design of that aircraft by the Grumman Aircraft Company. It was a truly state-of-the-art bomber. We attended those classes with our pilot counterparts. We were FRBNs (Fleet Replacement Bombardier Navigators), and they were FRPs (Fleet Replacement Pilots)— what acronyms! Eventually, ground school ended, and it was time for our first familiarization flights. Here, the pilots had a real advantage because most of them had been flying jet aircraft of some description (either trainers, if they were first tour people or some other fleet jet, like the A-4, if they were second tour types), and they were used to wearing and functioning in all the flight gear we had to wear. That was not true for the first tour NFOs. We only ever wore a flight suit and helmet in the aircraft we had flown in.

Now, all that changed instantly. For the first time, we were introduced to a g-suit to wear on the legs and lower body, designed to help us endure the gut-wrenching maneuvers to which we were to be subjected; a harness, to enable us to connect to the ejection seat; a survival vest packed with things to help us survive on the ground until help arrived; a helmet, of course, but now, with an oxygen mask attached. If you then add the cold weather clothes we had to wear (a veteran instructor told us: "Always dress like you'll have to walk home."), you can easily see that we looked like the Pillsbury Doughboy walking out to the airplane. Climbing up the ladder was initially a seemingly impossible job. Once in the cockpit, I couldn't understand how any of our instructors thought I could function since I could hardly move. Doing something strenuous, like maintaining eye contact with an adversary in a dog fight seemed ludicrous. Yet we all got used to it. And soon, we didn't even notice the equipment. In combat, I would have a lot more gear and weight, but I didn't know that then.

After many weather delays due to the runways being coated with snow and ice, which we tried to remove by having the more advanced FRPs taxing onto them and blowing the snow off, I finally was able to get my first hop in my fleet aircraft. Not only that, my pilot was the squadron CO, CDR "Whitey" Gooding. We took off and flew through the cloud cover until we were "VFR on top" (Visual Flight Rules on top of the clouds). Then the Skipper flew west to the Olympic mountains and the Pacific Ocean, then back east, crossing the Cascades, and on to Spokane and Coeur d'Alene, Idaho. He pointed out all the active volcanoes in the area like Mount Baker, Mount Hood, Mount Rainier, and of course, Mount St. Helens, which became very famous years later.

Then he demonstrated various flight characteristics of the aircraft, including how fast it could stop. At that time, the A-6A had two sets of speed brakes: wing tip and fuselage. The aircraft would retain the former, but the latter would be removed fairly early in its fleet life. We certainly slowed down with the wing tip brakes, and even more so with the fuselage brakes; but when he selected both of them simultaneously, I was glad my harness was locked, or I think I would have eaten the instrument panel! That FAM I ended all too soon, and we came back to the field to land and debrief the flight. After that, I drove home and couldn't wait to tell my wife about how unbelievably beautiful the area was, especially with the sun shining down on all those white clouds and snow-covered mountains.

Let this be a lesson to newlyweds with a pregnant wife. Telling her that story caused her to break down and cry uncontrollably. She had not seen the sun in months. The kids were still sick, the puppy wasn't housebroken yet, our bed was still broken, we still had the jalousie windows with the plastic on them, and she was even more pregnant. So my little tale of glorious nature and a spectacular airplane was not appreciated. I learned a very hard lesson that evening, but I did learn it.

The Navy's A-1 Skyraider—The Forerunner of the A-6 Intruder

Our class of FRPs and FRBNs had a class leader, by virtue of his seniority—a senior Lieutenant at the time—who took a personal interest in all of us. His name was Jay Troy Grafton, and he had flown A-1s in combat in Vietnam earlier and had then been the Flag Lieutenant for VADM Cousins, CTF-77 (the carrier task force assigned to the Gulf of Tonkin off the coast of Vietnam). One Friday, as we were all finishing up our planning for upcoming syllabus flights in the ready room, he invited the class to his house over at the Seaplane Base (NAS Whidbey actually had two locations, separated by Oak Harbor itself: Ault Field on the west side of the island, where all the squadrons were located and the Seaplane Base, where base housing, the commissary, exchange, etc., were located on the east side of the island on Birch Bay). I quickly called Peggy and asked her to find a babysitter. I drove home, picked her up, and drove over to LT Grafton's house. Peggy and Jay's wife, Sandy, hit it off immediately, and we were very jealous of his home but hopeful that we would soon get one like it. Those homes were ranch style with three bedrooms, two baths, and a fireplace. We thought they were very nice. It was a nice break for Peggy, who had been cooped up in that lousy trailer for weeks with all the snow, gray skies, and cold. These get-togethers at the Graftons' home became a regular part of our routine, and we certainly enjoyed ourselves at each and every one. But more importantly, most of that class would wind up together in VA-165, so we were already building a lot of rapport with each other, an essential ingredient for a combat squadron.

Eventually, our name finally came up, and we were able to move into base housing. There were three circles of these ranch homes for officers' families: Mountain, Rainier, and Cascade Drives. We moved into one on Rainier Drive while the Graftons were very close over on Mountain, and others from our class were similarly close by. So we began living together as neighbors, our kids played together, some of the elder ones acted as babysitters when needed, and our group became very close.

As part of the FRP syllabus, they had to qualify on the carrier with landings and takeoffs in the A-6 and also qualify with their visual bombing with real, operational, live ordnance. Neither of those things could be done near NAS Whidbey Island, so VA-128 established detachments. Our class traveled in Navy R4Ds (Douglas four-engine piston airliner, the DC-6) all the way to NAS Pensacola, Florida, where they qualified on board USS *Lexington* (CVT-16), an old Essex-class carrier from World War II, which was much smaller than the current fleet carriers and still had wooden decks. They had to be very precise with their lineup when coming aboard because just a couple of feet to the right, the starboard wing tip would hit the island structure. The wood tended to splinter, and we suffered several engine failures due to FOD (foreign object damage). I rode in the right seat for many pilots, just sitting there, as they hot-seated and occasionally hot-refueled; but that pace got a lot of pilots qualified in a very short time, and I racked up quite a few carrier landings—day and night.

An A-6 "In the Groove" with No Tailhook Down—A Touch and Go

Note the wing tip speed brakes deployed. The pilots created all that drag so they could land with more power on the engines to make them more responsive.

An A-6 "In the Groove": Note the Centered "Ball" on the Port Side of the Landing Area Indicating the Aircraft Is on Glide Slope This Picture Is Taken from the B'N's Side of the Cockpit.

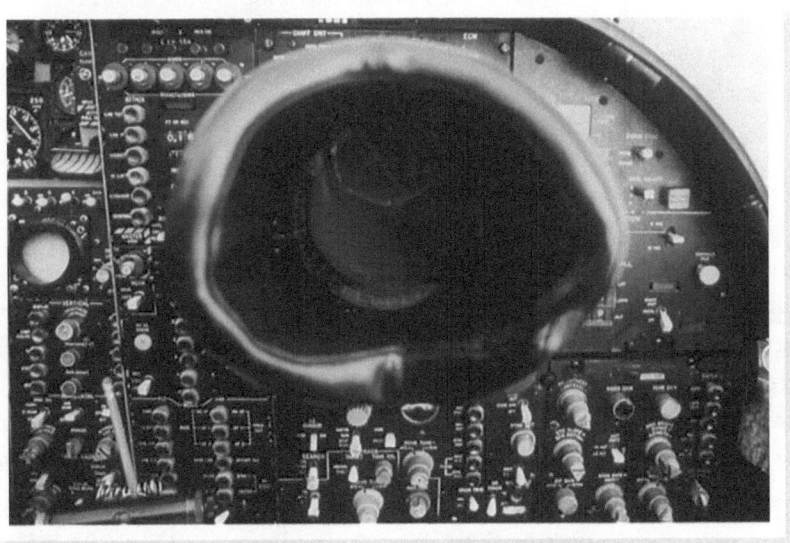

A-6 Intruder Bombardier/Navigator's Weapons System Panel

About this time, I was informed that I had been named a Distinguished Naval Graduate from NAOC and had the option of converting to the regular Navy from the reserves. I signed the papers immediately, so I now had USN, vice USNR, behind my name. Of course, I didn't make a penny more, but I now had the same commission I would have received had I stayed at the Naval Academy and graduated.

A VA-128 TC4C. This photo was shot in 1973, and this aircraft has the new TRAM optical pod under the nose. All A-6Es would eventually sport that pod.

The FRBNs had quite a few flights in both the Navigation and Weapons phases of our training in the TC4C aircraft pictured above. This especially configured Grumman Gulfstream sported the characteristic A-6 nose, which had to be that large because of the size of our search radar antenna and contained a complete cockpit near the tail with seats and radar repeaters all the way up to the cockpit. FRBNs actually got to operate the navigation and weapons systems under the tutelage of a qualified instructor before ever trying out those skills in the cockpit with a pilot who typically only had a rudimentary understanding of the DIANE (Digital Integrated Attack and Navigation Equipment) system and couldn't see the B/N's radar from his seat because of the hood, which blocked out the light (he had a repeater in front of his stick, but it was very small, and most pilots weren't very good at interpreting it). It was a very clever way to ensure that all FRBNs were introduced to DIANE in a standardized way and could achieve the best results from whatever was left of the system by the time he made it to the IP. You see, the instructors would pull circuit breakers to cause the student to lose parts of DIANE throughout the flight in order to evaluate how soon he recognized the failure and how well he dealt with it.

The Coveted Bull's Eye Patch for Dropping a
Bomb Right in the Center of the Target

This particular patch is one of the newer ones due to the wing's name. When I earned my first Bull's Eye Patch, the wing was known as COMMATWINGPAC (Commander, Medium Attack Wing Pacific). This was changed after the EA-6Bs hit the Fleet to reflect that fact.

Then we deployed to NAF Fallon, Nevada, for visual weapons. At Fallon, no one cared about our weapon system. It was all about getting the pilots qualified in visual bombing and rocket firing. The pilots also took this opportunity to "yank and bank" the A-6 so they could get familiar with its flight characteristics with and without a heavy load of bombs. We were even introduced to some of the ECM (Electronic Counter Measures) equipment on board the aircraft and flew against some of the simulated threats that Fallon operated on some of the ranges. I think I didn't accumulate more than thirty minutes of straight and level flying during that detachment, but it was something we FRBNs had not been subjected to before but had to learn to accommodate (more than one airsickness bag was filled during that detachment).

Those of us in the class who had not as yet been to SERE (Survival, Evasion, Resistance, and Escape) School were rounded up and sent to the one being operated right there on Whidbey Island, on the extreme eastern side of the Seaplane Base. At the time, the Navy operated three of these schools: Whidbey Island, Washington; Brunswick, Maine; and Warner Springs, California. We all felt that we were lucky because classmates had told us that Warner Springs had been picked clean years ago due to the number of survival students who had been through there. I had just been promoted to LTjg (Lieutenant Junior Grade, or an O-2).

Once again, our training consisted of living outside with classroom lectures and practical lessons in survival: edible plants, snare construction for small animals, and fire building for warmth, cooking, and signaling. We really were lucky because one day during each class, the students were allowed to dig clams on the beach at a negative tide. We collected quite a few, and the students with us who were from New England cooked them up. They made a fine stew, and absolutely nothing was left. But then, the time came to perform feats of evasion, so we were dropped off in the middle of nowhere and told that we needed to reach an extraction point by a certain time. If we made it, we got a sandwich as a reward. If we didn't, we were captured by the "black hats" and thrown into prison earlier. Needless to say, we all tried our best to get that sandwich. I didn't get caught, but I didn't make it to the rally point on time either. At the end of the time allowed, we all had to stand up and surrender.

Then, our time in the POW compound started, and the "black hats" acted out their roles to perfection. We were slapped around, interrogated, put in very small black boxes until our muscles all cramped up, and water-boarded—oh yes, we were! No one thought we were being tortured though. Of course, after twenty-four hours of this hell, it too came to an end. I remember the first thing I did was go to a local burger joint and load up on a burger and fries—wonderfully satisfying!

Graduation finally came for our FRPs, who had a shorter syllabus than the FRBNs, and they moved on to their operational squadrons (most went to VA-165 who was just returning from their second A-6A deployment on board USS *Ranger* (CVA-61)), leaving us behind to complete our weapons phase of training. At that time, FRPs and FRBNs had to achieve a certain standard in each of their bombing modes in order to graduate. That wasn't that hard for the pilots because they mostly had to become expert in visual dive bombing and high lofts, but the FRBNs had to achieve the standard CEP (Circular Error Probable) in each of four bombing modes (straight path, general dive, general dive toss, and high loft) in order to graduate, and our A-6As had a MTBF (Mean Time Between Failure) of something less than two hours. So when a student needed a full system capable aircraft in order to complete a syllabus flight, he might have to wait awhile to get one from maintenance, and then, he might have to abort before he completed that flight. It certainly slowed everyone down. I remember a FRBN in a class ahead of me who had been in the RAG for over a year before he graduated. Generally speaking, it took the pilots about six months and anywhere from nine to thirteen months for a FRBN.

All this training was absolutely indispensable, and we would find that it would serve us well in the months to come. By the time I graduated from VA-128, I felt ready to join my fleet squadron, and I too was assigned to VA-165 in the summer of 1969.

CHAPTER 3

VA-165
VA-165 BOOMERS HISTORY

The distinctive insignia worn by the Boomers consisted of special elements and significant colors. The green boomerang is the focal point of the insignia and signifies the squadron's ability to strike and return to strike again. The gray background was selected to portray the all-weather capability of the squadron and the aircraft. The gold compass card, aligned to the four cardinal headings, is emblematic of the worldwide commitments and global responsibilities of the Navy, which are supported by Attack Squadron 165. Central to the insignia is the white knight chessman denoting versatility and to indicate that the "Boomers, Have Weapons, Will Travel"—a parody of the old TV Western series *Have Gun, Will Travel* and used the paladin (or knight) on his calling card.

In January 1967, the Boomers moved to NAS Whidbey Island, Washington, where they transitioned to the A-6A Intruder. The Boomers became the first West Coast operational A-6 squadron and returned to Southeast Asia in November 1967 and again in 1968 as members of Carrier Air Wing Two (CVW-2) aboard USS *Ranger* (CVA-61). While embarked on *Ranger*, the squadron received the COMNAVAIRPAC Battle "E," the Meritorious Unit Commendation and the Navy Unit Commendation.

In February 1970, VA-165 joined CVW-9 aboard USS *America* (CVA-66), departing from Norfolk, Virginia, for their fifth combat deployment to Southeast Asia. They completed 9,009 combat sorties and dropped 7.3 million pounds of ordnance. For their outstanding performance during the 1970 combat operations, the squadron was awarded their second consecutive COMNAVAIRPAC Battle "E." Between September 1971 and August 1973, the Boomers and CVW-9 completed two more combat deployments aboard USS *Constellation* (CVA-64). They flew 2,600 combat and combat support missions during this period, delivering a half-million pounds of bombs and transferring nearly thirteen million pounds of jet fuel. For their superior performance, demonstrated courage, professional competence, and achievement of exceptionally impressive damage against heavily defended targets, the Boomers were awarded the nation's highest unit award, the Presidential Unit Citation. After nearly ten years of sustained combat operations involving six deployments, the Boomers returned to NAS Whidbey Island in October 1973 as the last squadron employed in the Southeast Asia conflict.

The fall of 1989 saw the Boomers filming in-flight, flight deck, and hangar deck scenes for the Paramount Pictures Corporation motion picture, *Flight of the Intruder*. VA-165 was decommissioned in May 1996.

Duty with VA-165

Upon reporting in the summer of 1969, I was assigned as branch officer of the power plants shop in the maintenance department. Unlike the Air Force, each Navy squadron had to be self-contained in order to move as a unit on board ship and function in an operational environment. The Air Force operates under a very different concept, based on a wing of similar aircraft. So one of the squadrons is a maintenance squadron. Our wings consist of different types of aircraft mixed in such a way so as to permit the carrier to complete its missions of sea control and power projection. I couldn't believe that the squadron would actually give me that job since I was so qualified for it with my previous experience at Pratt & Whitney Aircraft, who built the J-52 turbojet engines—military version of the JT8D engines on the Boeing 727, which powered the A-6. Obviously, the military is not always as dull-witted as the public is often led to believe.

I quickly was integrated into my new squadron, not in the least part due to the fact that we replacements had developed close ties in VA-128. So now, training started in earnest to mold our various personnel into a cohesive fighting unit. All of us, officer and enlisted men, were very well trained, but now we had to learn to function as a unit. Our skipper, CDR Dick Zick, turned out to be a great inspiration to us all, and he was instrumental in forging us into a weapon.

Now that I was in a fleet squadron, I had to team up with a pilot to form a crew. This was extremely important in the A-6 because the longer a crew flew together, the smoother they got—especially when everything wasn't working correctly. Remember that the MTBF of the DIANE (Digital Integrated Attack and Navigation Equipment) System was less than two hours. That meant that the B/N had a very small chance of having a full-up system by the time he reached the target. But we were all taught and adhered to this rule rigidly that once we passed the IP (Initial Point) in the run-in to the target, we would drop on it, no matter the flak, the missiles, or the degradation of DIANE. So flying with the same guy sitting next to you every flight created a smooth operation when we had to get creative to get our bombs off on the run. So now LCDR Jay T. Grafton and I teamed up. I was to fly with Jay for more than a year, and we became very close.

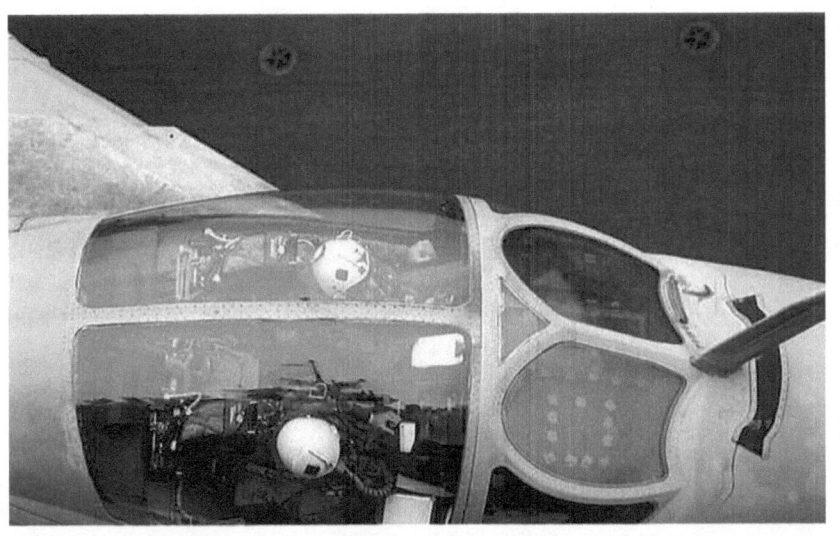

A-6 Cockpit Taken from "The Island" on the Ship

I also met a B/N who had made the previous cruise on Ranger, LT Bruce "Boxman" Wood, who, for some reason I never understood, became my Fleet mentor. He taught me many things about being a copilot, which were really not stressed in our formal training to date, and things I should remember in combat. Without his help, I would have had a much steeper learning curve once I got into actual combat. I owe him a huge debt of gratitude.

Interestingly, about this time, we received two additional replacements, who didn't wear our uniforms—two Air Force officers: the pilot was Capt. Larry Beasley and the navigator was Capt. Doyle Balentine. The former had recently flown with the 555 TFW—the "triple nickel" with Col. Robin Olds in command—in Southeast Asia. Larry, or Beez as he was known in the squadron, brought a lot of combat experience with him; and since he had been a MARCAD

(Marine Cadet) earlier in his life, he had experience landing on aircraft carriers. The navigator was Maj. Doyle Balentine, who had experience in F4s and B-66s (the aircraft equivalent of our A-3), which he had flown in combat in like Beez. Shortly after arriving, Beez was promoted to Major and became our operations officer, and he was a good one. The A-6 is a very forgiving airplane so that the crew has time to break out the PCL (Pocket Checklist, a pocket-sized version of the NATOPS (Naval Air Training and Operating Procedures Standardization) Manual) to review emergency procedures before proceeding. But there are a small number of emergencies which can occur, like an engine fire on takeoff or an accelerated stall into a spin, which the crew has to deal with from memory because there simply isn't time to reach for the book. So Beez had those checklists printed up in poster form and posted on the inside of every door to the commodes in the officers' heads in the hangar. So if you were taking your daily period of quiet contemplation, you could brush up on your emergency procedures at the same time.

During this work-up period, we made the usual visual weapons deployment to NAF Fallon, Nevada, and then had to fly to NAS Oceana, Virginia, to qualify on USS *America* (CVA-66), the ship from which we would operate during the squadron's next combat deployment with CVW-9 (Carrier Air Wing 9) or "CAG-9" in naval aviation parlance. This was a very strange situation. The Navy did not normally deploy a West Coast air wing with an East Coast ship and vice versa, but the rule certainly didn't hold this time. One would think that the Nation had one Navy, but that simply was not the case. Operating procedures and work-up training events were quite different. For example, the entire air wing had to deploy to the East Coast in order to complete work-ups with *America* because in the Atlantic Fleet, they would deploy to the Caribbean for about a month in order to complete all the training both the ship and the air wing had to master in order to be certified to deploy. On the West Coast, these evolutions were completed week to week with the ship usually being in port for the weekends.

The following squadrons composed CVW-9:

VF-92 (F-4J)
VF-96 (F-4J)
VA-146 (A-7E)
VA-147 (A-7E)
VA-165 (A-6A, A-6B & A-6C)
RVAH-12 (RA-5C)
VAW-124 (E-2A)
VAQ-132 (EKA-3B & KA-3B)
HC-2 Det 66 (UH-2C)
HC-7 Det 110 (SH-3A)[3]

The differences arose out of geography. The Atlantic Fleet had no live fire ranges anywhere near their air stations, and there really was no place for their ships to complete their drills because of the crowded shipping lanes. On the West Coast, we had several live fire ranges like NAF Fallon, MCAS Yuma, or even the ranges adjacent to Nellis AFB, Nevada. We could easily reach these places from a ship off the California coast. Other seemingly small variances in procedures around the ship were also prevalent, and of course, this gave rise to the ship complaining that CVW-9 didn't know what they doing with similar complaints about the ship from the air wing. We were not getting off to a great start as a team.

Those of us who had not done so, now had to go down to San Diego, California, and complete DWEST (Deep Water Evasion and Survival Training). After suitable classroom lectures, we all suited up in well-used Navy dry suits, which didn't fit very well. Then we were loaded up on an LCM-8 landing craft with a high tower on the stern and put out to sea. Once we were out of San Diego Bay, we lined up, climbed up to the top of the tower one at a time, were hooked up to a parachute harness, and told to jump. Upon entering the water, you had to roll over onto your back and let the Mike 8 tow you until one of the instructors told you to release your harness. This simulated a

---

3. The Detachment was not aboard *America* for the entire deployment. Rather, they cross-decked to relieving ships in the Gulf of Tonkin.

parachute dragging you across the water. This could have been a lot of fun were it not for the cold water and the ill-fitting dry suits we wore; because when you rolled over onto your back, cold seawater came pouring down the back of your neck and soaking the whole suit. What fun! On release of the harness, we then had to inflate the raft that was stowed in a seat pack hanging below our butts. Once you had the raft inflated, you had to get into it—a tricky maneuver—but it was much warmer in the raft than in the Pacific Ocean. Then, you just floated around and awaited rescue. After some time had passed, the helicopter came over, and when he indicated that he was going to pick you up next, you had to get out of the raft and prepare to get into the harness the helo dragged through the water to you. Touching that harness first could electrocute you. Then, we all flew back to the beach, received our certificates, and headed back to NAS Whidbey Island.

VA-165 had a long-standing (going back to the A-1 days) tradition of having all the officers assemble at the Officers' Club when ashore at the end of the work week on Friday afternoon to participate in the game of aces with five dice. As a matter of fact, there was a squadron instruction which laid out all the rules and responsibilities for it. One man was designated the Box Man, who had control of the strong box which contained all the money and dice equipment needed for the game. At this time, Box Man was LT Bruce Wood, my mentor. So he had the call sign Box Man. Everyone would sit down, and Box Man would order the first pitchers of beer as the game began. The losers had to pay him, and he paid for the beer as the evening progressed. If you were good with the dice, you never bought a drink.

After two hours or so, everyone would start to get hungry, and my pilot, Jay Grafton, would jump up and announce supper at his house. Then, there would be a mad scramble for the telephones as we all tried to call our wives to get babysitters. After a few Fridays had passed, our wise wives knew the routine and already had babysitters lined up, so they didn't have to scramble any longer. All of us then went home, changed, picked up our wives, and headed over to Jay's house. The menu was always the same: chicken on the grill, with rice and peas made by Jay's wife Sandy. Most Fridays we would sit in Jay's living room, watching flames climbing up the windows from his backyard deck and advise him to check the chicken. Of course, we always got the same response: "Aww, it's fine. Don't worry about it." And of course, by the time he took it off, it was so burned that I don't think the bones had any marrow left in them. So Fridays always turned out to be peas and rice. None of us cared. It was being together with our wives as a big family that was most important. Such things built our esprit de corps to otherwise unattainable levels. And that would pay real dividends when it came time to test our training and cooperation in real combat. I understand that this type of activity is frowned on in today's Navy, and I firmly believe that they are the worse for it. But then, today's aircraft drop smart bombs from miles away from the target and no longer incur any real stress over their targets, like we did and all the other aviators before us. We needed to be close and know we could trust each other. Today, it's like going to the office and coming back again.

A-6Bs and Cs

If preparing the squadron for combat wasn't enough, we now were assigned new aircraft. We took ownership of four A-6Cs and four A-6Bs. The former was to be a test platform for optical sensors which the Navy had to evaluate. It carried one LLLTV (Low Light Level TV) and a FLIR (Forward-Looking Infra-Red) sensor in a pod affixed to the belly of the aircraft where our centerline station (station #3) would normally be found. So those aircraft could carry six less bombs than the A-6A. Plus, that pod had a drag count of over 60, but we were never really told what it really was, so plugging the tables in the NATOPS manual to calculate things like max refusal speed on takeoff, fuel consumption en route, and range became difficult and more subjective. The A-6B was designed to carry and fire the Navy's Standard ARM (Anti-Radiation Missile). The Standard missile was, and still is, carried by the Navy's destroyers and cruisers. So it was big. But it was advertised as a quantum leap over the older Shrike ARMs which were currently in the fleet. The Standard missile would memorize the last position of the targeted radar and home to that point, even if the radar shut down. The Shrike just went ballistic and self-destructed when it ran out of fuel. No matter what they carried, when such suppression aircraft flew in combat, their mission was known as Iron Hand, and they used that as their call signs.

But having three different versions of the A-6 Intruder to maintain and operate caused VA-165 a great deal of trouble. For example, there wasn't time to train everyone on every platform, so aircrews were chosen for either the "C" model or the "B" model, and they had to be scheduled for those aircraft when we flew combat missions. Maintenance was worse, in many cases, because while the basic aircraft systems (hydraulic, fuel, electrical) were the same, the fire control systems were very different. In addition, since the Standard missiles were so expensive and so heavy, if the crew didn't fire them (none would be fired during our deployment), they had to be returned to the ship. That meant that at the first look at the "ball," that A-6B would be right at bingo fuel, and if they didn't catch a wire, they would have to clean up and fly off to their assigned bingo field (usually DaNang in South Vietnam). This gave rise to a future upgrade to the aircraft tailhook assembly, which would enable the aircraft to come aboard a few thousand pounds heavier, and that extra weight was generally fuel and would save a lot of aircraft from having to bingo after just one or two passes.

To provide US Navy squadrons with a defense suppression aircraft to attack enemy antiaircraft defense and SAM systems, a mission dubbed Iron Hand by the US Navy, nineteen A-6As were converted to the A-6B version during 1967 to 1970. The A-6B had many of its standard attack systems removed in favor of specialized equipment to detect and track enemy radar sites and to guide AGM-45 Shrike and AGM-78 Standard anti-radiation missiles, with AN/APQ-103 radar replacing earlier AN/APQ-92 used in the A-6A, plus AN/APN-153 navigational radar replacing earlier AN/APN-122, again used in the A-6A. Note the Standard ARM on the inboard port weapons station (#2).

Between 1968 and 1977, several Intruder squadrons operated A-6Bs alongside their regular A-6As. Five were lost to all causes, and the survivors were later converted to the A-6E standard in the late 1970s.

A-6C of VA-35 Black Panthers

Twelve A-6As were converted in 1970 to the A-6C model for night attack missions against the Ho Chi Minh Trail in Laos and Vietnam. They were fitted with a Trails/Roads Interdiction Multi-Sensor (TRIM) pod in the fuselage for FLIR and low-light TV cameras, as well as a "Black Crow" engine ignition detection system. Radars were also upgraded, with AN/APQ-112 replacing earlier AN/APQ-103 in the A-6B, and AN/APN-186 navigational radar replacing earlier AN/APN-153 in earlier A-6B. A vastly improved Sperry Corporation AN/APQ-127 radar replaced earlier AN/APG-46 fire control radar in A-6A/B. One of these aircraft was lost in combat, the others were later converted to A-6E standard after the war.

Training progressed as efficiently as possible, but it became apparent that the A-6C crews would not complete their syllabus in time to meet *America* in Norfolk before she deployed for Southeast Asia. So it was decided to leave those crews behind at NAS Whidbey with the four A-6Cs, finish the syllabus, and fly across the Pacific to meet *America* at NAS Cubi Point in the Republic of the Philippines. America loaded up and departed Norfolk in April 1970 and would not return until December of that year. We A-6C crews actually did not depart CONUS (Continental US) until Mother's Day 1970.

In preparation for our TransPac, we practiced with an EKA-3B from our air wing who had stayed behind to help us get to Hawaii, the longest leg of our trip across the Pacific Ocean. During those flights, we discovered that the A-6C could not maintain enough speed to stay in the A-3s refueling basket at high altitude due to our additional weight and drag. So we worked out a method of refueling in a toboggan-type maneuver where the tanker would drop his nose slightly and begin a shallow dive. Flying "downhill," the A-6C could manage to stay in the A-3s basket until the tanks were full.

Now that the four crews left behind had completed their training and we knew how to refuel this model from the tanker, it was time to catch up with the rest of the squadron and CVW-9 aboard *America*. So we packed up all of our gear and maintenance personnel, loaded them on Navy transports, and they left for the Philippines. Then, we had a final goodbye with our wives and families, showed up at the squadron with our light carry-on baggage, briefed our flight down to NAS Alameda in San Francisco, where we were to meet our A-3 escorts, and went out onto the tarmac to man our aircraft. Peggy walked out with me, and I was touched to see her kiss the engine nacelle of the starboard engine (on my side) asking the plane to carry me safely across that very large ocean. It was an emotional moment for us both. But it was time to "kick the tires and light the fires."

TransPac

Our formation flight down to NAS Alameda went quite smoothly on that Saturday morning, and we spent the rest of the day in briefings with our A-3 escorts. It would be a very complicated operation with twelve A-3s launching ahead of us. Along the way west, each of them would tank other A-3s in turn before turning back for Alameda, some would then tank us, until only our own KA-3B remained. That would occur somewhere about the midpoint to Hawaii. We had agreed that we would not try and stay in formation with our A-3 because our cruise speeds were so different. Rather, we would stay within radio contact range. The A-3s all had a celestial navigation capability. We did not. Rather, the A-6s would depend on our INSs (Inertial Navigation Systems) to get us across the ocean. Every hour, the B/Ns would cross-check each of our ground speed vectors to ensure none were very far out. It turned out that they agreed quite well throughout the TransPac.

An EKA-3B Refueling an F-8J of VF-211 in 1972

We had a very long flight on that first leg—close to eight hours of being strapped to a hard ejection seat all the way with just a relief tube for relief. One of our pilots, LT Brent Kirkland, lived in the Bay Area, and his mother had packed a wonderful box lunch for each of us. So we did have that to look forward to, but we found out that opening a can of soda above 37,000 feet was almost hazardous to your health because our cockpits were not pressurized to sea level pressures that high; rather, the environmental system maintained a pressure differential of 3 psi above 23,000 feet. So the inside pressure at our cruising altitude was about 12,000 feet. That lack of pressure has a spectacular effect on a newly opened can of soda!

Along the way, flying next to Jay, I started a chess game with a little plastic travel board I had brought along, but after a while, when I had him firmly beaten, he "accidentally" hit the board with his right hand, and pieces went everywhere. Some of them probably stayed with the airplane forever. So then, I had to amuse myself with doing calculus problems on our fuel usage. I don't think Jay ever got over that. It turned out that he had been appointed to the Navy Test Pilot School earlier and had been cut due to a problem with his poor math skills. Oh, well, I guess it is true that opposites do, indeed, attract.

As it turned out, we didn't need any fuel or navigational advice from our A-3, and we landed at NAS Barbers Point, Hawaii, safely. The next day, we were to launch early for the next leg of our journey to Midway Island, but the weather was hot, and we had to cancel because our A-3 escort did not have enough runway to safely abort a takeoff attempt, if something failed. But the day after that, we departed on schedule.

We made it to Midway with our KA-3D, filled out our logs, and took a break. The next day, we were on our way to Guam, with an en route emergency field on Johnston Atoll, which thankfully, we didn't have to use. Once we switched our radios to approach control at Anderson AFB, we were told that they were having an air show that day, which, of course, we hadn't known anything about. Then, they asked if we could do a flyby before we landed. Jay, acting as our O-in-C (Officer in Charge) replied that we would, and he briefed with our KA-3B that we would have him get out and take the lead, stream his refueling basket, and we would plug it and have our three wingmen fly in formation with us. So that's how we flew over Anderson for the first time. The management seemed very happy with our act.

The next day, we were off for NAS Cubi Point. Once again, the flight was flawless. Navigation by our four INSs was spot on, and everyone landed without a problem. We were finally reunited with CVW-9 and *America*, which we now called home. It was great to see our squadron mates again and hear about their trip "around the Horn" at the end of South America (our carriers can no longer transit the Panama Canal because they are too wide.) Apparently, we had missed some great liberty in Rio de Janeiro. But look at all the flight time we had bagged!

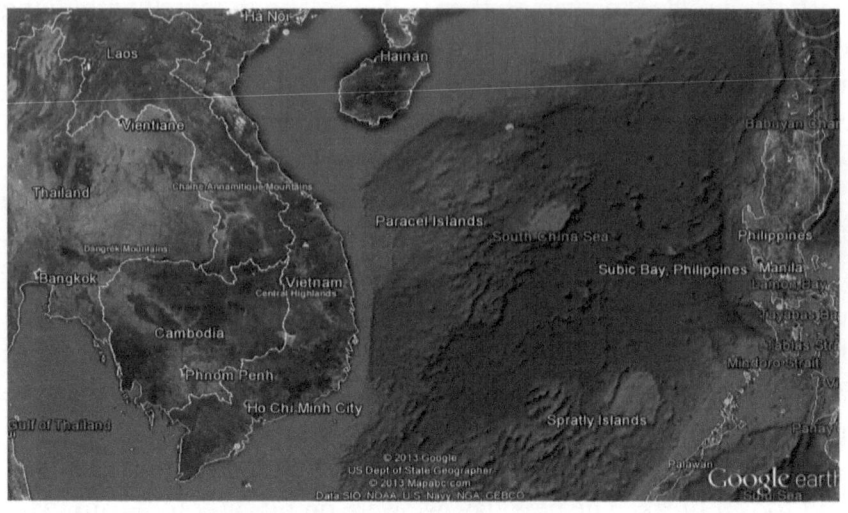

The Southeast Asia OPAREA

NAS Cubi Point, Republic of the Philippines

During our stay at NAS Cubi Point, we "nuggets" (first tour aviators) were ordered to JEST (Jungle Evasion Survival Training) School, which fortunately was right on the base. We learned about the many poisonous snakes (The flower and fauna are essentially the same in the Philippines and Vietnam, Laos, Cambodia, and Thailand.) and other deadly creatures we could come across if we had to eject. Probably the most deadly to us were the VCs and NVN Regular Army troops, so we spent some time in the jungle crawling around and discovered that you can remain completely hidden, even if the enemy is close enough to touch—a good thing to know. The final phase of the training introduced us to our Negrito guide (we were split up into small groups with one guide assigned to each). These are the native people of the Philippines, like Native Americans in our country, and what they don't know about the jungle isn't worth knowing. I was so impressed, I was trying to figure out a way to carry one of them in my lap in the aircraft. But failing that, I bought one of the bolo knives they sold, which they made out of old jeep leaf springs from World War II. The handle was made out of caribou horn, which when shaved, acts as a coagulant—a convenient thing to have attached to a big knife! Later, I had one of our parachute riggers in the squadron sew a closed pocket onto the outside right leg of my g-suit, so I thought I might have a pretty good chance of retaining it in an ejection.

My boss, the Maintenance Officer, in the squadron was LCDR John E. Grimes—about the saltiest guy I ever met. He had, like my pilot Jay, flown A-1 Skyraiders before transitioning to the Intruder, and he was definitely a product of the "old Navy." I remember when we first rejoined the squadron after the ship arrived, he had all his officers from the maintenance department meet with him in the ready room. After the agenda was completed, he announced that all his nuggets were to meet him at the brow (sometimes called the quarterdeck, the place where one could depart the ship down a ladder to the pier) at a specified time that night. He intended to give us our Fam 1 (Familiarization Flight 1) in Olongapo City. On the way to town that night, he announced that "If you wake up tomorrow morning in the gutter on Magsaysay Street with an empty wallet and a chicken sitting on your chest picking the barf out of your teeth, you had a great liberty!" Yes, John was quite a guy, and I really enjoyed working for him.

After a few days of R&R in Olongapo City, we departed for our first combat line period in the Gulf of Tonkin. As a nugget, I was assigned a bunk in one of the squadron's JO bunk rooms—no privacy but lots of camaraderie! During our transit over to the Gulf from Subic Bay (just a little more than a day), we had a series of lectures in our ready room from Air Force FACs (Forward Air Controllers) who briefed us on their procedures and what we could expect in Laos, where we would more or less confined for the entire cruise. President Johnson had declared that we would not bomb North Vietnam in 1967, so we were stuck with trying to stop the resupply of the Viet Cong and North Vietnamese Regular Army units in the south by interdicting the Ho Chi Minh Trail and a large portion of that trail ran through Laos, a place devoid of radar-significant targets. We B/Ns would spend many hours studying and taking radar scope photography so we could recognize our offset radar targets (distinctive limestone rock formations known as karsts throughout Laos).

We then picked up our sidearms and ammo. Since I was an expert with the Model 1911, 45 cal. semiautomatic pistol, that's what I chose, along with seven magazines of ball ammunition. I remember Beez carried a Colt Python .357 Magnum revolver with armor-piercing rounds, while my pilot, Jay, carried a toy-like snub-nosed .38 revolver full of flares. He always told me that contrary to our training to join up with our crewmate, he wanted me to stay away from him so that when I started the firefight, he would be going up to the rescue helicopter aboard the jungle penetrator they used; you had to know Jay. Then, we were issued gold coins, a blood chit (a silk sign, so it wouldn't rot in the jungle, in several Southeast Asian languages, which declared a reward for helping us get rescued), and morphine, in case we suffered a snake bite. (You had to amputate whatever the snake bit, so you'd have a chance to live. It's called primitive medicine.) Well, all that was not helping my anxiety over my first combat mission!

First Combat Mission

So the day finally arrived when all my training was to be concentrated on my getting to a target, dropping the bombs, and getting back to ship again. Yes, I was a nervous Nelly. The mission was to bomb with a FAC just south of the DMZ. Our flight leader for this three-plane strike was Major Larry Beasley. He very carefully briefed that this was to be a visual dive delivery on targets to be designated by our FAC and that, under no circumstances, were we to make more than one (that is 1) run. Everyone rogered up to his instructions, and off we went to suit up and man up. The launch, rendezvous, and flight into the northern end of South Vietnam was smooth. We were directed by the Air Force ABCCC (Airborne Command and Control Center), call sign Hillsboro, to head to a rendezvous with our assigned FAC, using one of the operating TACANs (Tactical Air Navigation Systems) in country, and switch to his frequency. We all did so and made contact with him immediately. He was flying in an OV-10, described the target, the run-in heading he wanted to use, the location of friendlies (there weren't any), and the safe heading to take in the event we might have to eject. So we all switched from a combat spread to a right echelon formation and watched Beez roll in on the target. Shortly after that, his wingman rolled in, and then we followed as the section leader. But halfway down the chute, Jay told me to turn off the Master Arm Switch on the ordnance panel because he had the wrong target and he was going to abort the run (that is, the *only* run we were supposed to make—remember the brief?). That was run number 1. Well, as things turned out, we actually made two more runs, until Jay finally thought he had it figured out and made a fourth run where we finally dropped all of our twelve MK-82 (500 lbs each) bombs. During all of this, Beez was screaming on the radio at Jay and me, asking what we didn't understand about one (i.e., 1) run. Our FAC must have been laughing himself silly. Meanwhile, I was imaging gunners on the ground refining their aim to blast us out of the sky on the very next run—each time. I wasn't happy either, but I may not have been as angry as Beez.

And the results of all this? The FAC reported that we had put all our bombs within 100 meters of our target (100 over 100, as they used to say) with no secondary explosions or fires, meaning, we moved the dirt around, but we made four runs to do it right! We checked each other over for hung ordnance and, finding none, headed back to the ship. It was a quiet flight. During the operational debrief in the ready room, the s——t really hit the fan! I thought Beez was going to have a heart attack right then and there, and I got it just as badly as Jay did for not stopping him. Yes, we really believed in the crew concept. After that, Jay and I had some private time and determined to never be that stupid again. That's probably why I survived.

Laos and the Ho Chi Minh Trail

It should be noted here that Laos was divided up into sectors, with the three largest divisions being Barrel Role, Western Steel Tiger, and Eastern Steel Tiger. The Air Force had the responsibility for the first two while the Navy had the third one.

The 7th Air Force, who was responsible for the Air War in the SEA OPAREA, was in the process of completing a project known as Igloo White within Steel Tiger. It was a multiphased effort to create a photogrammetric mathematical grid of the Laotian OPAREAs. This grid was to be tied to the latest Air Force Mapping Agency (the forerunner of the Defense Mapping Agency, which, in turn, morphed into the National Imagery and Mapping Agency, which at last morphed into the National Geospatial-Intelligence Agency, or NGA) geoid.[4] This was important because for the first time, geographical coordinates, along with the altitude of the point, could be passed along to others, and both parties could be assured they were talking about the same point on the earth. That was almost never possible in the history of warfare up to that point. Now, the principle is applied every time a smart weapon is to be employed.

In addition to establishing this grid, they were also implanting camouflaged sensors (acoustic and seismic) along various road segments of the Ho Chi Minh Trail with very accurate positioning within the grid. These sensors, mostly seismic, would transmit their data via a relay aircraft back to receivers at Nakhon Phanom RTAB (Royal Thai Air Base) situation along the Mekong River which Thailand shares with Laos (see SAT photo below). The data from the sensors were processed within Task Force Alpha Command Center at the AB and displayed on computer screens. Junior Officers (mostly female 2nd Lieutenants) manned these stations and would call out moving columns of trucks to one of the two Sparky FACs (one Air Force and one Navy O-3s) who were in secure (usually) radio contact with either LORAN (Long Range Radio Navigation) or A-6 Intruders—each officer working with airplanes from his own service. In the Navy's case, this was usually his own squadron, so he knew the crews and the capabilities of each very well. But this system was in its infancy in 1970, only the area right around the trail had been documented. Due to the unique characteristics of the A-6 weapons system, the Commanders of the 7th Air Force and TF-77 (the ships in the Gulf of Tonkin) agreed that when A-6s were on station (the

---

4. The geoid, simply stated, is the shape that the surface of the oceans would take under the influence of gravity alone.

smaller ships, or 27C class,[5] like USS *Ticonderoga* (CV-14) and USS *Oriskany* (CV-34) were much smaller and did not carry A-6 squadrons. Rather, they had either A-4 or A-7 single-engine, single-seat attack aircraft.), a B/N would be assigned to TFA. I had a tour there during each of my combat cruises. They were very rewarding and educational.

QU-22B Pave Eagle Aircraft

These small unpressurized aircraft flew an orbit over Laos all night to relay sensor data back to Task Force Alpha at Nakhon Phanom RTAB. These small uncomfortable aircraft were replaced in December 1971 with C-130Bs.

There were different missions assigned to the Navy and, in turn, the A-6s during this cruise: FAC, as discussed above; Commando Nail (bombing coordinates); and Commando Bolt (working with TFA). The latter two missions were under almost the exclusive purview of the P/Ns because they were used in bad weather in the case of Commando Nails and at night, regardless of the weather, in the case

---

5. Extended *Essex*-Class Carriers laid down at the end of or just after World War II.

of Commando Bolts. The B/N had to locate a radar-significant aiming point (usually a karst formation) and calculate the range, bearing, and differential altitude from that point to his assigned target. CNs then could be planned ahead of time on the ship, but the CBs were quick reaction strikes against convoys or other activity of interest along the Trail, usually at night. So the B/N never knew where he would be called on to bomb other than somewhere along the Trail. That required him to study a lot of radar scope photography, along with his charts, so that he could interpret the radar more accurately. In contrast, our fighter crews had nothing to study but the performance characteristics of their planes and the MiGs they might someday engage. Their preparation for a mission was very brief.

Typical Laotian Karst Ridge Suitable for an OAP (Offset Aim Point)

To overcome this difficulty, the Air Force established a system of DMPIs (Designated Mean Points of Impact) associated with each of their strings which were implanted densely enough and positioned accurately enough to use as "strike strings." If an operator detected movement along a string she was monitoring, she would advise the

FAC (either Air Force or Navy) who would call his next strike aircraft in the queue and, in the case of the A-6s, get the B/N to start typing in the data for that DMPI, while his pilot maneuvered the aircraft so he could make the run on the correct heading (roughly aligned with that road segment). While they were doing that, back at TFA, the operator would keep the FAC advised of the activity she saw on her string. She usually could give a pretty good estimate of the number of trucks and their speed.

Of course, based on those parameters, the convoy would either be short of or passed the DMPI by the time the aircraft dropped its bombs, so the FAC would advise the strike aircraft on whether to drop long or short by a certain amount.

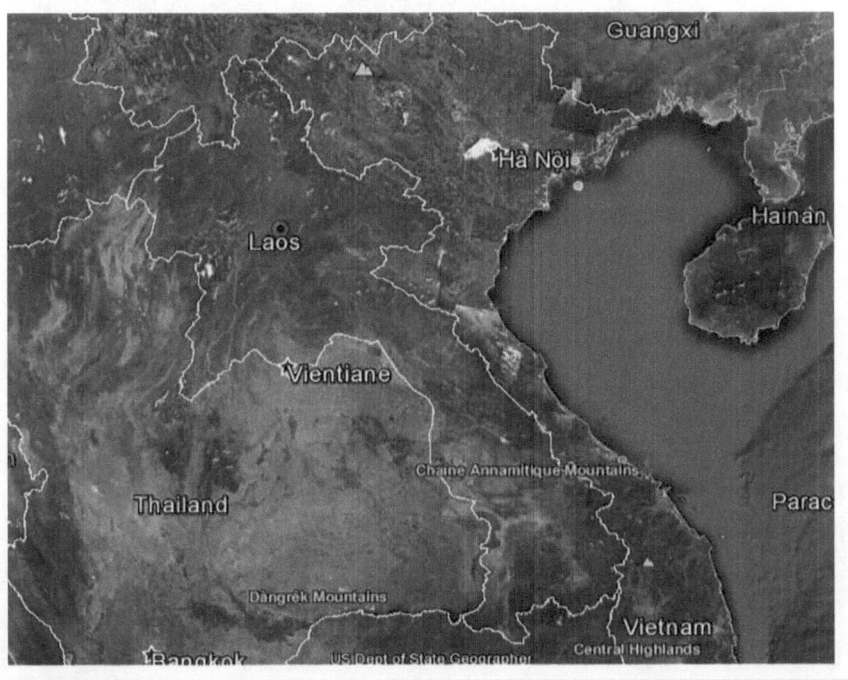

Laos Today

The bulbous top part of the country was known as Barrel Roll while the lower elongated part was known as Steel Tiger. The western part was reserved for Air Force Ops, and the eastern part was the Navy's responsibility.

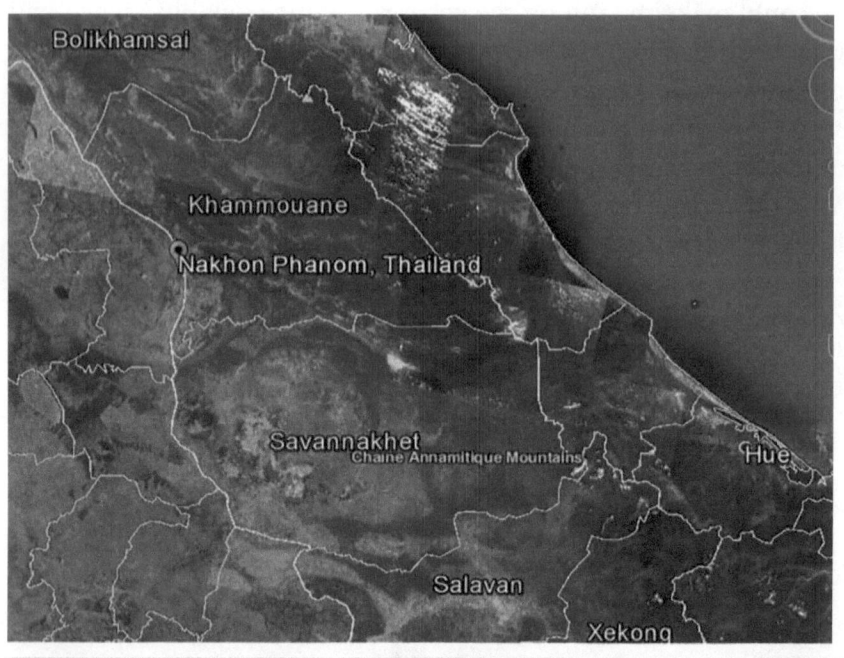

Nakhon Phanom, Thailand.

This town was home to the 7th Air Force's Task Force Alpha at the Royal Thai AB. Data from all the sensors implanted along the Ho Chi Minh Trail were sent there for processing and were used by the Sparky FACs to put strikes in on logistics operations moving along the Trail. In the case of the A-6, which carried the AMTI (Airborne Moving Target Indicator), as well as the A-6C's optical and ignition sensors, the aircraft could, theoretically, at least, actually see the convoy and bomb it directly. However, there were problems with this. After a while, even when secure radio was used, the convoys would stop before the A-6 could release on the DMPI (We heard later that the North Vietnamese actually used signal lights, which they turned red when they heard static on our frequencies—all you could hear if you didn't have the key to decrypt the transmission.) so there would be no moving target for the equipment to detect.[6] When the B/N realized that he had no moving targets, he had to switch his scope back over to the regular radar display, reacquire his final aimpoint, and begin tracking it so he could correct the ground speed velocity vector calculated by the computer with inputs from the INS and/or Doppler radar. All this time, the pilot had to fly the aircraft as smoothly and accurately as he could in accordance with steering queues the computer would provide him on his VDI (Vertical Display Indicator)—a device that looked like a TV screen with a roadway, ground texture, clouds, and all his attack symbology. At that point, the B/N would be told whether to drop long or short based on his estimated ToT (Time on Target). He would add that data to the ballistics computer and continued to keep his cursors (range and azimuth) on the aimpoint until the computer sent the release signal to the bomb racks. Once the bombs left the aircraft, the B/N would call, "Bombs away," and the pilot would add power and climb up to a safe altitude, rolling the aircraft inverted so that both of them could look at the ground through the top of the canopy. Then, they had to report their results. Typically, you'd want to see secondary explosions or fires, indicating something had exploded and/or begun to burn. The jungle wouldn't do that, so it meant the crew had successfully executed their attack on that convoy, and yes, people had just died or were maimed. It was part of the job. And just maybe, we gave a GI or Marine down south a better chance of surviving his tour.

The Commando Nail mission was almost the same, except the target was a set of coordinates with a description (the B/N was never given the altitude in those days, so he would usually pick it off an air navigation chart—more on that during the discussion of the next cruise), and he would do all the planning needed to execute a full system attack against

---

6. Then our first deployment with the A-6C was made during the Southwest Monsoon season in SEA (generally, June–September), probably not the best time of year to evaluate optical sensors. No B/N that I talked to in VA-165 was ever able to use any of the extra sensors carried in the A-6C in actual combat, although they seemed to work fine over the Gulf. I picked up *America* at about 80 NM on FLIR.

that target. As the photograph below reveals, visual bombing during the Southwest Monsoon was usually not possible, so FAC missions were scarce. Some days, only the A-6s and the E-2 Hawkeye air control aircraft would launch, although our F-4s would launch every day to go up north and fly BARCAP (Barrier Combat Air Patrol) missions to ensure the North Vietnamese would not make an air attack on our ships.[7]

A Picture Ed Took of His Wingman During a Commando Nail Mission Just South of the DMZ. Note the Weather.

---

7. Our Air Wing Commander, or CAG as he was called in every wing, was a fighter guy, and he had decided that we would hang no bombs on his fighters. They would carry their air-to-air missiles (Navy F-4s had no gun) and be ready to engage MiGs. Of course, that cruise, they never saw one but spent all their time up in the northern part of the Gulf flying their BARCAP race track patterns until it was time to return to the ship. And then do it all over again the next day. By the end of that cruise, the fighter jocks were screaming for bombs!

Boomer 503 is dropping on our bombs because his system was down, although his radar worked. The B/N in 503 that day was my mentor in VA-165, second cruise B/N LT Bruce "Boxman" Wood. Later he told me he thought I had done well, and it meant a lot, coming from someone I admired so much.

Unfortunately, due to the cloud cover, we almost never were able to observe any secondary explosions or fires. That did not please the Intel guys back on the ship. But we didn't lie to them just to make them happy or inflate our combat results for the politicians, either.

During the planning stages for a mission, the B/N would work out all of his backup data in the event of some form of system failure, which we have seen, was almost inevitable prior to reaching the target. While he could usually make some sort of system attack with almost any failure of some part of the system, the B/N had to be prepared for a MRL (Manual Range Line) attack in the event of a computer failure.

In the A-6A, B, & C models, the computer's heart was a rotating drum with read/write heads on it, which had to spin at an unbelievably high RPM (12,000?) in order to operate. Given the level of heat and humidity in SEA during the Southwest Monsoon, both were extraordinarily high, and the memory drums often stopped turning—a fatal error of the computer. Those aircraft also had rotating number dials for the numerical displays, and they were also prone to sticking. So many times, the B/N didn't have access to certain numbers in a readout because they were stuck. So MRL attacks were made quite a lot. The B/N would work out an attack azimuth which would give him the best view of the OAP he intended to use—preferably beyond the target itself so they wouldn't fly over it before "bombs away." Then, he would calculate the altitude of the attack and add the slant range of the fall of his bombs from a table created by NWC (Naval Weapons Center), Dahlgren, Virginia, plus ½ of the length of his "stick" (the length of the bomb load on the ground). He would dial that number into his radar, which would fix the range line at that range. This would theoretically put the midpoint of the stick on his target, if all the flight parameters were maintained by the pilot.

Of course, due to wind, the B/N would have to talk the pilot onto his azimuth line on the radar, which also wouldn't move. Looking into the scope, the B/N would see the cursors fixed (the range line at the value he had calculated and the azimuth line through the axis of the aircraft) and plowing along the ground as the aircraft flew. He had then to identify his OAP and direct the pilot to turn slightly as required to keep his azimuth line running through that point. Often, with experienced crews, this would, toward the end game, result in hand signals from the B/N to the pilot, who could tell from experience how much to turn—all the while, trying to maintain the preplanned altitude. When the OAP reached the MRL (Manual Range Line), the B/N would say, "Bombs away," and the pilot would press the pickle button on his stick. As incredible as it may seem, this method really did work, if the crew could do it. One night with no computer at all, Jay and I performed this maneuver on a "suspected truck park" and achieved four medium secondary explosions.

LT(jg) Engle in Boomer 504 Aboard USS *America* (CVA-66) in the Gulf of Tonkin

TO NORTH VIETNAM AND BACK AGAIN

Note the charts beside the B/N's console and the canopy. Radar scope photography was kept on his kneeboard.

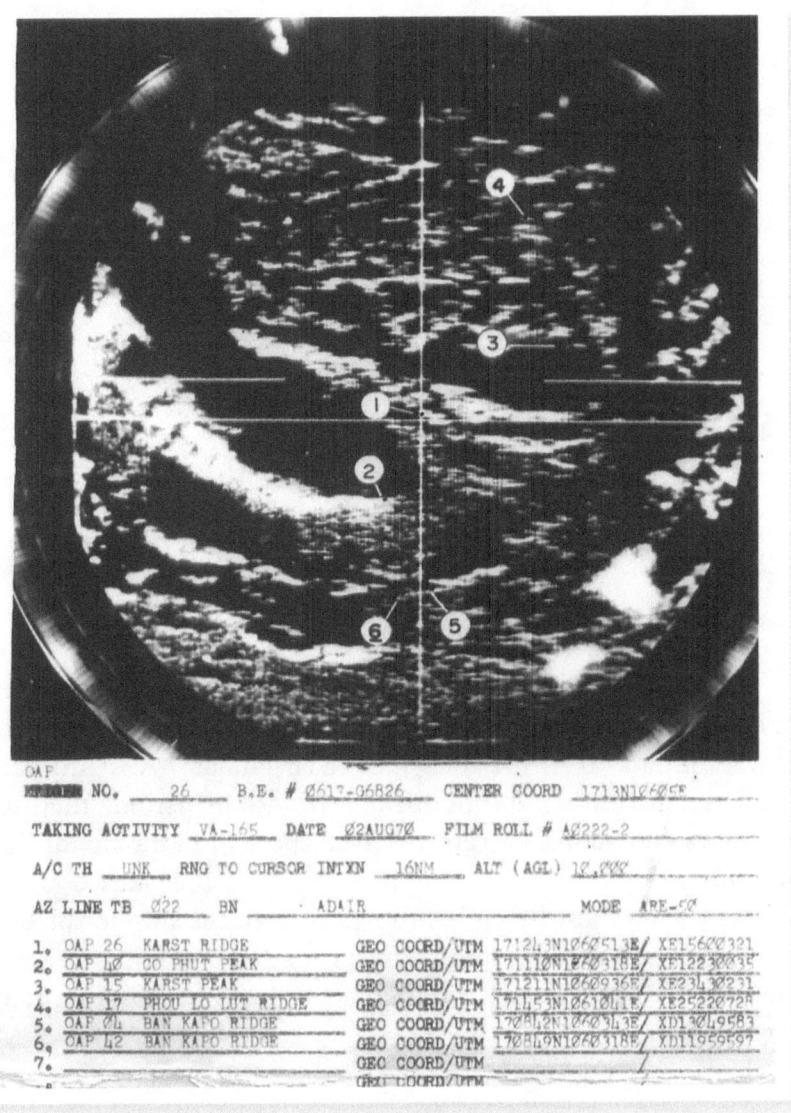

Kneeboard Card of RSP (Radar Scope Photography) Showing OAP 26

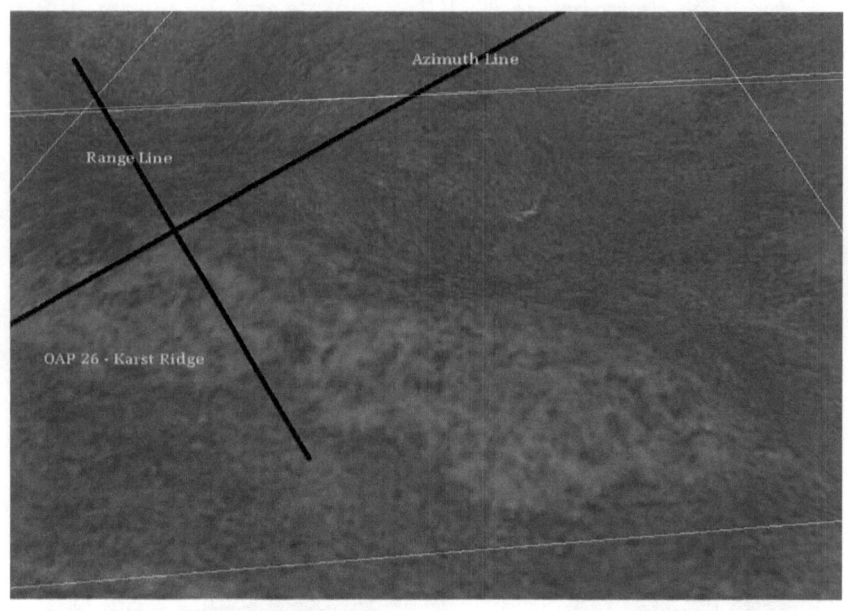

OAP 26 in Laos Today with Azimuth and Range Lines Approximately
Matching the Placement by a B/N during System Attack

Enemy response during these missions was almost nonexistent. In the South and in Laos in 1970, the North Vietnamese had neither SAMs (Surface-to-Air Missiles) nor radar-guided AAA (Antiaircraft Artillery), so during the Southwest Monsoon period, they really couldn't see us because we either stayed above or in the clouds. It was becoming very easy to be complacent. The feeling started creeping in that we were just flying bomb trucks from the ship to the beach, delivering our payloads, and flying back again, land, maybe watch a movie in the ready room, and then get up the next day and do it all over again.

When fall finally arrived, the weather began to clear, and we were "fragged"[8] more often to work with the FACs flying over Eastern Steel Tiger. Occasionally, these very brave men would fly out to visit with us on the ship. We always took first-class care of them and learned to work with them much closer. A few of them even got rides in one of our aircraft, if the mission was noncombat and not a maintenance test hop. They were from the 23rd TAS (Tactical Air Support Squadron), stationed at RTAB Nakhon Phanom, call sign Nail followed by a unique number, which they never changed. So many times, when we checked in and got their call sign, it was someone we knew well. A very positive and effective relationship developed between us, and it resulted in a lot of positive results from our visual bombing efforts. They always liked the bomb loads we hauled over to them because they worked with a lot of Air Force F-4s, which didn't carry near the bomb load of the A-6. Some of our B/Ns even flew with them during their tours with TFA. When they returned, we could get detailed info on how they flew and operated. It really was a great fit between us.

During this cruise, due to the political climate, we only flew missions in Laos and sometimes South Vietnam. A few of our crews did actually get the opportunity to do some close air support with Army FACs in South Vietnam, when their units were being hard-pressed by the Viet Cong and/or Regular North Vietnamese Army. When those missions were undertaken, our SOPs (Standard Operating Procedures) from CVW-9 went out the window because American lives were at stake. Generally, we would not fly lower than the top of the automatic weapons effective altitude because that was our greatest threat in those areas. But when American lives were at stake, all that changed, and putting our bombs precisely where they were needed became the priority. On those missions, we were also

---

8. The Navy received a "fragment" of the overall Air OPORDER issued by the 7th Air Force every day which covered our missions and targets for the following day. So the phrase "fragged" was born to describe a mission to which a sortie had been assigned. Unlike the Army, we weren't talking about a disgruntled soldier throwing a grenade into his officer's tent.

authorized to make multiple runs and most did so, dropping only two or three bombs a pass, while carrying anywhere from 12–18 Mk 82s.[9] The Army FACs loved our bomb trucks because we provided them with a lot of in-close firepower over an extended period.

One night, after dropping our bombs, we rendezvoused with the Skipper, CDR Dick Zick. It was a moonless night, with few clouds, and an ocean of stars in the sky. Jay was flying in parade formation on the Skipper's right wing somewhere near the provincial capital of Hue in South Vietnam in a left turn when he announced he had a bad case of vertigo. He told me he was absolutely convinced that we were inverted and heading toward the ground. Now, I had been trained in aviation medicine about this phenomenon and knew the only way for a person to shake it was to concentrate and trust his instruments. Jay couldn't even look at his because he was in parade formation on the Skipper's wing. So I started telling him, in the calmest voice I could muster, what they said: "We're in a gentle left turn at 20° of bank in an upright attitude," etc. It worked. Jay calmed down and was ready to shoot the Case III approach to the ship when we got back. We were given terrific training, and it really helps to have a copilot.

CVW-9 did suffer some losses during this cruise even in the benign environment in which we flew, but they were more operational losses than combat losses. For example, we would carry Mk-82s with both a mechanical nose fuse (M-904), much like those used in WWII, and an electrical tail fuse. The latter had reliability issues. For example, there was a 1 in 10,000 chance that one of them could detonate at the expiration of safe arming delay time, which would just be a few seconds. Since bombs actually fly with the aircraft which dropped them for quite a while before they begin to increase their separation, we were restricted from dropping them in a SPL (Straight Path Level) attack, unless the pilot executed a 4 G breakaway after "bombs away." One of our crews apparently forgot that restriction and did not execute the breakaway maneuver. Well, they found one of the 1 in 10,000 failure fuses, and it detonated just below the aircraft. While they suffered a lot of damage, they were able to nurse the

---

9.   500 lb LDGPs (low drag general purpose bombs).

airplane into Da Nang and actually walk away from it. We sent in a maintenance crew to survey the damage, and they declared it "strike damage" (damage sufficient to not be economically repairable—to be stricken from the operational inventory). So that airplane was put on a barge and sent out to us on *America*, loaded onto the hangar bay, and shipped back to CONUS when we returned home when the cruise ended. It never flew again.

Typhoon

One day, we learned that the ship had to depart the Gulf of Tonkin and head out into the South China Sea for maneuvering room because a typhoon was approaching. Furthermore, we learned that Da Nang, which only had one very long North-South runway, was closed due to excessive crosswinds. That meant that we had to have so much fuel in order to fly to an alternate field in Thailand that we would be too heavy to land on the ship: we either had to land or swim. What a choice! In addition, Jay and I flew off at night for our target, which really wasn't worth the trouble, and had to make a Case III nighttime recovery. Flying back, we were surrounded by clouds, even at high altitudes. St. Elmo's Fire glowed on the windscreen and leading edges of the wings which began to make our radio crackle.

Despite the interference, we were able to contact the ship and got a vector for our marshal position and flew there to begin to set up for our push (penetration) time. Jay, of course, was flying instruments, and I was heads up in the cockpit, when I saw an A-4 in plain view fly right across our flight path through a hole in the clouds. I immediately called CATC and told them our marshal pattern was intersecting with another ship's. They apparently didn't know that and had to reset everything to maintain separation. Meanwhile, we were burning fuel and getting closer and closer to empty. Remember, we already had to fly a lot farther both to and from the target that night, so our fuel state was beginning to be a concern.

Finally, we were given a new marshal pattern and push time, and Jay hit it right on the money. I never understood how he figured it out, but he always got to our push point with no more than a few seconds of error. So down we came through those clouds. At times, I couldn't see our wing tip lights. And of course, we were glowing like plankton in the Caribbean. When we hit 5,000 feet, I called "platform," and Jay slowed down and "dirtied up" (i.e., dropped the landing gear, put out the slats and flaps, dropped the tailhook, and deployed the speed brakes, which I couldn't see clearly). Flying on instruments, Jay put our aircraft right in the groove as our approach controller gave us small corrections all the way down. Now, a carrier instrument approach has minimums of 100 feet and ¾ mile visibility, so at ¾ of a mile, the approach controller always tells the approaching aircraft to "call the ball" since that is the point to take over visually. Jay and I had a longstanding agreement that he would never break his instrument scan until I told him that I had the ball, where it was (high or low), and where we were for lineup (right or left and how much). But this night, when the approach controller told us to call the ball, I couldn't see it, so I said nothing, meaning Jay would continue to fly instruments, which he did. Several seconds went by until I finally saw the ball and the deck. I called, "Ball," and we immediately touched down. I know Jay never had a chance to acquire the ball himself, but he had us set up so well, we landed perfectly. When I got out of the cockpit, I was tempted to kiss the deck, but I resisted. It never felt so good to be back aboard!

HO, HO, Uncle HO!
Can Your SAMS Come Out to Play Today?
By Hugh Replogle, CDR, USN, Ret

For the SE Asia deployment in 1970, VA-165 got a collection of A-6 "variants." In addition to eight A-6Cs, we also got three specially configured A-6 aircraft that were wired with a system to fire the "Standard[10]-ARM (Anti-Radiation Missile). These were standard

---

10. The word refers to the missile, which the Navy surface fleet had developed initially for air defense of the Fleet. This is the same missile body, which destroyers and cruisers launched. It was so big, the A-6 was the only aircraft in the Fleet which could carry it, and they carried two on a typical Iron Hand mission.

A-6 aircraft that were equipped with special sensors to detect and locate antiaircraft defense system radars. These three aircraft were designated A-6 B-PAT(s) (for Passive Angle Tracking).

The Standard ARM was a "super-Shrike," designed to home in on designated radars emitting a signal. In these aircraft, the B/N would set up the sensors to detect radars (usually the "Fan-Song" radars associated with the Soviet Surface to Air (SAM) missiles that North Vietnam used) that were "emitting" and possibly tracking our aircraft or some other aircraft. Once detected, the B/N would "tune" the missile to lock onto that radar signal, and then the missile could be launched to fly to and dive on (and explode twenty feet above) the detected radar site—whatever it might be, from a search radar to any antiaircraft tracking and guidance radars. The idea was to take out the enemy air-defense radars, without which their air defenses would be greatly inhibited.

The missile could fly a couple of flight profiles and could reach out seventy miles or better to attack a radar site that it had been "tuned" to home in on. Even if the radar site shut down, the missile's "memory" would continue to try to fly to the last-remembered targeted position, and *boom*! Maybe one less enemy radar system site—maybe. The North Vietnamese (possibly with other nation's technical advisors) knew about this retaliatory capability and did not like it much. That psychological threat was a key to our effectiveness.

Five crews were specially trained to fly the A-6B "birds" on the missions where they were needed.

The "Standard-ARM" missiles were *big* and *expensive* (and heavy). The A-6Bs launched mostly on what were called Iron Hand missions primarily, in support of photo-reconnaissance RA-5C aircraft which were ordered in for special photo sweeps of particular targets or areas that higher authority wanted high resolution imagery of. Our job, in the A-6Bs, was to cover their flight track and attack anything that tried to take a shot at them with electronically controlled AAA (Antiaircraft Artillery) systems.

The A-6B crews, in conjunction with the RA-5C crews, worked out a system where, with two A-6Bs with Standard-ARM missiles, we could cover the RA-5 aircraft in such a way that we covered the area in front of him and the area behind him at all times. We made an effort to use a discrete IFF code and let it "slip out" who we were. We also came up on the communications frequencies and talked it up so the "listeners" (North Vietnamese and friends) would know that we were the Iron Hand (ARM) shooters and what we were there for.

Over the course of the six months on station in the war zone, we A-6B crews escorted numerous photo recce missions and additional strike missions.

We never fired an ARM missile.

The photo birds and other aircraft under our escort were *never* taken under fire by any electronically controlled AAA system. None of the photo birds ever sustained any battle damage, and at the end of the cruise, they all went home alive.

Without having to expend one very expensive missile, the electronic air defense radar systems over North Vietnam declined to "radiate" for the time we were escorting the photo pilots doing their mission or other specialized missions.

Mission effective?

The CAG was ambivalent:

"What the hell did you accomplish?"

"You never launched an ARM on anything."

"Ya' got no BDA (Battle Damage Assessment) on anything!"

The CO of the RA-5C squadron was pleased. All his aircraft and crews went home.

Was the mission a success? You decide.

Note by Ed Engle: The reader should note that these A-6B crews had to return their missiles to the ship due to their expense, and that meant that they were at or below Bingo fuel (minimum fuel to reach an alternate airfield ashore) for their first landing attempt because every pound of missile was a pound less fuel. That's pretty gutsy stuff, and they deserved high praise for their efforts, but like many things in the Navy, they were never recognized for their bravery.

Task Force Alpha and Home

Line period melted into line period, and I found myself with TFA over in Nakhon Phanom during the last one. Our new Administrative Officer, my pilot, Jay Grafton, wrote me a set of orders authorizing me to catch a MAC (Military Airlift Command) flight out of Bangkok if I couldn't get back to the ship before they departed for CONUS. It turned out that I couldn't get from NKP, as we called it, all the way to the other side of the country, Bangkok, and work my way back to the ship before she had sailed, so I very soon found myself on a MAC charter flight operated by Continental Airlines. While they served no alcohol on the flight, we did have good-looking flight attendants and comfortable seats for our long flight back to CONUS. We stopped for a leg stretch and fuel on Midway Island after over eighteen hours of flight time from Bangkok. We were all glad to get off the plane for a little while. Then, we took off for Travis AFB, California. For some reason, I was shocked when we crossed the beach at San Francisco Bay: there were no bomb craters—anywhere! My rational brain told me that that was the way it should be, but I had been staring down at so much torn-up real estate over the last seven months that it just looked odd.

After we deplaned, I found someone with whom to share a cab into the San Francisco International Airport and got a seat on an Alaskan Airlines flight to Seattle. I called Peggy, gave her my arrival info, and boarded the plane for the final leg of my journey home. It was a great homecoming, except that I found I couldn't sleep because there were no ship noises and the birds would wake me up because they seemed strange—not the mechanical sounds of fans, tie-down chains hitting a steel deck, or the screams of the bomb elevators, but the birds. I suppose it's about what you get used to. But it was certainly great to be home and try and get reacquainted with my wife and the kids, who were now almost 6, 4, and 1½ (Jeannine, Steven, and Greta, respectively).

Rebuilding and Retraining

In those days, after a carrier would return from a cruise, the ship would go into restricted available while she detached crewmen and accepted new ones, and the squadrons she had carried followed suit. So when the rest of VA-165 returned from their around the world cruise, I happily stepped up to take on the duties of SDO (Squadron Duty Officer) every few days to give those guys the chance that I had had earlier with their families. Bachelors tended to complete their introduction back into CONUS society elsewhere—many in Seattle. Of course, we also began transferring officers to new positions in other places in the Navy, processing others out to civilian life, and accepting new officers and men into the Squadron. It was a time of great transition, and I found myself now assuming the role of the veteran in the Squadron, while I watched my mentors depart for other positions.

Strangely, and I have never learned why this happened, our Air Force officers were replaced by a new pair. The pilot was Capt. Lee Hiser, and the navigator was Maj. Sid Dodd. Stranger still, Sid moved into the house next door to us on Rainier Drive, and our wives became fast friends as did Sid and I. Sid had come from F-111s—an Air Force plane which was designed to go in alone, fast, and low, just like the Navy's A-6, only much faster (it had afterburners and could go supersonic). Neither Jerry, Sid's wife, nor Peggy had had any sisters, and they each fell into that role easily.

Dan Graham joined the squadron while the ship was transiting back to Norfolk. He was tasked with getting our A-6Cs ready to transition to VA-35 based at NAS Oceana, Virginia. During this period, he was able to get himself designated a maintenance test pilot. Very early in this period, he found that an aircraft declared "ready to fly" had a control pushrod missing. That got the current QA (Quality Assurance) office fired and replaced by Dan, who was a senior LT due to his being kept in NATC (Naval Air Training Command) to teach air-to-air tactics.

Up until this point, VA-165, as well as most of the A-6 Community, was still strongly influenced by the old heavy attack

(A-3s) and ASW (S-2s) communities due to many of their pilots transitioning over to the A-6. In their old aircraft, they almost always flew solo missions, and therefore, so did we. That was all to change because we had a new CAG, CDR Gus Eggert, who was given top priority to integrating the new Top Gun concept of overall air superiority into Air Wing 9 using the new Top Gun graduates (like LT Randy Cunningham of VF-96) to help develop a new air superiority attitude in the Wing. Dan was instrumental in transitioning VA-165 into this new philosophy, writing the SOP (Standard Operating Procedure) for A-6 section (two aircraft in formation) takeoffs, which was later placed verbatim into the NATOPS manual.

I, however, was still flying with Jay, and Dan's B/N was a nugget named Mike Flanagan. By now, Jay had become a division (four planes in two sections) leader, and the squadron did its best to schedule sections and divisions together for training missions. So Dan and I rarely flew together. But there are exceptions to every rule, and the following is one of them.

For some reason that I do not remember, Dan and I were scheduled to fly a single plane night low level to our bombing range at Boardman, Oregon, through the Cascade Mountains. I remember gearing up in the locker room when one of our new pilots, LT Mike Eddy, recently joining us from A-4s, said while he strapped on his g-suit, that if anyone had told him a year ago that he would be flying a low-level mission through the mountains at night, he would have told them they were nuts. Yet here he and we were getting ready to do just that. While we had several aircraft on this event, we flew in stream (separate takeoffs and separation on the route). Dan and I launched and headed east into the Cascades.

Typical Valley in the Cascades Looking East

Once we let down into the mountains, I was concentrating on my radar picture to provide terrain avoidance to Dan, but I noticed that the shadows I was looking at didn't seem long enough, and checking our altitude, I noticed that Dan was flying at around 1,000 feet AGL (Above Ground Level). It took a little while for him to trust me, but he eventually did, and we continued at some pretty low altitudes. I looked up from my scope once out the right side of the aircraft and saw ridgelines of granite flying by well over my head, so I immediately stuck my head back in the scope. We eventually got down to Boardman, dropped our bombs, and flew IFR with Seattle Center back to Whidbey Island and debriefed. It was to be a very important training mission for Dan and I when we got back into combat.

TO NORTH VIETNAM AND BACK AGAIN

Scene from the B/N's Side during a Low-Level Training Flight

Remember, we did this at night too.
Our new CVW-9 consisted of:

VF-92 F-4J
VF-96 F-4J
VA-146 A-7E
VA-147 A-7E
VA-165 A-6A & KA-6D
RVAH-11 RA-5C
VAQ-130 Det 1 EKA-3B
VAW-116 E-2B
HC-1 Det 3 SH-3G

Morale in VA-165 was extremely high. We had won the first two Navy Es for excellence awarded to the West Coast A-6 squadrons, and everyone felt we were part of a very special and elite group. After watching the interviews of the veterans of the real *Band of*

Brothers, I would say that we felt much as they did. If you had to go to war, you really wanted the very best guys around you—and we certainly had that. Our deployment with the rest of Air Wing 9 for visual weapons training at NAF Fallon, Nevada, 16–30 July '71, only made our morale stronger and raised VA-165's esteem in the eyes of the squadrons remarkably. On the 30th, we flew over to NAS North Island in San Diego, California, to start workups with our new ship USS *Constellation* (CVA-64). This lasted from 2–31 August, and we were generally in port on the weekends, so some of the families came down from Washington. My family drove down with Sid Dodd's in their big station wagon, and we had a great time. One night, since Jerri had never been on a ship, we took our wives to supper in Ward Room 1 (the formal one). I'll never forget Jerri's reaction when we arrived on the pier (Sid was driving). He stopped the car, and she said, "Well, where is the ship?"

Sid pointed to the island with the big "64" painted on it, and Jerri said, "That's the ship? I thought it was Building 64!"

We had a wonderful evening and gave our families a first-rate tour of the ship before heading back to the motel.

Jay and I had fused ourselves into a real team. He had even taught me how to fly the aircraft from the right seat, and by setting the throttles to Auto, I actually landed the aircraft on a straight-in approach to NAS Whidbey Island (Ault Field), so I knew if he were hit, I could get us both back to the ship and then eject him with some line I carried to pull his ejection handle before I ejected myself. Landing on the ship was not possible from the B/N's seat, but ejecting nearby would increase our chances of surviving. I think we both felt a lot better about our new plan and my new training.

Breaking the Sound Barrier

By now, I was a designated full system maintenance test B/N, which meant that I would fly an aircraft which had to be tested due to either major maintenance it had undergone or if it were newly introduced into our inventory as an acceptance test flight. There were also maintenance test certified pilots. Both types flew randomly together, as the schedule worked out. We would almost never fly with our regular crewmates on these test flights. The squadron had gotten in a newly reworked aircraft from NARF (Naval Air Rework Facility) Alameda, California, and it was undergoing inspections by the various branches of our maintenance department and would soon need an acceptance test flight. LT Jim Workman and I were assigned to the job. As I recall, we briefed this flight on a Thursday afternoon, but maintenance did not release it for the test flight. The same thing happened on Friday and Saturday. Then, on Sunday morning, the SDO (Squadron Duty Officer) called Jim and I to come in and perform the test flight. Neither of us thought it would actually be released, but it was; and we soon found ourselves airborne on a crystal-clear, dry, sparkling Pacific Northwest Sunday morning with just about no one else in the sky with us, flying a beautiful acrylic-painted A-6A with no stores on the pylons at all.

We soon completed all of our tests, which included engine shutdowns and relights at about 40,000 feet. I called Seattle Center and requested a high-speed descent back to Ault Field on Whidbey Island. They eagerly approved, and Jim pulled the nose up, dropped the left wing, and put the plane into a nearly 90° dive straight at the tower at Ault Field. Down we came, accelerating rapidly with the engines at 100 percent power. Suddenly, I noticed a rumbling noise I had never heard in the almost 1,000 hours I had in the aircraft and noticed vapor streaming over the canopy from the metal canopy bow just behind the windshield, but nothing seemed to be out of limits, so we continued until Jim pulled up, I called the tower, and we flew downwind into the break for a visual landing on the duty runway. We taxied in, declared the plane ready for operational flights, and went to the ready room for the debrief. The SDO was furious at us because he had been getting calls from the wing duty officer about our "booming" the tower (i.e., flying by the tower at supersonic speed to hit it with the leading and trailing edge shock waves). Jim and I just laughed, reminding him that the A-6 Intruder had no upper speed limit since it was "drag limited" (i.e., it had too much drag and too little power to exceed Mach 1). So we went home.

That was not the end of it, however. Later that night, I got a phone call from Jay, who was now our ops officer, and he said he had been called in about the complaint. He had calculated our flight data in conjunction with the state of the air at the time of our dive and discovered that, in all likelihood, we did, in fact, break the sound barrier and boomed the tower. To the best of my knowledge, we were the only ones to have ever done that, so Jim was labeled with the call sign Boom Boom for the twin supersonic booms. Jim and I were to room together for the next cruise on Connie.

New Tactic

Another thing we did in VA-165 to improve our tactics against moving targets was to experiment with glide bombing at OLF Coupeville, the field we used to prepare for landing on the ship located just a short distance from Ault Field. One of our pilots, LT Dave Waggoner, drove his pickup truck over to the field one night with a handheld radio, while Jay and I flew over there to try and find and "attack" him with our system. He was easy to locate, and I was able to lock him up with our tracking radar while initiating a full system mock attack against him. Jay started down in a shallow dive from about 5,000 feet AGL with the engines at idle and continued down until the bomb tone went off, indicating that the computer would have dropped our bombs. At that point, he went to 100 percent on both engines and climbed out. We performed this profile multiple times, and Dave told us he never heard us until we started our climb, but by then, the bombs would have been on their way. This became our tactic of choice for attacking movers along the Ho Chi Minh Trail at night.

KA-6Ds

A KA-6D Landing Ashore: Note the Refueling
Basket Stowed in Its Housing

To replace both KA-3B and EA-3B Skywarrior during the early 1970s, seventy-eight A-6As and twelve A-6Es were converted for use as tanker aircraft, providing aerial refueling support to other strike aircraft. The DIANE system was removed and an internal refueling system was added, sometimes supplemented by a D-704 refueling pod on the centerline pylon. The KA-6D theoretically could be used in the day/visual bombing role, but it never was, with the standard load-out being four fuel tanks. Because it was based on a tactical aircraft platform, the KA-6D provided a capability for mission tanking, the ability to keep up with strike packages and refuel them in the course of a mission. A few KA-6Ds went to sea with each Intruder squadron. Their operation was integrated into the Intruder squadrons, as A-6 crew were trained to operate both aircraft and the NATOPS covered both the A-6 and KA-6D. The fully-fueled

KA-6D carried 26,000 pounds of JP-5 in internal and five external tanks. During our deployment on Connie, one of our crews transferred 23,000 pounds in one mission (launching early to top off the departing fighters, refueling those returning, and landing immediately afterward—a Yo-Yo mission.)

So before long, it was once again time to deploy to SEA. My last night at home before moving the squadron down to San Diego to move aboard Connie, Peggy just wanted to cuddle, and that's what we did for most of the night. It was sweet, and it helped her face the future without me. The ship, with CVW-9 aboard, departed San Diego on 1 October 1971.

Second Combat Deployment

During our transit to the Philippines, we endured many lectures on topics from aircraft and ship recognition to MiG performance characteristics to effective rates of fire and ranges of AAA guns and the various SAMs we thought the Russians might have given to the North Vietnamese. These lectures, usually followed by quizzes, were seemingly endless. But by the end of October 1971, we finally did arrive in the Philippines and tied up at the carrier pier at NAS Cubi Point in Subic Bay. We had flown off a few aircraft, and the flight crews got to fly a bit to knock the rust off our skills. But by 4 November, we were once again in the Gulf of Tonkin.

My first mission with Jay this time was with a FAC, dropping twelve MK82 LDGPs and achieving no results on a riverbank. This time, though, we were carrying a Shrike ARM because there had been rumors of SAMs along the Trail this time. The next day was pretty much the same with no results due to smoke. So the war at this time, at least to us, wasn't very exciting. We just loaded up our "bomb truck," flew over to somewhere in Laos, dropped everything we had, and flew back—usually with no BDA to speak of.

On 12 November, I left the ship and traveled to RTAB Nakhon Phanom to once again act as a Sparky FAC.

This time, after getting settled in, I was introduced to a PhD-type from the Air Force Map Service in St. Louis, Missouri, who asked me to document all of the radar OAPs the A-6 B/Ns were using along the Trail. He sat me down in a big chair with a binocular-like device attached, a huge machine that reminded me of an x-ray machine. I had control wheels to move the stereo pictures around until I got the OAP I was looking for under a reticule etched into the viewer. Once I had it, I hit a button, and a diamond stylus punched a small hole in the film while recording the exact latitude/longitude and altitude of that point. Then, I would move on to the next OAP. I kept at it until I had everything entered into their database.

Then I compared some of them with the results from their computer for bearing, range, and differential altitude between the OAP and the DMPIs which I had with me on a kneeboard card. I remember in one case the range difference between the data on my kneeboard card and their database (a photogrammetric mathematical data base) was some 3,000 feet! I remarked to the PhD that I had obviously done something wrong, and we'd have to figure that out and fix it before we could use the data operationally. He responded by asking why I thought I had made a mistake since the data on my kneeboard card had been measured from charts produced from pre–WWII French surveys.

This and further technical discussions with him revealed that charts do not permit the kind of precision measurements which we required for bombing. Back on the ship, the Intel guys would not make measurements from the photographs and light tables they had; because just about the time they would get everything aligned, a catapult would fire, and the shuttle would hit the water brake, shaking the whole ship and knocking their photos out of alignment with the computer. So we were forced to use charts to measure everything. Now that I knew that couldn't be done and expect to gain any kind of accuracy, I began searching for an alternative.

Connie left the line and spent 21–28 November in port at NAS Cubi Point.

After I returned to the ship, which was now back on the line on the twenty-ninth, I brought this up with the squadron, and we decided to have the senior B/N on the last event of the night, take all the next day's Commando Nail targets with him and have the Sparky FAC B/N on duty at NKP run all of them through the computer and provide the airborne B/N with all the offset data for the next day's runs. It was amazing how our BDA improved! We began achieving great results on almost every run now. Despite what many opponents of the A-6 concept said about our accuracy, it was never the bombing system. It was all about mission planning and the lack of tools provided us on the ship to do it properly. Worse yet, the A-6 Community had never realized the problem, and the subject was not being taught in the RAG. While the Community probably remained ignorant of our discovery, VA-165 used the new precise method and achieved greatly improved results for the duration of this cruise.

VA-165 Officers Taken on the Flight Deck of
USS *Constellation* (CVA-64) Early Spring 1972
LT Ed Engle is circled on the left. LT Dan Graham is circled on the right—just as they would fly in the A-6. LCDR Grafton is standing behind LT Engle without the hat in the back row. Major Sid Dodd is on the far left, and Captain Lee Hiser is the fifth officer from the right in the back row.

Connie was back on the line by the twenty-ninth, when I rejoined them from NKP. All through the month of December, we had lousy weather and mostly were unable to work with any FACs. System bombing above the clouds usually resulted in RNO (Results Not Observed) for our BDA reports. On 12 December, Jay and I were flying way up north in Laos on a weather reconnaissance for CAG, who had been having the Air Wing fly "Blue Tree" missions. These were basically a photo reconnaissance by one of our RA-5Cs into North Vietnam, supported by a heavy package of fighters and attack aircraft. If they were shot at, the RoE (Rules of Engagement) allowed them to shoot back, and they always did. On this day, we also carried sixteen Mk 82 LDGPs, which I dropped on a Commando Nail mission, but it was another RNO WX (Weather). However, during our flight, we received MiG alerts and got some SA-2 radar indications on our ECM (Electronic Counter-Measures) gear. Missions were definitely getting more exciting!

One night, returning from another routine mission, Jay flew what I thought to be a good pass, but we boltered (i.e., failed to catch a wire) and flew off the deck to enter the pattern downwind for another look at the deck. Jay was always fond of gamesmanship, and this flight proved to be no exception. He told me to cheat on telling the ship our fuel state. At that time with the A-6A, we were fairly severely weight restricted for carrier landings and couldn't come aboard with much fuel. So we were already on the low fuel side for the first pass, and each additional pass would typically cost about 1,500 pounds of JP-5. That didn't leave the fuel for many passes at the deck. But this particular night, I was telling the ship that we were only burning 500–1,000 pounds for each pass, which was a bold-faced lie. Jay was confident he could get aboard, so why would I argue with him? Unfortunately, despite three more passes, we didn't get aboard, and the ship bingoed us to Da Nang (this was the last recovery of the night, so we would have to spend the night). Jay immediately cleaned up the aircraft, added full power, and started climbing for the airfield while I broke out the checklist and reviewed our bingo flight parameters. I believe we leveled off at 42,000 feet. By now, our fuel was almost exhausted, and the Low Fuel light came on with over 100 NM to go to our bingo field. Things were getting tense!

But the A-6 was a peculiar aircraft: the tables told you how much fuel the aircraft would burn under certain conditions, but at high altitude, we always burned a great deal less than the tables said we were supposed to. This night was no exception. At 42,000 feet, we seemed to be making fuel, despite that glowing Low Fuel light. I contacted Da Nang approach control, but Jay talked to them. He told them to give him line up but ignore his glide slope because he was going to come in high and drop down steeply at the last minute. They agreed, and that's what he did. I felt like we were making a visual dive run on the end of the duty runway, but he greased the aircraft onto the tarmac, and we taxied free of it quickly since one of our RA-5Cs was behind us. As it turned out, the Vigilante flamed out on the taxiway before he could get onto the parking ramp, and we didn't.

We arranged to have the aircraft serviced by the Marines there, and we proceeded to the BOQ (Bachelor Officers' Quarters), which was a Quonset hut filled with bunk beds. Jay and I found an unused pair. I hung up my .45 on the head of the bed and tried to get to sleep, despite the rocket attack that was going on somewhere on the perimeter. I kept thinking we might have to hoof it to the slit trench, but the firing never came any closer, although I can't say I got a lot of sleep.

The next day, the ship gave us a "Charlie" (ramp) time; and we launched, made our time, and trapped on the first try. I don't know what happened with Jay the night before, but whatever it was, he had purged it from his system by the next morning. So our mission from the night before finally came to an end.

It was about this time that LT Randy Cunningham, a pilot in VF-96 and one of the new graduates of the Top Gun School at NAS Miramar, California, shot down his first MiG on a flak suppression mission in support of an RA-5C Blue Tree mission in North Vietnam at an airfield near their border with Laos just south of Barrel Roll. According to Randy, he was just pulling out after dropping his bombs on a flak site near the airfield when he saw something moving just above the jungle canopy. He rolled his F-4 upright and identified the mover as a MiG-17. He armed his AIM-9 Sidewinder air-to-air missile, got good tone, and fired. The missile ran true, and the MiG crashed.

The weather continued to be bad in Southeastern North Vietnam, even though we now had authorization from the Nixon Administration to start bombing up there to remove that area as a logistics sanctuary for the Regular North Vietnamese Army and the Viet Cong. So our CAG, CDR Gus Eggert, and several of the squadron skippers devised a plan to fly alpha strikes[11] into that area above the clouds, using A-6s as the pathfinders.

I flew the last event on Christmas Eve, Overhead Tanker,[12] with one of the nugget pilots, whom I don't recall, but we didn't make a great landing. He apologized to me all the way to the ready room, but I told him I really didn't care if the landing was pristine so long as we landed without breaking either the aircraft or ourselves. I don't think that stopped him from fretting about it, though. However, when the LSO arrived to debrief our pilots from the last recovery, he was wearing a Santa Claus suit and gave them all "OK - 3 Wire" grades—that's a 4.0 GPA.

The ship and air wing took Christmas off. Oddly, the weather was absolutely clear with unlimited visibility—the first day with that kind of weather in weeks. Most of us were sorry we didn't launch some alpha strikes up north on Christmas instead of taking it off. The ship hosted a "steel beach picnic" on the flight deck with charcoal grills and hamburgers and hot dogs and Aloha shirts and shorts

---

11. The alpha strike was a maximum effort strike devised earlier in the war before President Johnson's bombing halt was called in 1967, to fly a large number of aircraft in a fairly tight formation with each aircraft separated by a distance calculated to provide mutual support while minimizing the threat from the SA-2 SAM systems.
12. That mission is tasked with providing ready fuel for aircraft who are having trouble getting aboard. The extra fuel gives them more looks at the deck. Unfortunately, because of the skill of CVW-9 pilots, we wound up dumping most of the JP-5 so we could get light enough to land, rarely tanking anyone.

just like at home—sort of. VA-165 had a great party in our ready room.

Jay and I flew our first Pathfinder mission on 27 December. We had three A-7s on our wings, and we dropped sixty Mk-82 LDGPs on a POL facility at Quang Khe getting moderate 57mm radar-guided AAA during the run. Of course, our BDA was RNO WX, because our small window of good weather had closed. We flew another one of these on the twenty-ninth, dropping forty-six bombs this time on the Ta Tien POL facility with no reaction from the enemy noted, and RNO WX as a result. Interestingly, we discovered on the latter mission, with F-4Js on our wings, that they couldn't keep up with us when we hit our IP and started inbound to the target at full power (480 kts or so) without going to zone 1 afterburner (their J-79 engines had a total of three zones of afterburner); and they were only carrying six Mk-82s each, while we had twenty-two. We were slow to start with but didn't get a lot slower when they loaded us up.

Unfortunately, on this same day, our operations officer, LCDR Fred Holmes, and his B/N, LT Bill Burton, were shot down after being hit by an SA-2 Guideline missile which literally blew them out of their aircraft. LT Burton actually saw the warhead exploding below and to his right, but before he could initiate the ejection sequence, he found himself with his parachute deployed. He was rescued by a CSAR helicopter that was flying just off the coast near Vinh, NVN searching for the crew of a fighter that had been shot down an hour earlier when A-6 parts and a white parachute started coming down from the clouds nearby. The helo picked up LT Burton, and he was taken to the North SAR destroyer and then back to the Connie. After a couple days in sick bay and several debriefings, LT Burton was transferred back to CONUS. LCDR Holmes's orange-and-white-paneled parachute was spotted going into the cloud tops, but he was never seen under the clouds and was never recovered. His status was MIA until he was declared KIA well after the war ended. I attended the memorial service his wife organized when I was with VA-52.

These were very dangerous missions because aircrews couldn't spot the SAMs being fired on the ground. Rather, by the time they flew out of the undercast clouds, their boosters had already dropped off, and they were accelerating toward Mach 2. It didn't give you a lot of time to perform evasive maneuvers. Several A-7s had been lost in addition to our aircraft. Cooler heads prevailed, and this tactic was abandoned, and we went back to flying our usual mixture of Commando Nail, Bolt, and FAC missions. Since LCDR Holmes was gone, Jay was moved from administrative officer to operations officer once again.

Connie pulled out of the line for some R&R in the Philippines, 2–9 January '72.

I flew my next combat sortie the first day of our new line period, 10 January. We were supposed to work with a FAC over in Laos, but en route, we received ECM indications of a SAM launch while we were transiting at 20,000 feet in Laos! While we never saw them, we were diverted to Da Nang to debrief with 7th Air Force about the incident, and while we were there, we met an Air Force F-4 crew who apparently had been the target. The pilot told us he bent the airplane around at 10Gs. I don't know much about the F-4, but I'm quite sure he overstressed the airframe. We were definitely getting the impression that we weren't winning this war.

Four with Two Bombs

Jay and I flew a Commando Bolt on 26 January and were switched over to an Owl FAC (nighttime equivalent of the Nails), flying O-2s—the military equivalent of the Cessna 310—to probe a road segment. Our secure UHF radio capability was down so we had to use an encryption wheel we all carried to pass information like road segment location, etc. When we raised the Owl, he told us he had seen four trucks moving down this particular segment just a few minutes ago and wanted us to fly up it and see if we could detect them. Our B/N Sparky FAC at TFA advised us to "attack from Mount Vernon to Sedro Woolley"—a bearing reference to two towns not far from our base on Whidbey Island, and we were pretty sure the bad guys wouldn't know that. Frankly, I had little hope that we would be able to find anything because I never had before.

Jay flew around to get set up on the correct bearing while speaking with Owl, who told us he would hold high above the target while we made our run. He also told us to tell him before we dropped. Since I was running AMTI, I set up the ordnance panel for our 2 Mk20s, deselecting the 12 Mk 82 LDGPs. As Jay flew up the correct bearing to the road segment, he was in a shallow dive with the engines at idle, just like we had practiced back at Coupeville. I was getting very nervous because the range to the bombing point was rapidly approaching, and I had not detected a thing. Then, all of a sudden, at the bottom of a 10NM PPI display, a popcorn ball appeared. All I had time to do was slew the range cursor down to it with both rate buttons and step the system into attack. While doing that, though, I heard the track radar lock up on the target; and the Mk 20s (500-pound cluster bombs containing 220 small mortar-like projectiles, which could penetrate armor) dropped just a few seconds afterward—we were almost too close to be able to hit the target.

Jay instantly went to 100 percent on the engines and started a steep climb, screaming at me to set up the ordnance panel for the Mk 82s. We had rolled inverted as I was doing that, and I could look at the ground through the top of the canopy. Just a few low clouds were around, we could see the ground pretty well. We watched the bomblets go off like hundreds of Fourth of July sparklers, and I remember I had enough time to say, "Oh, sh——t!" when nothing happened after that. But then, the secondary explosions started, and we got four medium ones, evenly spaced. By then, Jay was looking for blood, so he rolled in "hot" and dropped the twelve Mk 82s we still had, once again pulling up in a steep climb. All kinds of death and destruction was unleashed as those 500-pound bombs exploded on the ground, but we achieved no results—not even a small fire. Jay was not happy, but I was ecstatic. About this time, Owl called and asked us if we had dropped. Both of us had completely forgotten about him, and we had flown through his altitude four times! He told us that when the Rockeyes went off, he almost stalled out, thinking he was being hosed down by a ZSU-23 (automatic, multi-barreled, Soviet-designed AAA gun). We didn't see the necessity to tell him we almost had a midair collision with him four times! So with just two Mk 20 Rockeyes, I had killed the four trucks he had seen. I loved the Mk 20 from that moment on.

On 28 January, we flew a Commando Nail up to Mu Gia Pass with two Jason's (call sign for VA-147) flying as Iron Hand support, due to the increasing SAM threat. We were carrying eight Mk 82 LDGPs and eight Mk-36 DSTs (the latter was a magnetic mine-fused version of the Mk 82). The Jason's bombed on our wing with an additional A-7 for a four-plane formation. We made two runs, dropping the Mk-82s on the first run and the mines on the second. We left a huge sustained fire behind.

On the thirty-first, we hooked up with a Nail FAC since TFA was down. He had spotted some trucks parked under some trees. We dropped our whole load of twelve Mk 82 LDGPs and two Mk-20 Rockeyes, and he reported fifty small secondary explosions and one sustained fire—not a bad night's work!

Hong Kong and the Year of the Rat

Connie left the line on 2 February for Hong Kong and a ten-day port visit. The ship's special services people had put together a trip for our families who flew over on a charter jet to meet us there. What a great birthday present for me. Peggy was waiting when we arrived on 4 February, and we had a great time. It was terrific to be together again. I'll never forget, it was the Year of the Rat; but after just five days, we were all ordered to return to the ship. Everyone I talked to thought it was a drill to see if we could actually emergency sortie from a port of call with so many people ashore. I remember, while awaiting the last officers' boat to take us out to Connie (our carriers have to anchor way out from Hong Kong Harbor because it is so shallow), I told Peggy we'd probably be back the next day. Boy was I ever wrong! It turned out the Regular North Vietnamese Army had swarmed across the DMZ and invaded the South. The war was heating up.

A New Pilot

We got back to the line on the ninth, and I flew a FAC mission down in the tri-border area (South Vietnam, Laos, and Cambodia) with twelve Mk 82 LDGPs in a four-plane division. Together, the FAC reported we had achieved 100 percent of our bombs within 50m, 75 percent within 20m, and two 5m road cuts. I guess that was better than our usual RNO WX but not much. When we returned to the ship, I discovered that was my last flight with Jay. I was too senior to be flying with the Ops Officer, so I was introduced to LT Phil Fossum with whom I would fly until I left the Squadron.

After flying some combat support missions (tankers), Phil had convinced the Skipper, CDR Tom Conboy, that he was safe around the ship and could be trusted to fly a combat mission, so we were fragged for a FAC mission on 12 February in Cambodia. I told Phil then, that our relationship was going to be fruitful one since, in all the time I had flown with Jay, never had we bombed in Cambodia. It turned out our target was a bridge which was being used by North Vietnamese Regulars to maneuver against the South Vietnamese provincial capital of An Loch, between Saigon and the Cambodian border. Our sixteen Mk 82 LDGPs made sure they wouldn't be able to use it again until they could repair it. Later that day, we flew back to Cambodia to bomb some bunkers with a FAC, but our electrical fuses failed, and the first few were duds. The rest, Phil couldn't get any closer than 40m—not a great mission.

We flew our first Commando Bolt mission on the night of 14 February. TFA ordered us to probe (something only the A-6 could do due to our AMTI capability) for movers, but I couldn't find any. So we dropped our twelve Mk 82 LDGPs and two Mk 20s on a fixed target but received no secondary activity, although we did receive a good bit of AAA—Phil's first. That night in the ready room, Phil asked me how he would know if he had executed a SAM break properly (I guess the AAA had got him thinking about how much worse it could get). He had received the same training as all of our other pilots, so he knew what to do; although a pilot can't practice against a live missile until the day it shot at him in anger. So looking into his eyes, I said, "Well, if we're here watching the movie after you performed your maneuver, you would have done it correctly."

I don't know if it helped, but I knew he would have to do it himself for the first time before he gained any confidence. Oh, and of course, he had to do it right or we wouldn't return to the ship or home at all.

My relationship with Phil was warming up very quickly, because on the sixteenth, we dropped sixteen Mk 82 LDGPs just above the DMZ in North Vietnam and experienced a good bit of 85mm AAA fire (black puffs similar to German 88s in WWII) and a SAM (orange smoke), though it was not aimed at us. On the eighteenth, we flew with a FAC against the North Vietnamese incursion into the South through the tri-border area. We flew in a section of A-6s with sixteen Mk 82 LDGPs each and managed to destroy a building and four KIA (Killed in Action). On the twenty-third, we carried our first LGBs (Laser Guided Bombs), but we had to rendezvous with an Air Force F-4 who had the equipment to illuminate the target since the A-6 wouldn't get its own illuminator for years to come. But ABCCC could not hook us up, so we dropped our conventional bombs and brought the LGBs back to the ship.

On the twenty-fourth, we were back at night on a Commando Bolt with TFA. I found nothing moving during our run in, so I dropped on the DMPI (now using our precision OAP data) with the corrections provided by the Sparky FAC. We dropped our twelve Mk 82 LDGPs, reset the ordnance panel, and dropped the Mk 20s on top of them (The latter were high-drag weapons, so they had a much shorter slant range, and we had learned the timing to get them to drop among the bombs. It covered the target area quite well.). We took over a hundred rounds of very accurate 37mm fire during the run, which almost took us out. The next night, working with TFA, I again was not able to detect anything moving, so we dropped on the corrected DMPI with the same load and got three small secondary explosions and a small sustained fire with no enemy defensive reaction. We flew several other missions with LGBs, but we never dropped any of them due to an inability for the 7th Air Force to hook us up with an illuminator.

On the first of March, on a Commando Bolt, we ran a fixed target for our wingman whose system was down and then were assigned to probe a road segment. Once again, I could not find anything moving, so we dropped on the corrected DMPI with our typical load of bombs and Rockeyes. We received a lot of accurate 37mm fire but managed to achieve five secondary explosions. We then left the line for a little R&R in the Philippines.

But before pulling in to port, the ship and air wing performed a nuclear strike exercise. We really hadn't paid too much attention to this part of our mission with all the actual wartime strikes going on all the time, so it was a good thing to get some practice, thinking about how to do it as a wing with nuclear weapons. Launch times in this type of operation are absolutely critical because each aircraft must hit each target at the specified time or we would start blowing up our own aircraft, so a smooth flight deck evolution is essential. Phil and I had a later time, so we were parked back near the aft end of the island with electrical power on the plane but no engines turning. So we were in a position to watch the whole show. One of our aircraft was parked up on Cat 2 (port side bow catapult) waiting for the ship to turn into the wind to start the launch sequence. Since the first launch was so critical, we were all sitting up there for quite a while before that time came.

For some reason, our Cat 2 aircraft had set his parking brake even though he was attached to the catapult. So of course, when he got the signal to start engines and complete his checklist, he forgot about the parking brake. Right at launch initiation, the catapult officer fired him off. Phil and I watched as clouds of smoke enveloped the aircraft, and as it blew back to us, we could smell rubber. Like every other carrier pilot, he retracted his gear as soon as he cleared the ship. In this case, he was very lucky that pieces of tire didn't jam his gear doors. Now, since this was an exercise more for the ship than the aircrews, we simply rendezvoused and headed in to NAS Cubi Point. One of our flight checked the Cat 2 aircraft over and couldn't see any damage, so the flight leader ordered him to land last, and the rest of us went in, landed, and supervised the downloading of our weapons—at least I did, because B/Ns had to sign for them, not the pilots. By and by, our Cat 2 aircraft came into land with his tailhook down to catch a wire on the field since he had two blown main tires. At least, that was the plan. When he landed, it turned out he still had his parking brake on, so he touched down on his magnesium wheels, which instantly caught fire and caused him to lose control of the aircraft on the runway. Fortunately, it came to a stop pretty quickly, and he didn't damage the aircraft any further. Of course, he had wheel fires which had to be extinguished with a special chemical we called Purple K since water would just cause the magnesium to explode, and I think his wheels had ground down almost to the axels. Yes, the A-6 was one tough bird!

Connie was in port from 2 to 15 Mar and then returned to the war.

Back on the line once more, we were working with a Nail FAC in Laos carrying sixteen Mk 82 LDGPs who found us a truck. While we scored 100 percent within 100m and 50 percent within 25m, we did not hit the truck, but we received about twenty rounds of 37mm and five rounds of 85mm fire for our trouble. I guess Phil was a bit rusty from the R&R. We actually found out a bit later that, with our M904 mechanical nose fuses on our bombs, we had to put one within 17ft ($\approx$3m) of a truck in order to destroy it. That was because, even though we would set the fuses for "instantaneous," since they were mechanical, there was always a bit of delay before they fired, causing the bombs to penetrate into the dirt before exploding. Had we been using air bursts or reliable electrical fuses, our BDA against trucks would have been a whole lot better.

The next day, we launched with eight Mk 82 LDGPs and eight Mk 36 DSTs, the latter being the magnetic mine version of the Mk 82. Once again, we rendezvoused with a Nail FAC who wanted us to cut a road for him. While Phil missed with the bombs, he put the mines within 5m of the road segment and two of those were right on the road—a pretty good mission. The missions we flew the next several days were very similar. We dropped a combination of Mk36s and Mk 82s with M346 mechanical long-delay fuses which were all set to different times; I never knew the times in case I was shot down and captured.

Finally on the nineteenth, we flew a Commando Bolt. That night, TFA didn't seem to have their act together, and we couldn't get onto any movers, but the fixed target the Sparky FAC gave us turned out to be golden. Our wingman had no system, so we took him in on that target on our wing (the pilot would pickle his bombs when he saw mine come off using the weapons system). We were both carrying twelve Mk 82 LDGPs and two Mk 20s and dropped them together as described earlier. I must have made a good run because we scored five large secondary explosions.

An A-6 Intruder Heading Home Carrying a
Refueling Store on the Centerline

On the twenty-first, we rendezvoused with our Nail FAC, and we brought ten Mk 82 and two Mk 84 LDGPs to the party. The latter were 2,000-pound bombs which the ship's gunner was trying to get rid of. They were really designed to knock down buildings and industrial areas, not jungle targets. Anyway, Nail had an IDP (Interdiction Point) for us, and Phil scored a 6m road cut and a road slide—beautiful visual bombing. An old vet couldn't have dropped them better. Nail was very pleased. Once again, it was time to leave the line for a little R&R. This time, for a change, we went to Yokosuka, Japan.

About this time, I heard from my detailer that I was going to get PCS (Permanent Change of Station) orders to an operational test and evaluation staff in San Diego, California. I immediately wrote home to Peggy who was overjoyed with the news. This time, we were determined to buy our first home, and it would be in Southern California.

Yokosuka, Japan

USS *Constellation* (CVA-64) with Carrier Air Wing Nine (CVW-9) embarked arrived in Yokosuka, Japan, on 25 March 1972, scheduled to depart on 6 April for San Diego following a six-month combat deployment to Southeast Asia (SEA). The "fly-off" from the Boat to the West Coast Home Naval Air Stations was scheduled for 16 April. Many officers and men had taken advantage of the opportunity to order motorcycles in Japan through the Navy Exchange, and those motorcycles were being loaded into the available space in the somewhat depleted ordnance magazines for the trip back to the CONUS (Continental US) since we didn't need the space for bombs anymore.

Along with the lessened need for magazine space, the Air Wing also needed less personnel and, therefore, several air crew, among others, were able to precede the carrier to the States. Among those departed from VA-165 (Boomers) were LCDR Jay Grafton (LT Ed Engle's regular pilot) and LTjg Mike Flanagan (LT Dan Graham's regular B/N).

Naval Air Facility Atsugi, Japan, is a US Navy joint use airfield about twenty-five miles from Yokosuka and is a quiet alternative for liberty away from the Boat. The train ride between the two bases for knowledgeable commuters is about two hours. For planning purposes, three to four hours would be recommended (also a realistic time for driving). At about 0900 on 1 April, LT Graham was at breakfast at the NAF Atsugi Officers' Club, and he responded when a phone call was announced for "any officer from Air Wing NINE." The caller was the CVW9 Command Duty Officer and he asked, "Who else is there, Grumpy?" and then said for all to Return to Boat ASAP! LT Graham responded by acknowledging the April

Fools' Joke and the CDO replied that "The motorcycles are going back onto the pier" and that all officers were to be on board by 1400! LT Graham and the other officers were able to beg for helicopter transportation from a Marine squadron at Atsugi and were back at CVA-64 before 1300.

During this same in-port period, I had traveled to Kyoto, one of the first capitals of ancient Japan, with several other squadron mates, for tourist activities away from Yokosuka. Of course, the entire time in Kyoto, the group speculated about whether we really would be heading back home to CONUS. That question was clearly answered when we arrived on the pier next to USS *Constellation* to find it full of motorcycles. That was a bad sign!

Extended

The ship sailed at 1630 beginning what was to be a forty-seven-day at-sea period with all re-supply and re-arming accomplished by underway replenishment from surface ships, aircraft, and helicopters. We arrived on Dixie Station in the Gulf of Tonkin (the southern operating area of CTF-77, the northern area was known as Yankee Station) on 6 April.

On the seventh, Phil and I flew a FAC mission down south but could find none with whom to work. So we had to drop our bombs on a backup target with RNO as a result. This wasn't exactly a thrilling mission for which we were extended. On the ninth, we had a similar experience. At this point, we were beginning to think we had gotten better training at Fallon.

On the ninth, Phil and I were launched at dusk to work with a FAC, but we couldn't find any, so I set up to drop on a Commando Nail target provided to me by ABCCC. We were carrying twelve Mk 82 LDGPs and four Mk 20s. I had always heard that twilight, both morning and evening, are bad times to fly because the guys on the ground can see you, while you can't see them. I was to learn the truth of that statement on this mission. The Commando Nail went OK, but we couldn't see anything on the ground where we dropped, although we got hosed down pretty well by a 37mm gun during our run-in. Now, Phil had blood in his eyes, and all he wanted to do was kill that gun. He told me he knew where it was and climbed up to dive-bombing altitude, while I reset the ordnance panel for the Mk20s. Reaching his perch, he rolled in, and I started to call out his flight data on the way down. All of a sudden, the air was full of tracers seemingly coming right at us, and Phil broke off the attack for some reason. I turned off the Master Arm on the ordnance panel and asked him what the hell he was doing. He said he had the wrong location of the gun on that run, but he now knew for certain where it was. So back we went to our perch with the Master Arm on, and in we went. This time, as I was calling out the flight date, I noticed tracers between me and the stall fences on my wing—I mean, that is getting too close! And what did Phil do, instead of dropping our Rockeyes, he aborts the attack for the second time! I was furious, but now, we had no more time and had to get back to the ship to meet our recovery time. On the way home, Phil told me he broke off the attack the second time because the tracers were so dense, he couldn't see his gunsight reticule clearly. And I thought the tracers between me and stall fences was too close! I made sure he knew from that moment on that if you commit to a run, you drop your bombs, no matter what. He never did that again.

When we returned to the ship with our four Mk 20s, I got an earful from my ordnancemen (I was the Avionics/Armaments Division Officer at that time) about bringing bombs back, forcing them to have to unload them, and on the last event, which would extend their work day for hours. They all knew I had a reputation for never bringing back ordnance and should have known it wouldn't have happened unless I had a damned good reason. I suppose they didn't stop to think about that, and their comments were like throwing gasoline on the fire still burning in me over Phil's actions and what they almost cost the both of us, so I let them have it with both barrels. The next day, I went down to the shop and explained what had happened, apologizing for my apparent overreaction, but cautioned them that they really should find out what happened before passing judgment.

On the tenth, with a FAC with whom we had never worked, "Rash 12," we bombed a Regular North Vietnamese troop concentration about 60NM north of Saigon with sixteen Mk 82 LDGPs. We hit the FAC's smoke, but he couldn't see the results under the thick foliage. Maybe we did some good. Who knows?

The next day was almost a carbon copy. This time, the FAC was Chico, and the mission was in support of the defense of An Loc again. We had a three-plane division for him, each carrying sixteen Mk 82 LDGPs. We hit his smoke, but he couldn't see anything just like yesterday—RNO foliage. On the twelfth, we rendezvoused with Chico again. This time, we had a three-plane division for him, each carrying sixteen Mk 82 LDGPs. When we reported in, he asked our flight lead to confirm our ordnance. He wasn't used to so much from so few. While he was delighted to get our ordnance and we hit his smoke, he couldn't see anything just like yesterday, but he did give us 100 percent within 5m. We continued bombing around the vicinity of An Loc and actually dropped on tanks and armor with "Sun Dog 14" on the fourteenth, and got 0m error as a result. At this same time, on another mission the same day, our Air Force Captain, Lee Hiser, was called in to support the command post in An Loc itself, who reported a Russian tank (T-72?) coming down their street. Lee rolled in and put a Mk 82 right into the engine compartment. Those guys were sure appreciable!

Breaking the LBJ Bombing Halt

The fifteenth of April was a stand-down day. In the morning, VA-165 CO, CDR Tom Conboy, launched in an A-6 to fly to *Kitty Hawk* (CVA-63), on Yankee Station, with CDR Gus Eggert (Commander Air Wing Nine) in his right seat (normally the B/N's seat). They returned that afternoon and called a meeting to announce that three carriers (USS *Kitty Hawk*, USS *Constellation*, and USS *Coral Sea* (CVA-43)) would each be launching A-6 attack aircraft for a coordinated night strike on SAM sites around Haiphong, North Vietnam, in preparation for B-52 strikes which would follow immediately.

Kitty Hawk had VA-52, Knightriders, embarked, while *Coral Sea* had Marine A-6 squadron, VMA(AW)-224, Bengals, embarked. The *Kitty Hawk* class ships were assigned three targets, and the *Coral Sea* just two. These attacks were the first scheduled for Route Package 6 since President Lyndon Baines Johnson declared a halt to the bombing in the North in 1967! Since the aircraft were coming from three separate aircraft carriers and they would be flying single-plane low level routes at night with no lights, conflict resolution, to avoid mid-air collisions, would be accomplished using time over target (ToT) and the geographic separation of ingress and egress routes. So the planning had to be closely coordinated.

As the senior of the three squadron commanders involved, CDR Tom Conboy and his B/N, LT Don Ohnemus, were to take the first (Honeybee One[13]) of the eight targets and were therefore scheduled for the first time-over-target at 0328 hours (over the Gulf of Tonkin, 0428 over land). Boomer XO, CDR Jim Seely, and (USAF exchange B/N) MAJ Sid Dodd had the second CVW-9 target (Honeybee Two), and VA-165 Ops Officer, LCDR John Shutt, and LCDR Gary Parten had the third Honeybee mission. Three additional Boomer crews were assigned as "manned spares" and would each man an airplane and, if needed, would launch to replace one of the primary aircraft. Two of the "spare" crews had each flown together as a crew during the deployment.

Although LTs Dan Graham and Ed Engle were both seasoned combat aircrewmen, each with designations as division lead qualified, they had not flown together in combat and were therefore assigned as the last "manned spare" crew. Their regular crewmembers were already back home, but LT Engle had acquired a new pilot, LT Phil Fossum, but the CO would not let him fly the mission because he had not been with the squadron very long. So when the CO asked with whom he would like to fly the mission other than his regular pilot, LT Engle chose LT Graham because they had trained together in CONUS flying low level missions at night in the Cascade Mountains of the Pacific Northwest and had developed a high degree of confidence in each other's ability. "Grumpy" and "Smutty" were

---

13. "Honeybee" was the call sign for Air Wing 9.

assigned an aircraft that had only recently been acquired by the squadron (from the Marines) primarily because it was to be delivered to a repair depot for scheduled major maintenance. So while they fit the bill as a required "spare," it didn't seem that Management had much faith that they would actually fly one of the missions.

The six *Boomer* crews all participated in the actual strike planning with each primary crew working mainly on their own target. In the process of doing the planning, LT Graham noted that he had, in fact, extensively planned the Honeybee One target (an SA-2 site known as VN-99) during Replacement Training; and the attack plan that he had proposed was adopted by the group. All planning material was completed and each of the "manned spare" crews carried copies of the target materials for all three missions, which the B/Ns had to study closely so they could find those targets with just radar. Since they weren't radar significant, they would have to use the system of progressive OAPs which they had developed in raids along the Ho Chi Minh Trail. The below graphics are recreations to the best of the author's knowledge of the VN-99 target located just southwest of Haiphong proper.

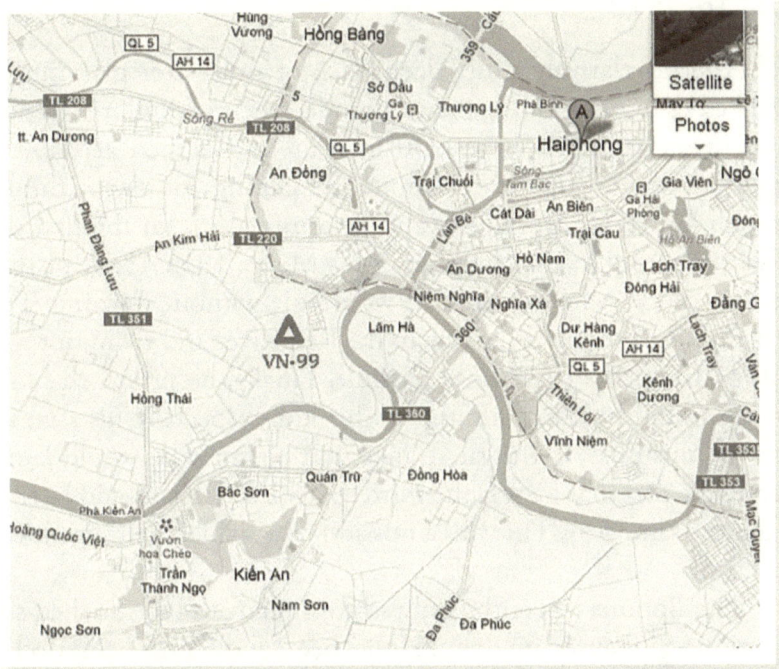

Approximate Location of our Target, a SA-2 SAM Site Named VN-99

A Recent Satellite Image of the Target Area

April 16, 1972

After a relatively short sleep (lack of time after planning and severe cases of nerves), the crews attended the mission brief at about 0100 in preparation for a 0230 man-up and launch at 0300. LT Engle lay awake for the few hours remaining for sleep, thinking through his SERE procedures and determined to, for the first time, fly with a round in the chamber of his Model 1911 45cal. pistol, so the first enemy who approached would die without warning. Then, he determined to make his way to the Red River and swim out to the Gulf of Tonkin as covertly as possible. Finally, he promised himself that he would be a better father to his kids, especially his son, if he survived this mission. It was strange, but he knew he would launch, despite the fact that he was the third spare. LT Graham said later that he felt the same way. This was a mission from which neither expected to return.

The Boomers were the only strike aircraft to be launched so all attention was focused on them. Honeybee 2 and Honeybee 3 declared themselves "sweet," but Honeybee 1 announced that his aircraft was "sour." The Air Boss asked for the status of the spares. The crew for the first spare declared their aircraft INOP and were immediately followed by the second spares' call of "sour." While both LTs Graham and Engle tried very hard to find something wrong with Boomer 503, the aircraft, the weapons system, and the ECM gear were all sweet, so they reported their status and assumed the Honeybee 1 mission. As scared as they both were about this mission, once the flight deck crew broke their tie-down chains down and they started to taxi, they were too busy to think about the fear anymore and had to get to work. This was clearly a case of the training taking over. They were launched from about a hundred miles from the coast-in point south of Haiphong, North Vietnam, into a black night with no visible horizon.

An Artist's Conception of a Typical Intruder
Mission into North Vietnam

The following is a running narrative recreated from a cassette tape recorder carried by LT Graham, who had it wired into his headset:

0310   Both: Inbound to NVN, used features on Hainan Island for radar update of the navigation system. Descended from 5,000 feet to about 1,000 feet.
0312   Both: Performed "practice attack" to ensure no surprises with the bombing system
0314   Ed: Noted numerous surface contacts; Descended to 450 feet AGL.

0318   Ed: Noted surveillance radar "looking at us"—appeared to be from off shore (Could have been a US Navy frigate).
0320   Dan: Saw "flares" ahead—either SAMs or Standard ARMs fired from VA-53, Knightrider, A-6Bs.
0320   Ed: "48 miles to target."
0322   Both: Lots of small boats fishing with lights created the visual impression of the coastline, but the radar told the truth.
0322   Ed: Master Arm On.
0323   Ed: Speed up to 450 KIAS, Hdg 337.
0325   Dan: Made call "Honeybee 1 will be 1 minute early."
0326   Both: AAA and strobes off to left.

NOTE: All during our ingress to the target, the VQ-1 EP-3 (call sign Deep Sea) kept broadcasting: "SAM, SAM vicinity of Haiphong" on GUARD (243.0 MHz), which all military planes monitored all the time. The problem was that the GUARD receiver overrode everything else, including our ICS (Internal Communications System), which we absolutely had to have to communicate at those altitudes and speeds over enemy territory at night. So Ed secured the receiver. This could have had severe consequences if someone had been shot down, but it was absolutely necessary at the time. Fewer calls from Deep Sea would have eliminated the necessity of shutting them off.

0327   Ed: Seeing his OAP a little better asked, "Can I make a correction? Guess not!" as 14 Mk20 Rockeye released with just 1.2 sec safe arming delay fuses. That short a fuse lit up the entire belly of the aircraft like strobe lights! The Ballistics Computer freeze data revealed bomb release was 120 feet above the target.
0327   Ed: RT Hdg 140.
0329   "They're shooting down there!" (Flash underneath aircraft, probably the fuses, which we didn't think about until later.) Heading 170 for egress from the target area.
0329   "Break hard right, high terrain!" (may have been boats with no terrain radar fill-in)
0330   "Coming back down" (to 600 feet).

0331 "Flares off to the right" (Later, they were determined to be two SAMs, which exploded a few hundred feet off our right wing.)
0332 LT Hdg 150.
0333 Honeybee 2 calls "Feet Wet" (meaning their aircraft was over water and out of the SAM threat envelope).
0334 Honeybee 1 calls "Feet Wet."
0335 76 NM to the boat: Observe lots of AAA.

Time Unknown Rendezvous with Honeybee 2 who has no radio receiver. Led him down to the "ball" on CCA approach.

B52s were observed high above heading toward Haiphong, as Boomer 503 came around for their own pass at the deck.

Crews were met on the flight deck by one of the Air Wing Flight Surgeons who issued them medicinal brandy! That never happened before or since! It must have really been a tough mission!

A "Small Boy" frigate was fairly close to the NVN shore because they had been told to anticipate about a third of the A-6s to be hit during this mission. No aircraft were damaged. Fifty-five SAMs were fired, but because the A-6Bs with the Standard ARM were active, the NVM SAM sites minimized their radar radiations and fired the SAMs and AAA without continuous radar guidance.

The mood in the ready room was exuberant. Winston Churchill once said that the greatest event in a young man's life was to be shot at and not hit. All the crews endorsed that sentiment that morning. I have never used illicit drugs, but I can't imagine that they would give a higher high than we felt that morning. After all the debriefing, we all went up to the "dirty shirt" (one could wear a working uniform like flight suits) wardroom for a cheeseburger and fries.

As we were eating, they were joined by the fighter crews from VF-96 and VF-92, which never happened—ever. So suspiciously, they asked these guys why they sat down. The answer: "You guys are f——ing crazy! We counted 55 SAMs shot at you from our BARCAP orbits and didn't need you to have your IFF on to follow your route of flight. We just had to follow the AAA!" The Boomers gained a lot of respect from our fighter guys that morning.

The reports on SAM activity showed that the Honeybee 1 targeted SAM site did not fire any SAMs for at least two days while airstrikes were conducted in that area multiple times daily, culminating in the mining of Haiphong Harbor. That was about as good a bomb-damage assessment as the Navy could get, considering that the bomblets held inside a Mk 20 canister didn't make big craters—rather the intent was to damage the radar and missile components. Some members of our squadron received newspapers from home a week or so later with headlines: "B-52s Strike Haiphong—No SAM Reaction." Not a word was written about the reason for their not experiencing any SAMs, whether we were that good or they had just shot up all their ready missiles at us, we'll never know, but the attack had the effect the Seventh Air Force had sought. Once again, Air Force public affairs people were at least a lap ahead of the Navy's.

Now all of us on that mission were qualified to become members of the Red River Valley Fighter Pilots' Association, formed earlier in the war by the Air Force in Thailand to discuss and develop effect tactics against the air defenses in North Vietnam. To become a member, one had to perform at least one mission in Route Package 6 North Vietnam.

We were both awarded Distinguished Flying Crosses for the mission. Our decorations had been submitted as Silver Stars but had been downgraded to DFCs because there was no discernible BDA.

The Distinguished Flying Cross

So went the Boomers' 16 April Practice Fly Off. The Real Fly Off wouldn't occur until June 29!

About this time, I started reading J.R.R. Tolkien's *The Hobbit* and *The Lord of the Rings* trilogy. I would read them in my bunk at night (or at least after my duty day had ended because sometimes it was daytime) after my shower—if there was enough water. They enabled me to leave the Gulf of Tonkin and Connie for a little while every day, and that was very therapeutic.

Showers, however, on an "oil burner" (vice today's nuclear-powered ships) were always iffy. We had to make water from the evaporators in the engine rooms, which depended on the seawater to condense the used steam back into liquid water, and when that seawater was over 90°F, the operation was not very efficient, and the margin of available water, which we used a lot of to operate the steam catapults, would shrink until the ship would have to go on water hours: water was made available only to the galleys and the officers' messes. Even when we had water available for showers, we were all expected to take Navy showers: (1) get wet, (2) turn off the water, (3) soap up, (4) turn on the water, (5) rinse off, and (6) turn off the water. The problem was that more than once, the engineers would turn off the water just after step 3. Imagine sweating heavily all day and finally getting into the shower and then not being able to rinse the soap off. Ahh, I don't miss it. But then, we all knew we lived like kings compared to our Army brothers in country. I can only imagine what those poor guys went through each and every day of their tours.

The War Continues

On the eighteenth of April, Phil and I were back working with a FAC down south bombing a VC compound west of Phu Cat. Results: RNO smoke and foliage.

On the nineteenth, things changed dramatically, and all the carriers now on Yankee Station began launching three Alpha Strikes every day. These were all daylight, dive-bombing deliveries with a maximum number of aircraft from each carrier, flying in the defensive Alpha formation. My first one of these was as #2 to our Division Lead and XO, CDR Jim Seely (who would go on to become a Vice Admiral), and his B/N Major Sid Dodd. There were six A-6s in our division, which was, in turn, part of a larger flight composed of A-7E bombers, A-7E Iron Hand, F-4J fighters for flak suppression, and CAP. There were a total of thirty aircraft in the formation. The target was the railroad yard at Vinh in North Vietnam. Our division of four A-6s was tasked with hitting the repair yards, while the other section was tasked with hitting the POL storage tanks nearby. The A-7s had similar targets about the complex.

Four of the A-6s were carrying ten Mk 83 LDGPs (1,000 pound) bombs while the other section of two carried twenty-two Mk 82 LDGPs—all with M-904 mechanical nose fuses set on instantaneous, while the A-7s were carrying six Mk 82 LDGPs each, and the Iron Hands, of course, had Shrikes. Approaching our CIP (Coast-In Point), which was very close to Vinh, because it is almost situated on the coast, we began to receive radar indications of SAMs and some AAA. Before we reached the CIP, the first SAMs were launched at the strike group.

At that time during the war, the North Vietnamese had learned that the standard US tactic against their SA-2s was doing a barrel roll about its flight access. But in performing that maneuver, the aircraft, loaded with bombs, would lose several thousand feet in altitude. So they would launch a second missile a few seconds after the first and aim in initially lower than the first to catch the aircraft as it came out of its avoidance maneuver with the first one. That was bad news for us, but there was some good news. They had also learned that we dropped chaff just before we broke into the barrel roll, and their very good proximity fuse liked those chaff clouds better than our radar return. So they would detonate on the chaff. In 1972, they weren't using their proximity fuses any longer. Rather, the operator had to merge the transponder from his missile with the skin return from his target. And he had to do that with the target maneuvering hard (at least 4Gs), popping chaff, and transmitting deception signals to his receiver. That made his job extremely difficult.

So with the sighting of the first *Guideline*s heading up to us, the entire strike group went into that high G barrel role. Our aircraft went into a stall shutter, while we were flying wing on the XO, and I was afraid we would fall out of the sky, but our trusty Intruder hung in there and kept flying with all that weight on her wings. During the maneuver, Phil asked me if I had the SAMs in site. He was always trained not to lose sight of the missile once it was in the air. I told him that I didn't because of our position on the left wing of the XO's aircraft but not to worry because I knew that Jim Seely would never lead us into a SAM. Just fly his wing, and we'll live. He did, and we did.

We had at least one more of these before we got to the target. During one of them, I remember watching the Iron Hands launching their Shrikes while the SAMs were coming up in the opposite directions. I definitely got the impression that the Shrikes weren't very effective.

About this time, we had reached the target area. Understand that the only set of eyes looking for our target was the leader's. So when he signaled us to cross under and go into a right echelon formation, we knew he had it in sight because we couldn't roll in from our current finger four formation (which we copied from the Luftwaffe in WWII known in German as a *schwarm*). So from the right echelon, at about

13,000 feet, Sid "kissed us off" (hand signal meaning he was leaving the formation) and the XO rolled in. Phil then had to continue for a few seconds, so as not to dive directly behind lead, where we would catch all the flak which was shot behind him. I looked down, and the sky was full of 85mm bursts. It was breathtaking! We had about a 10° spread to the right of the XO as we hurtled down the chute in our 45°, 500kt dive. As I was calling out the dive angle, altitudes, and airspeed to Phil, I saw the XO's bombs go right through the building he was aiming at and explode inside. It was unbelievable! We hit our pickle altitude about that time, and I yelled at Phil to pickle but break right because the XO had, predictably, broken left. Most A-6 pilots did that because they had much better visibility to that side.

As we started our 6G pull up to the right (I lost sight of the stall fences on the wings because of the vapor the compressed air on the tops of our wings was creating), I looked down to my five o'clock position and saw our bombs hit the rail yard just to the right of the building the XO clobbered and saw, to my amazement, that railroad cars were being slung aside as if they were HO gauge toys. I had not known to that point that a 1000-pound bomb could do that. I didn't have too much time to contemplate that beautiful sight, though, because I suddenly heard a very sickening *chink* metallic sound. We had been hit by some of that 85mm shrapnel. I immediately told Phil to steer 090 and ease off on the Gs, as my eyes went down to the hydraulic gauges. We really had no idea how badly we had been hit—only that we had. Between looking at the gauges and listening for scavenging pumps, indicating we had lost hydraulic fluid, I was pretty busy. There were no indications of fire, so that was a great thing. A fire would have caused us to eject very close to the target area, and I was pretty sure that the enemy would not be very happy with us after what we had just unleashed on them.

Once we reached our "feet wet" position, we rendezvoused with a couple of planes from our division and had them look us over; we still were seeing no indications of any damage in the cockpit. They couldn't find any leaks or other signs of damage, so we pressed on to the ship and formed up for our Case I recovery. We landed normally, and I reported the aircraft down for battle damage to maintenance, but they couldn't find anything wrong either and put the plane back on the flight schedule. It flew the next two alpha strikes that day, but when the plane captain was putting on the pitot tube cover, which is located up toward the top of the leading edge of the rudder, he found a hole in the top of the green boomerang on the starboard (my) side. The shrapnel must have been inside the rudder, but since it was causing no problems, they slapped ordnance tape on it, and the plane kept flying.

About this time, our RA-5Cs from RVAH-11 were restricted from flying up into the North Vietnamese Route Packages which had significant SAM threats because their XO had been hit by one during a post-strike BDA (Bomb Damage Assessment) photo reconnaissance mission. He got the plane back to the ship and managed to land it, but it was taken to the hangar bay and declared a "strike" (damaged beyond repair). I went down to look at it, and I counted eighty-eight shrapnel holes in the tail section! RVAH-11 had been flying these missions since our Air Wing started flying the Blue Trees earlier in the cruise. They would wait until the smoke settled over the target area and then come screaming in supersonic on the deck with cameras snapping away. They had to keep their wings level because of the cameras and couldn't take any evasive action. Of course, by the time they flew through, all the enemy personnel were waiting for them, and they usually drew a lot of flak, but the SA-2 proved to be very effective where the AAA had not been. As fast as they flew (their F-4J escorts couldn't keep up with them, so they always used two sections: one to escort them on the way in and the other to pick them up on the way out), they couldn't outrun the Mach 2+ *Guideline* missile.

The RA-5C 603 from RVAH-11

So now all of our post-strike BDA photography would be taken by RF-8s flown from USS *Coral Sea*. The film cans then had to be flown aboard Connie and Kitty Hawk by helicopter and then taken to the IOIC (Integrated Operational Intelligence Center), which had been designed to integrate directly with the Vigilante. It was a giant step backward for our intelligence capabilities.

On the twenty-third, we were back on Dixie Station and flew all the way to the Gulf of Thailand in Cambodia to work with a FAC with fourteen Mk 82 LDGPs. It was a 600NM round trip for us, and we made five runs with him since there was no flak reported in the area, but results were RNO. Upon returning to the ship, we were told they wanted to run an air defense exercise with our flight being the bogies. Two F-4Js from VF-96 launched to intercept us, and we flew an ACM (Air Combat Maneuvering) exercise with them until they ran out of fuel and had to land. Their flight time was much less than an hour. We had flown 600NM, made five runs, completed the ACM exercise, and landed in our sequence—last except for the E-2 and the tanker. What a comparison between aircraft! OK, they go fast.

The next day, we were working with a FAC in the defense of An Loc again. We dropped fourteen Mk 82 LDGPs within 15m of his smoke and got RNO smoke for our reward. The next, we returned with the same bomb load, dropping on a bridge, which we missed, but we got a medium secondary explosion for our trouble. But we had to return with no radio on the wing of one of our flights, always a pain. On the twenty-sixth of April, we were way down in the Mekong Delta, bombing a VC position with the same load. This time, our flight was credited with four bridges destroyed, three damaged, and three sampans sunk. On the twenty-seventh, it was back to the An Loc defense again with the same load, and the Army FAC had us rolling in on an automatic weapons and mortar site. The flight achieved 100 percent on target with a 15m CEP but RNO foliage.

On the twenty-ninth, our flight leader lost his radio transmitter, so Phil took the lead and rendezvoused with our Army FAC near An Loc again: same results. On 1 May, back on Yankee Station, we flew a FAC mission 25NM west of the South Vietnamese provincial capital of Hue against an IDP. The flight was carrying sixteen Mk 82 LDGPs and achieved one 50m road slide and a 10m one to go with it. On May 3, we were placed under our own control in the Ashau Valley, carrying sixteen Mk 82 LDGPs. We found a bridge with a white object near it we could not identify. We hit the bridge and the ground. Somehow, this sortie didn't seem worth the cost. But interestingly, while we were finishing up, a thunderstorm closed in, and it got so dark, I actually turned on our thunderstorm lights in the cockpit. I had never used them before, and I never would again, but that day, they really helped.

On the seventh of May, we rendezvoused with a FAC over the southern part of the Ashau Valley, a known hot spot for the VC and now the Regular North Vietnamese Army. We had sixteen Mk 82 LDGPs, and our FAC had two trucks for us. Phil did very well on his run, getting 100 percent within 40m, 50 percent within 20m, and a medium secondary explosion, but by the time we got there, the trucks had fled. The significant thing about this mission was getting there. After launch and rendezvous, our flight of two headed west and encountered a huge line of thunderstorms as far as we could see North and South, and the tops appeared to be around 50,000 feet. So we could neither fly around nor over that front. We would have to penetrate it—never a good idea. Since I was senior, we took the lead, and I went into the hood. Immediately, I found I could easily see the densest part of the clouds which all looked the same to the naked eye, so I called for our wingman to get up close in parade formation and stay with us. Then I gave Phil steers through that cold front around the bad parts. I did sneak a peek outside during a relatively clear period on the radar and noticed our M904 mechanical nose fuses were glowing with St. Elmo's fire. I asked Phil if he knew whether that might be bad, but he didn't know any more than I did, so we pressed on. Obviously, because I am writing this, we were successful in navigating the cold front, and St. Elmo's fire is not a danger to the M904 mechanical nose fuse.

We flew this sort of mission all over South Vietnam until 10 May, when all hell broke loose up North.

10 May 1972

The ninth of May closed with CVW-9 getting fragged for three alpha strikes up near route package 6 for the next day. Planning continued late into the night, but Phil and I were scheduled for the third go and didn't have an early brief, but I felt like something big was in the wind, so after the crews for the second strike left, the ready room to proceed to the flight deck, I went to CATCC (the Carrier Air Traffic Control Center) to watch their mission unfold. Watching the NTDS (Naval Tactical Data System) displays and listening to the various radio frequencies they had on speakers (e.g., strike primary and the fighter squadron discrete channels) provided me with a pretty good overview of what was happening.

I watched our strike proceed into their target, the railroad yard near Hai Duong in North Vietnam, and the SAM calls were furious.[14] Then, we heard AAA calls when they got closer to the target. Then, I saw our A-6s drop their bombs and head out for the coast. Since we had no gun and never carried air-to-air missiles throughout the war, we had no reason to hang around. But the A-7s did have a Mk-60 20mm Gatling gun and sometimes carried AIM-9 Sidewinders, so they tended to hang around the target area looking for something to kill. With all the bombs dropped and our A-6s already starting to call "feet wet," I was about to leave to get ready to brief for the next launch, when all these open triangle symbols (Λ) appeared coming down from Hanoi. The symbol was NTDS speak for "bandit," an enemy aircraft. I don't recall how many there were, but I was impressed by the large number (later, the Navy figured out that there were twenty: fourteen MiG-17s, two MiG-19s, and four MiG-21s). Of course, I couldn't tell from the display what kind of MiGs they were, but I was very interested in the fact that the North Vietnamese hadn't bothered to launch them at our strike package until after the bombs had fallen. I always thought air defense was supposed to prevent bombs from falling—just goes to show you that I was never in tune with the oriental mind.

On the one hand, I was very happy that our A-6s had gotten out of there before it turned into "fun in the afternoon with the MiGs," but now I was concerned about the rest of our aircraft. We still had a lot of A-7s and F-4s around the target area. I actually have an audio recording of this engagement, but today, even I can't figure it out, because there are so many people yelling into their radios at the same time, and it's pretty clear they're all scared. So here's the best summary I can provide, much of this learned later from the crews who were actually in the engagement:

- All of our fighters from both VF-92 and VF-96 were engaged. Several MiGs had already been shot down.
- An F-4 from VF-92 (call sign Silverkite) with their XO, CDR Harry Blackburn, as the pilot ran into a flak trap and

---

14. For a more detailed account of this strike, see *One Day in a Long War, May 10, 1972*, by Jeffrey Ethell and Alfred Price, Random House, New York, NY, 1989.

was shot down—only the RIO (Radar Intercept Officer), LT Steve Rudloff, ever showed up at the Hanoi Hilton, although two parachutes were seen over the target area. No one could say what happened to their CDR Blackburn, but later, we learned that Steve Rudloff had been blinded in the cockpit fire which erupted after they were hit, and then had badly injured his ankle on landing.

- One of the guys I had graduated with from AOCS, LT Tom Blonsky, was the RIO in a VF-96 fighter flown by LT Matt Connelly that was desperately trying to shoot down a MiG which had jumped one of our A-7s. When he finally got off a shot with a Sidewinder, the MiG-17 pilot broke hard into the missile, and it passed him without exploding, but the shot had gotten him off the A-7's tail, and he departed for home. But they finished the day with two confirmed MiG-17 kills.

- One of our A-7s who was down low trying to find a suitable target to strafe was jumped by a MiG-17, and he couldn't shake him while the MiG's tracers were whizzing past his cockpit. An A-7 couldn't out turn an A-6, and the A-6 couldn't out turn a MiG-17. Up at a higher altitude was another A-7 who saw all this unfolding beneath him, and he thought, *A MiG for me, probably the only A-7 to ever shoot one down.* Then, as he prepared to roll in, he remembered that his airplane had a weight in it where the gun should have been, and the ship had stopped putting Sidewinders on the A-7s, so he was just like us—nothing to shoot back. But he kept his dive coming, and the MiG driver, apparently seeing him in his mirrors, broke off the attack and flew home.

- LTs Randy Cunningham and Willie Driscoll, flying in a VF-96 F-4J (call sign Showtime) assigned to flak suppression was hotly engaged with MiGs, after dropping their four Mk 20s.
    - Randy already had two MiGs to his credit and shot down two more early in this fight.

- Then, he engaged what I would call a "MiG Master" who knew just about as much about what his MiG-17 could do as Randy did about his F-4J, and that *was* about all there was to know for both of them. Both knew that if they broke off the attack, they'd probably get nailed.
- They tangled horns in repetitive rolling vertical scissors until they ran out of energy, dove, picked up energy, and went back again into the vertical—a deadly cycle. But the MiG-17, much like the Luftwaffe's ME-109s in WWII, had limited fuel because of its small size, so the MiG Master had to break off the attack first and try to return to his base. When he did, Randy was on him in a flash and sent him into the next world. That made his fifth kill and that made him a MiG Ace, the first one of the Vietnamese War.
- Now, it was time to head home, but an SA-2 missile site locked him up, and the missile detonated just abeam his tail section. I was listening to his wingman talking to him about his problem, and it was clear that he was trying to stay with as long as he could to get "feet wet." His aircraft would start an uncontrollable climb. Then, he would kick the rudder over hard to roll inverted (his elevators were not working), dive, pick up airspeed, and start climbing again. The problem was: every time he did it, he would lose several thousand feet, so he was getting lower all the time.
- Eventually, as he neared the Gulf, the damage had progressed to the point where he had lost just about all control, and his aircraft entered an inverted spin. He stayed with it for several revolutions in an attempt to ensure they were over water, but his wingman yelled at him to eject, which he and Willie eventually did. Now, our A-7s flew over them in the water and

kept the fishing boats away, which were approaching to capture them, by strafing in front of them.
- Very soon, the RESCAP (Rescue Combat Air Patrol) helicopter flew over to them and retrieved them both. I greeted them on the flight deck when they returned. The Navy withdrew them from combat then and there and sent them on a speaking tour of the SEA airfields before flying them home. Randy received a Navy Cross, and Willie another Silver Star.[15]
- As our aircraft were going "feet wet," most of the fighters were screaming for fuel. Our duty tanker was being flown by our XO, CDR Jim Seely and Major Sid Dodd, and they listened as every "manager" in the Gulf was giving the fighters different vectors to him (Connie's tanker control, *Red Crown*, and the E-2). So the XO got up on the frequency and told them all to shut up. He then calmly reported his position and told them he was popping flares (these were countermeasures we carried against heat-seeking missiles). The flares enabled the fighters to effect very efficient rendezvous and get their fuel. Later, I found out that one guy plugged the XO with less than 500 pounds of JP-5 remaining. In an F-4, that's about enough to wet the tanks. But thanks to our XO and Sid, the Air Wing lost no fighters due to flameouts.
- Summary: At the end of this mission, we had lost two F-4Js: one to flak and the other to a SAM. We had another damaged due to same 85mm flak. We had gotten good bombing results on the target, and the Air Wing was credited with 7½ MiGs (the ½ is for a probable, not confirmed), and we had the first MiG Ace of the War. Over all, it was an outstanding mission.

---

15. They had each gotten a Silver Star for each of the first four MiGs because that was CTF-77 policy. It was not that liberal when it came to the bombers, though.

Phil and I went on the next and last Alpha Strike of the day. We dropped twelve Mk 36 DST mines up near Hon Gai Island, where the North Vietnamese operated patrol boats. This was a tricky mission because to drop mines, you have to remove the wind drift from the equation so your mines will fall along the planned "mine line," and the crew has fairly stringent airspeed and altitude restrictions so as not to damage the mine components in the bomb. But when configured this way, the Mk 82 is fitted with Snakeye Retard fins which pop out when they leave the aircraft and slow the mines down just like a parachute. We had to drop manually because our system died, and as we began to egress, MiG calls started coming up from just west of Haiphong. Of course, our fighters on BARCAP, most of whom had not been in on the big MiG kill of the previous mission, were getting very excited, like sharks with blood in the water. As we listened, we heard a VF-92 F-4J actually shoot a Sparrow (radar guided air-to-air missile) at a VF-96 F-4J. Fortunately, the firing aircraft realized the error and turned off the target illuminator to make the missile go "stupid." Phil and I thought, *If these guys are shooting at their own type aircraft, what chance have we got?*

VA-165 Ordnancemen Loading Mk-82 Snakeyes (Notice the fins)

Mk82 Snakeye Retards Being Delivered

Continuing south at max speed and low altitude, one of our destroyers appeared broadside to us with his guns trained at us. Phil thought it would be great to fly over them, but I cautioned him to give them several hundred yards' clearance as we passed. With the near-friendly fire incident to which we had just listened, I didn't think we needed to participate. The ship didn't shoot, and we continued back to Connie for a Case I recovery.

The next day, since CTF-77 had started mining the harbors in North Vietnam, we flew a coastal patrol mission with four Mk 20s to ensure the enemy wasn't using small wooden boats to unload the freighters now anchored outside our minefields. It was a fun mission. We flew about 100 feet above the water to avoid SAMs and never got below 500 kts. We passed Russian ships, Chinese ships, and others from the Warsaw Pact. But none of them even had anyone on deck. They showed us no activity at all, and we saw no sampans. So we flew the patrol and returned to Connie with our Mk 20s still on the wings.

Mining Dong Hoi Harbor

On the thirteenth, we were fragged to mine Dong Hoi Harbor in North Vietnam. I worked with our mine warfare officer LT Ralph Griffiths in CVIC (Carrier Integrated Intelligence Center) to lay out the mine field with the three A-6s with sixteen Mk 36 DST SERs each provided us for the mission. We chose a long axis line, which roughly mirrored the centerline of the harbor and two shorter crossing lines (see the next graphic). During the briefing (this time I was the flight leader), I carefully explained that we would rendezvous overhead the ship at 10,000 feet where each B/N would check out his system before we split up and proceeded individually to the target. It was nighttime, so individual approaches were a good idea. We then set individual ToTs so we would have no flight conflicts over the target area, but those times were close because we wanted the air defenses to have as little time as possible to react. We would be first because we had the longest axis to fly and would be exposed to the most ground fire.

Dong Hoi Harbor, Vietnam Today

    The green lines represent the approximate mine lines of our two wingmen, while the red line is ours. The yellow circle was the position of the automatic weapon.

    The launch and rendezvous went normally, but I found that I couldn't get my computer to work, despite my best efforts while the others seemed to be OK. So I told Phil I wanted another couple of orbits of the ship to try and get my system straightened out, so I sent the other two on their way. That turned out to be a big mistake! After two more orbits, I still hadn't gotten the computer to work, so I told Phil, we would go with the MRL backup I had planned. I would give Phil steers to get the aircraft on a crab angle which would eliminate any drift from our mine line due to crosswinds, and I would tell him to pickle when the range line reached a prominent point to the south of our target area. So we headed out on a heading of 270 (due west toward the coast). My thought was that I would locate the coastline with my radar and give Phil steers until I could get him on the line to start our run. But I soon discovered that my search radar antenna was stuck in the full down position, so my range was very limited—about 10NM. About this time, Phil saw very bright lights near the area he thought was Dong Hoi Harbor. I looked up and discovered that they were flares. I remember thinking that I knew we had them. I had dropped plenty. But I didn't know the North Vietnamese had them. It was not a good omen for us since we had that very long axis to fly, and we couldn't fly lower than 200 feet nor faster than 350kts because of the restrictions on the mines.

Eventually, I found Cape Mui Ron, which was just to the North of Dong Hoi and started setting Phil up on our mine axis with a series of course corrections, while he descended to our preplanned attack altitude. As we were approaching our drop point, I looked up and saw several 57mm rounds fly above the canopy. Phil said later that he had seen them and just dropped a hundred feet or so to reach our run-in altitude, and they flew over us. The azimuth was good, so it was quite accurate. Now, I had managed to get my azimuth line to stop drifting from the aimpoint, so I had solved the crosswind, and we had reached the correct range, so I told Phil to pickle, and the mines started coming off. It was the longest run I had ever made, and it was like daylight outside! As I recall, we were in our run for almost 10 seconds, which is an eternity under those conditions.

As we neared the end of our run, I saw a bridge out to my two o'clock position, and at the south end, all of a sudden, a tremendous white light appeared. In it, I could see the gunner and loader in a pit surrounded by sand bags. Suddenly, the sky was full of white tracers, which I had never seen before. And they were coming straight at us. There were hundreds of them (and remember, there's a tracer only every so often in a belt of machine gun ammo), and there was no bearing drift relative to the canopy bow on my side, which meant they were coming straight at us. I don't know how big my eyes were, but I said nothing, just waiting for those damn mines to finally free us. At that point, I found I had become very calm, almost serene. I knew I had done everything I could to save us, and I had lost, and we would surely die. I put my head back against the head rest on my ejection seat and closed my eyes, awaiting the inevitable.

Suddenly, they passed just overtop the canopy, and we received no damage. I couldn't believe it, but the last mine had come off the rack, and I screamed at Phil to break left and get us out of there, which he did as fast as he could. Later, as we reached our marshal position to get ready to start our Case III recovery to ship, I apologized to Phil for not saying anything about the automatic weapons fire, but he told me he knew about it because of the bright illumination it made in the cockpit. Boy, that was close! I was tempted to kiss the oily, non-skid-coated steel deck after we climbed down from the cockpit, but I thought that would be too dramatic and resisted the temptation.

Too Close to the Guidelines

The next day, the fourteenth, Phil and I were back at the Alpha Strike. This time, the target was a POL storage facility south of Nam Dinh. Our four-plane division was carrying eighteen Mk 82 LDGPs each, and we scored good hits on the target, receiving no enemy reaction around the target which we thought very strange. However, as we were egressing at about 500kts, we received the whole sequence of SA-2 launch signals all the way from search to track in very quick succession. With all the SAMs we had seen launched, we had never seen them use all their modes in sequence like that, but the only things that really mattered were that the site was very close at our five o'clock position and they were preparing to guide a missile at us. I called all that out to Phil, as I pulled myself around to look out over the starboard elevator. Very quickly, I saw a huge cloud of dust, followed by a guideline missile with booster take to the air, shortly followed by a second. Frankly, my initial reaction was "How could they be a threat? They're so slow!"

Then, the boosters dropped off, and it seemed like they accelerated to Mach 2 immediately—very impressive! We now have a fundamental problem because Phil can't see them, and he's driving the plane. I know that I am going to have to call his break into them so we can out turn them. So I wait until I think they are close enough, and then I scream at Phil to break right *now*! That maneuver should have put our velocity vector at right angles to the missiles', but Phil, instead, chose to break left (remember, how A-6 pilots always wanted to turn to the left?). Well, that did for me. I could no longer see them since we just turned away from them, and they are closing really *fast*! So just like the night over Dong Hoi Harbor, I knew there was nothing more I could do, and I became very serene and put my head back in the head rest and closed my eyes waiting for the explosion, like the one that took out our Ops Officer back in December.

Then, I felt the Gs come off the aircraft and sensed we were straight and level, although I couldn't figure out how that could have happened. It was time to get back to work. First, I called "Feet Wet" as we transited out of the SAM envelope, and then I had to start talking Phil through CTF-77's elaborate "Return to Force Procedures." They consisted of flying to certain points, squawking a particular code on our IFF, then proceeding to another point and altitude, changing the squawk, etc. These were not things you wanted to ignore because our own ships would shoot at us. Finally, we got back to Connie and got into the overhead rendezvous circle for A-6s in preparation for a Case I recovery. Once, we were established in that circle, things calmed down a lot, and I looked over at Phil and said, "If you ever break left when I tell you to break right, I'm going to kill you. Forget about the enemy."

He had his dark visor down over his face, and his oxygen mask covered the lower part of it, so I couldn't see any of it, but he answered in a very thin voice, "You know, I always thought SAMs were white. They're not white. They're camouflaged and have black numbers!"

Then, I yelled at him all over again. I have no idea how close those two missiles came, but if he could see the numbers, they were way too close. The only thing that saved us that day was our ECM gear and chaff (since they weren't using their VT fuses). Had they used those fuses, there would have been a different outcome, and I wouldn't have survived to write this memoir, and you, the reader, wouldn't know anything at all about a couple of guys who simply failed to come home from that mission.

"The Boat" from the Pilot's Perspective during a Case I Recovery.
The picture is from a VA-34, Blue Blasters' cockpit,
but it's very close to what I was looking at when I had
my chat with Phil after the SAMs missed us.

Area of Vietnam between Haiphong and Thanh Hoá

More Alpha Strikes and the End of Cruise—Finally

The next day, 17 May, we flew another big Alpha Strike, this time against the Thanh Hoá Railroad Yard. Ever since the air war had begun in North Vietnam, the bridge at Thanh Hoá had been a key target for every air wing which ever deployed to the Gulf of Tonkin. Now, a bridge is a difficult target for gravity dumb bombs because they are so narrow and the structure is not solid. Many sorties had been launched against it, and they all failed to drop it, but most resulted in high losses of aircraft and men. In fact, the approaches to the bridge on both sides had been so badly cratered that the bridge had been rendered useless for the most part. But the Navy had a biding desire to drop it, no matter what. One Admiral, whose name I can't remember, was said that the world had a crack in its crust, and that crack was held together by the Thanh Hoá bridge. If we ever succeeded in dropping it, the world would split apart.

One of the reasons for recommissioning USS *New Jersey* (BB-62) was to employ her sixteen in guns against that bridge, but by the time the ship had gotten into the war, President Johnson had declared a bombing halt in North Vietnam, and she couldn't be used for that purpose. By the time we flew this Alpha Strike *New Jersey* was back in mothballs. But we were all glad that we wouldn't have to bomb the bridge but would get to see it.

The strike launched and rendezvoused smoothly. Our division leader, LCDR John Shutt, and his B/N LT Gary Parten, led us into our position in the strike formation with no problems, and we proceeded to the target. Each of our A-6s carried ten Mk 83 LDGPs, while the A-7s and F-4s carried smaller numbers of Mk 82 LDGPs. As usual, some of our flak suppression fighters accelerated out ahead in afterburner and rolled in on the guns they could see.

Nearing Thanh Hoá, the strike leader radioed "batter up" to the group, advising us that he had the target in sight and signaling it was time for us to shift to the right echelon formation from our normal Alpha formation. About this time, we were coming under some pretty significant 85mm AAA fire. Phil crossed underneath John and Gary's aircraft, while the second section slid out to the right to give us room. So there we were in our right echelon waiting for John to roll in with flak bursts all around, when he started pulling up his nose and dropping his left wing, so we followed him in that maneuver. But then, he stopped and held that awkward position, continuing to turn over the target area for another 270° before he rolled in. The reader must understand that up to this point, none of the pilots had seen the target because they were flying formation and had to watch the aircraft they were guiding on intently, and the B/Ns' visibility was restricted because we were in a left turn. So none of us knew what was going on, and all of our aircraft were in a stall shutter from all that weight and our attitude. Suddenly, John and Gary rolled in and so did we with about a 5° spread in azimuth.

As soon as he rolled out, Phil saw the target and started tracking it with his gunsight, while I called out the usual flight parameters. While we were reaching our 450/500kt dive parameters, I looked across the circle we had been flying in and saw so many 85mm bursts at that part where John had originally initiated his dive that I couldn't see the ground, and I thought, *Maybe that's what the old WWII vets meant when they said, "The flak was so thick, you could get out and walk on it."* We reached our pickle altitude, dropped our ten 1000lb bombs, and beat feet for the coast. Oh, yes, I did see the bridge, too. It was still there, but the approaches at both ends looked like a moonscape. While we had a lot of 85mm fire, there were no SAMS fired at us.

On the nineteenth, Connie departed for Singapore, a port none of us had been to before. It was a nice change. We had to anchor even further out than we did in Hong Kong and take a charter boat into the city. On the way, we passed many Chinese and Russian ships loaded with trucks and other war materials. We all thought it would be easier to sink these ships right here and now rather than try to catch those trucks once they got loose in the jungle. Politics, of course, prevented that. Singapore really was a great liberty port, but all too soon, we were headed back to the Gulf of Tonkin.

We returned to Dixie Station, and on 1 June, Phil and I worked with a FAC against a VC position. We were carrying fourteen Mk 82s and achieved 80 percent within 20m, but RNO foliage. On the third, we were on another FAC mission, but the weather was so bad, we couldn't effect a rendezvous with our FAC and had to dump our bombs just north of An Loc, along with most of the other aircraft from our wing. Again on the fifth, we were fragged to work with a FAC, carrying eleven Mk82s and three Mk 43 TDDs (Time Delay Detonation). We had no radio and had to bomb with another aircraft but achieved 20m CEP. On the sixth, with fourteen Mk 82s, we found our FAC in some pretty bad weather (the Southwest Monsoon was setting back in) and dropped on three different targets but got RNO foliage for our trouble. We flew these sorts of missions every day but began carrying VT fuses on our Mk 82s because the targets started to be troops in the open. These fuses had small radars in the nose and would detonate at about sixteen feet above the ground, maximizing the blast and fragmentation effect. Of course, we had to use the Snakeye Retard fins on the bombs in order to get the noses pointed at the ground so the radar could work. On the eighth, we and many other aircraft caught 130 VC in the open about 45NM southwest of Can Tho. The FACs promised to send our BDA along after they collected it all, but if we ever got it, I never heard about it.

As it turned out, we flew our last combat mission on the thirteenth of June (remember, we were originally scheduled to fly off to NAS Whidbey Island on the sixteenth of April). Phil and I bombed a mortar position west of Saigon with fourteen Mk82 SERs and VT fuses, achieving 8m CEP, and destroying a store's cache and leaving a secondary medium-sustained fire. Connie left the line for the last time after recovering our last event and headed for Cubi Point. From there, she sailed back to Yokosuka to pick up the motorcycles we had there. Since I already had PCS orders in hand, I was detached from VA-165 in Japan. I traveled up to Yokota AB where I was able to catch a C-141 flight back to CONUS. I sat in a wed seat, with my feet on a J79 engine, but I didn't care. The next day, we landed at Elmendorf AFB outside Anchorage, Alaska, and I got a seat on an Alaskan Airlines Boeing 727 to Seattle-Tacoma International Airport, where Peggy picked me up to drive down to San Diego to buy a home for our next duty station. What a road trip that was! I had not expected to survive this cruise, yet here I was alive and well with my beautiful wife. Life was good.

VA-165 finally executed their fly-off to NAS Whidbey Island on the twenty-ninth of June.

For their accomplished during this deployment, USS *Constellation* (CVA-64) and Carrier Air Wing 9 received the Presidential Unit Citation, the highest citation which can be awarded to a unit. It was very rarely given to aircraft carriers and their embarked air wings.

Post Combat Thoughts on the Effectiveness of the Intruder

The Intruder was never rated very highly by the various DoD bombing surveys which were conducted during the war. This was primarily due to the lack of education within the Navy on the issues concerning charts, chart-making, geodesy, and offset targeting. The latter, which we did so much of in Southeast Asia, was critically dependent on having made precise measurements of range, bearing, and differential altitude between the radar aim point and the target, which were not radar significant in that war. As I found out at TFA, the charts we were provided had been printed from pre–World War II French survey data using crude surveying tools. Some errors, as discussed above, were in the thousands of meters in location, with significant altitude errors on top of those. In a straight path level attack, which was our common "full system" mode, one foot of vertical error results in one foot of range error with respect to getting a bomb on the target. So if the B/N made an altitude error of as little as twenty feet, his MK82 bomb would not be close enough to kill a truck, and he had to read those altitudes by visual interpolation of contour lines on a chart based on old inaccurate data.

In general, these things were not understood. Later, while working in Washington, DC, a geophysicist at DMA (Defense Mapping Agency) explained to me that charts were worthless for precision measurements because of the way they were made. He added that DMA had made a movie, years before, describing how they were not to be used the way we used them in Vietnam. Neither I nor anyone I knew in the A-6 Community had ever seen it. It existed, yet the Navy seemingly had ignored it. In order to make such measurements with precision, one had to use a DDPDB (Digital Point-Positioning Data Base), a product that they created with lots of high definition stereo imagery and a lot of computer processing. So the Navy had developed an aircraft which they could not utilize to its full potential because they were ignorant of the means and methods required to actually derive the radar offset data needed in a jungle environment against soft targets. It was a revelation which haunted me for years, but I was able to do something about it in the end (see Project *Challenge Athena* below).

So I was lucky enough to have been able to fly a premier carrier-based bomber in combat but was not provided the tools to properly engage the targets I was assigned.

CHAPTER 4

PEGGY ENGLE'S VIEW FROM THE HOME FRONT

The events portrayed in this chapter happened over four decades ago and in all probability are not in the correct chronological order. Nonetheless, these things actually did happen and are truly related to the best of my ability.

Upon arriving at NAS Whidbey Island in the worst winter in over sixty years, we found there was a waiting list for base housing. The only "furnished" housing available was two trailers. One was in worse shape than the other, so we took the better of the two, and it was a bit of a horror. Jalousie windows which let cold air into the place and a propane heater whose tank had to be filled every ten days or so during that miserable winter are just two examples of why that place was so horrible. While in that trailer, we acquired a black Labrador puppy. In a snowstorm, someone had abandoned her at about six to seven weeks old, and while we didn't want a dog, we couldn't let her freeze under the trailer. She grew to be about ninety pounds and was an escape artist.

When we finally got a three-bedroom house on base, things got much better. Once on base, we began to make more friends with fellow squadron mates. There were several calls asking for a "fourth." Since I never learned to play bridge, I couldn't get invited. So bridge lessons were needed, and having learned to play the game, my life was saved when the squadron deployed. Having three young children can really get overwhelming without any fellow adult company. The bridge parties were something to help all of us cope. Since we had a limited income, we would pack up our children and go to the hostess's home for a game. The children played with the other children in the house, and the wives set up our game. In one particular month during the deployment, we played about forty times (morning game and after-supper game). Coffee was served in the morning and cheap wine was the usual beverage at night. We all took turns providing snacks.

We watched the news every evening and were frequently upset by what was being reported. We were also distressed by the anti-war demonstrations. For me, telling myself that I'd know if my husband was shot down or killed seemed to help, although that was misguided to be sure. There were no computers back then, and the Navy didn't have the ability to allow embarked personnel to send electronic messages home anyway. All contact was either by regular mail—slow—or by phone when the ship reached a port. Long distance was rather expensive, so most of our communication was via written letters. The time between writing to my husband and getting a reply was usually a week to ten days, not bad really, considering they were over 10,000 miles away. If I needed additional funds to make ends meet, I was pretty much on my own. Sometimes, that meant I'd spend less on groceries or go without such things as a trip to the beauty parlor for a haircut. The children usually had all they needed but not a lot of extras. The Navy pay was not very good at that time, but then things were also a lot less expensive.

Being mother and father was not something I'd been prepared to be, but there was no option. My three decided to push me as soon as Dad went away. Their misbehavior lasted until I got to a point that a spanking for all was required. Later, it came out that our son ran the show, advising his sisters to not cry, which didn't help at all.

Living in base housing, we were fortunate that utilities were included. An additional benefit was that if the water heater ruptures, a maintenance man was sent out to replace it. If anything went wrong with the house, the Navy always had someone ready to help.

Our escape artist Lab got loose so frequently in the housing area that the Shore Patrol finally told me if she got out once more, they wouldn't return her to us. In response, I went to The Western Farmers feed store in Oak Harbor and purchased a horse tether. I also advised the children to be more careful about where she was when they opened a door to go out. Those measures did the trick, and we managed to keep our dog. She was a big part of our family. Our son would lie on the floor with his head on her side, twisting her hair and sucking on his thumb until he fell asleep.

Whidbey Island is not a warm place. Summer lasted about two weeks. Being from the mid-Atlantic region, I had always been into sunbathing. There was a small ditch behind our house, and my friends and I would go into it to cut the wind and try to get a tan—pretty desperate! We usually took some wine and cheese along with the suntan lotion. Sunscreen was not part of the plan. Screening that weak sun was the last thing any of us wanted to do.

The thing I missed the most while Ed was gone was having an extended family around me. The squadron became my family as we did lots of things together. For example, we painted mushrooms on driftwood to sell at Officers' Wives' Club fund-raisers. We got together once a month at the Skipper's house to have a meeting. If you had a problem, you could usually get help there. We had garage sales. We tried to get together for supper out once a month, usually at the Officers' Club, because it was a lot more affordable than going to a restaurant in town. Most of us were far away from our extended families, so the support of the squadron made life bearable.

The six-month cruise we were promised turned into a thirteen-month cruise. The sad part was that the extensions were done one line period at a time. It was a tradition that we have a party when the ship departed the combat area, and our squadron would be on the way home, out of harm's way, off the line. The first party was relatively tame. The day after the party, we all found out that they were not on the way home. They would be flying for another line period (roughly a month, but they could vary quite a bit). The second party came and went and still the squadron was extended. We had a party every month until the final real party. One of our outings to the Officers' Club got a bit out of hand. For some unknown reason, it seemed like a good idea to throw our empty glasses at the fireplace. Unfortunately, there was a copper cover over the stone work that took a lot of hits from errant glasses which failed to land in the fireplace itself. The Club sent our men the bill to replace it. They paid it, but the Club never did replace that copper cover. The last time I was there years later, it was still dented. At the final party held at the Skipper's home, the Oak Harbor Police parked outside and stayed there driving any impaired wife home until all of us were safely home. There were quite a few of us who needed the service, and we all appreciated their efforts.

When the planes flew in, we were all dressed in our best clothes.[16] The children were clean and waiting for their fathers. We usually had banners. I think I kissed the plane and gave thanks. The whole town of Oak Harbor had "Welcome Home" sings. It was an unforgettable experience, and the townspeople themselves made it extra special.

Being home while your husband is away flying against people who are doing their best to kill him is a difficult thing to live with. Add to that having to deal with small children and not having your family nearby can make you feel very much overwhelmed and alone. The squadron, however, made all the difference. We were able to lean on each other and provide one another with that adult contact which is so critical to mental health. I will never forget my sisters in VA-165 and VA-52, and I thank them today for all their help and friendship.

---

16. Author's note: I didn't fly in with VA-165. This memory was from our VA-52 fly-in after the war.

CHAPTER 5

THE OPERATIONAL TEST AND EVALUATION FORCE

My new job was with DEPCOMOPTEVFORPAC located at NAS North Island in Coronado, California. That was such a complicated acronym that Peggy had to practice writing it out, so she could get it right on the checks she spent at the Commissary and Exchange. It stood for: Deputy Commander Operational Test and Evaluation Force Pacific. Our headquarters, where the Commander of OPTEVFOR resided, was in Norfolk, Virginia. So the Deputy Commander was responsible for all operational testing on the West Coast.

We found a nice three-bedroom, two-bath home, surrounded by a low-maintenance garden, on Tee Bird Lane in San Diego on the north mesa overlooking Fashion Valley. It was a beautiful starter home for our family, but it was not a dog-friendly yard for our black Labrador retriever, Heidi, but we were lucky to place her with a nice family on Whidbey Island, so she wouldn't have to leave the only home she ever knew.

My new job was a really interesting one: I was to be a project officer in the Radar and ECM (Electronic Counter-Measures) Division of DEPCOMOPTEVFORPAC. The downside to the job was that I was to spend a good deal of time at sea doing operational testing of various systems. I learned a lot about the surface and subsurface Navy in that job going to sea in both types. I even had the opportunity to help another project officer, LCDR Wally Clough, a surface warfare officer, work out his test plan for the Ægis Weapon System, since he didn't have a feel for aircraft fuel requirements, and his test plan called for some very high speed runs in complicated patterns.

As Wally and I became friends, he told me he had been part of the minesweeping operations, which the US had promised the North Vietnamese as part of the peace deal signed in Paris. Since I had dropped more than a few of them, I was interested in what he had to say about his operations. Then he informed me that the Navy told the sweepers that most of the mines were duds, planned that way from the beginning to make the sweeping operations easier and safer. I was stunned. The more I thought about how close Phil and I had come to death in order to press home our mine attack in Dong Hoi Harbor, the more angry I became. Risking death to drop duds? What was my Navy thinking? I experienced my first burst bubble of enthusiasm for the Navy at that time, and it wasn't pleasant. The Management didn't seem to care about providing the Fleet with the best equipment they could to help them fight and win. It was hard to believe, but that fact would be reinforced in the months and years to come. It seems that people at the top really did care more about the politics and the programmatic than they did our Fleet.

LCDR Wally Clough and I Planning the Aircraft
Target Profiles for his Ægis Testing
Note my handlebar moustache. It was legal under
the uniform regulations established by our Chief of
Naval Operations, ADM Elmo R. Zumwalt.

Peggy and I became certified divers, and Wally had bought and lived on a ninety-seven-foot wooden schooner built in the '30s in Nova Scotia. Since he and his wife really liked abalone, they invited Peggy and I to go out with them many Saturdays to fish for the tasty little crustaceans off Point Loma. At that time, sport divers were allowed to fish for them, but that has long since changed. I don't think we ever went out on one of these trips when we didn't catch our bag limit. I got pretty good with a spear gun and managed to bag a nice selection of game fish at the same time.

Keeping the promise I had made to myself to be a better father to my kids, and especially my son, my eldest daughter joined the

YMCA Indian Maidens, while my son joined their Indian Guides. Peggy and I were very active with those programs and life in our neighborhood was really good for the kids. They had quite a few friends, and we took many family trips to the beach.

Entertainment and great restaurants were readily available, and Peggy and I took advantage of it. We really had a good time in San Diego, despite the fact that I was still at sea a lot. But I was having trouble dealing with the effects of all the near-death experiences I had in conjunction with the memories of those comrades who didn't get to come home like I did. I would slip into black moods and become almost suicidal. I didn't seek death, but I didn't turn away from it either. Today, I suppose I would have been diagnosed with PTSD (Post-Traumatic Stress Syndrome), but in the 1970s, I was just glad no one was spitting on me. People really didn't care what any of had been through, except those who actually attacked returning vets. I still feel rage at how despicably they acted, and personally, I will never forgive Jane Fonda and all her left-wing friends.

I really had not expected to reach the age of thirty since I concluded I couldn't possibly survive two combat cruises. Despite the odds, February 1974 arrived on schedule, and with it my thirtieth birthday. Peggy knew I was having a lot of trouble adjusting to life again and dreaded reaching thirty, so she threw me a birthday party that I will never forget. She made it a champagne brunch and invited a small group of our closest friends over. The food was incredible. The company was great. We drank all the champagne in the house, took a nap, and got up, bought more, and started all over again. What a birthday! What a wonderful wife I had. Her concern helped me through those dark days, and I will be always grateful to her for her love and understanding.

One of the officers with whom I worked in the Division was getting ready to retire, and he was the project officer for the WLR-8, the new ECM system which the Navy intended to install in the planned USS *Los Angeles* (SSN-688) Class submarines.[17] It was an important project, but it had been plagued with technical difficul-

---

17. SSN-688 was commissioned on 13 November 1976, and decommissioned on 4 February 2011.

ties, which had caused him to put the project into *deficiency* status several times, extending the testing period, and of course, increasing the cost. The command felt there was a good chance that he would, in fact, retire before the project completed OPEVAL (Operational Evaluation), which it had to do in order for the Navy to fund its procurement according to DoD regulations. So I was named as his assistant and had to very quickly get up to speed on both the system and the test plan he had written.

The unit we were testing had been installed on the USS *Sargo* (SSN-583),[18] homeported at Pearl Harbor, Hawaii, and we were advised by the Developer that the unit had passed TECHEVAL (Technical Evaluation) and had been certified ready for OPEVAL. So it was time for us to head to Pearl Harbor.

---

18. SSN-583 was commissioned on 1 October 1958, and decommissioned on 21 April 1988.

USS *Sargo* (SSN-583)

The project officer, our ET-1 (first class electrician's mate) technician, and I arrived in Honolulu and secured rooms in the Pearl Harbor BOQ and BEQ on Saturday before heading down to *Sargo* who was alongside at the Submarine Base. When we arrived, there were "yard birds" (shipyard workers) all over the boat, and the periscope was pulled out of the sail (the WLR-8 antenna was mounted at the top of that mast). That wasn't the condition we expected to find our project submarine in the weekend before we were to start OPEVAL. After going aboard, we discovered that the Captain had ordered the periscope pulled because it had been leaking when they dove, and he wasn't very happy. We let the shipyard and the Captain worry about that part, and we went back aft where our equipment was located, and our tech got to work running diagnostics and checking out the system.

That took an hour or so, and by the time he was finished, he was sweating and didn't look too well. He told us he had a real problem with claustrophobia. What a time to find that out! The project officer and I decided we couldn't let me go out to sea on that boat, so it would just be the two of us. He would stay ashore and provide such support as he could from there.

Finally, Monday rolled around, and it was time to get underway. It turned out that SUBPAC had a few staff officers aboard so they could keep their submarine specialty pay, so as a Lieutenant, I was assigned to share a berth with a machinist mate in enlisted berthing. This is known as hot bunking, and since he was a bona fide member of the crew and I was a foreigner, he had the bunk priority. I got to use it when he was on watch or working. Otherwise, it was his, and I had to stay up whether we were testing or not. As we cleared Pearl Harbor and transited into deeper water, it was time to dive, and never having been on a submarine at sea before, I wanted to be in the control room when we did. So I pretended to be some bulkhead paint over in the corner to watch this whole evolution. The Captain ordered the boat to dive, the klaxon sounded, and orders started flying around as ballast tanks were opened to the sea, and we started to slide beneath the waves. Unfortunately, just as the sail slid under, seawater started pouring down around the periscope tube all over the

Captain and XO; that's right, the same tube the yard birds were supposed to have fixed on Saturday. The air in the control room turned blue immediately as the Captain decided to tell everyone how he really felt about the shipyard, so I decided it was time to go check on my equipment and chat with the sailors who would be operating it.

Our gear was fine, and the sailors from the Pacific Fleet seemed confident in their ability to operate it. Since the boat had planned on doing some local training south of Pearl Harbor, we wouldn't be transiting over to our OPEVAL area in the Pacific Missile Test Range near Barking Sands off the west coast of Kauai, so I had plenty of time to get familiar with the equipment and its operation. Unfortunately, on Thursday, one of the crew came down with an attack of appendicitis, and the Captain had to head back into port to get him to the hospital. That event turned out to be very fortunate for me, as later events will reveal.

Once in port, the Captain decided to have a morale-building party with the officers and crew, and our little group was invited. Unfortunately, as the festivities were switching into high gear, my project officer announced that he would buy the crew a keg of beer if they would cut off half my moustache when we left for Barking Sands on Monday. They, of course, thought was great news since I was an "airedale" (surface and subsurface Navy's name for aviators) anyway. I had very different feelings about it. After all, I was under orders to go to sea with these guys, and now, I was going to be attacked when I did because my project officer, the guy I was trying to help move into retirement, had led them to do it. After he thought about it, he even agreed. Then he decided that since I knew my way around airplanes and the bulk of our testing was going to be with P-3s from NAS Barber's Point on Oahu, that I should run the test services from the command center at Barking Sands. I called my wife that night, after I had made travel arrangements for myself and my tech, to ask her to meet me there, but she said she didn't have any money and simply couldn't do it. I was disappointed, but there was nothing I could do about it and got on the plane for Kauai on Sunday to move in and get ready for operations starting on Monday.

He and I arrived at Barking Sands Command Center bright and early Monday morning, and while we were awaiting *Sargo*'s arrival, we familiarized ourselves with the command and control systems in the Center. I spoke with the SDO of the P-3 squadron which had been appointed to provide our airborne radar sources for our equipment on the boat. Everything seemed to be in readiness when *Sargo* checked into Barking Sands Control.

It didn't take long for things to go wrong. Immediately, the range reported that they could not pick up the transponder they had installed on the boat to facilitate tracking its exact position during our OPEVAL. Despite everyone's best efforts, the transponder remained dead. Unfortunately, this meant that in order for the ranges tracking radars to gain a "skin paint" track on the target submarine, *Sargo* would have to operate "broached" (i.e., with her sail partially exposed above the water). In a seaway, like we had running at the time, that is the most uncomfortable position for any submarine. Their hull shape is not designed to dampen motion, so they roll and pitch like crazy. Now, I was glad once again for a whole different set of reasons that I was not aboard. So was our ET-1, by the way!

So after much time wasted, and that meant money for the developer, who was represented by a Commander who was in the Command Center with me, I was finally able to get an aircraft over the OPAREA and begin executing our test plan. Unfortunately, our gear seemed to be deaf and dumb. No one working the gear on the boat could pick up the aircraft's radar emissions. I talked with the flight crew to ensure their gear was working properly, and they confirmed that it was. So the problem seemed to be with the WLR-8, and our operators on *Sargo* then had to begin troubleshooting everything, so I had to send the aircraft back to Barber's Point since there was no sense in incurring more costs just to have be orbit the area. The day wore on, and it became quitting time for the government civilians manning the Center, and they asked me if I would authorize overtime. I turned to the developer with the recommendation to continue working until we got some usable data since we had already invested in a full day of range services as well as the aircraft, but he decided to cut it off, so we secured for the day.

My ET-1 and I had a light supper at a little roadside Japanese noodle shop on the way home, so we didn't get back to the motel until 2000 or so. I walked up to the desk to ask for my key, and the clerk told me it had been picked up by a woman. Now, that was a surprise. I asked who it was, but the clerk couldn't describe her. I think my ET-1 was just as curious as I was because he walked with me up to my room. I knocked on the door since I had no key, and Peggy opened it! Now I was really surprised! Of course, I was very happy to see her, but she was a bit miffed with me because (a) I was late and (b) there were strange cigarette butts in the ashtray. Thank God, they didn't have lipstick on them! They belonged to my ET-1. It was a good thing the developer's CDR refused to pay for overtime that night!

She had no money left, so I fed her and gave her some cash, so she wouldn't be destitute while we were working. While she ate, she explained how she had managed to get to Kauai and find me; I had not told her where I was staying because she said she couldn't come. It was quite a story. My Division Head had called her to ask what she wanted to do about my paycheck he was holding for me (yes, in those days we still received government checks; direct deposit was unknown). So he agreed to drop it off at our home. She deposited it into our account and started writing checks. He told her where I was staying on Kauai, and she booked a flight to Kauai with an overnight stop in Honolulu. She found a dump of a motel to spend the night since she brought very little cash. The next day, she flew out to Kauai and hired a cab to take her to my motel. That took the rest of the money she had, so she had to wait in my room until I got back from work. Hence, her anxiousness at my tardiness. But once again, Peggy proved herself to be very resourceful and not a little courageous. I was very pleased that she had joined me since neither of us had ever been to that island before. We had a great time, when I wasn't working, and got to see most of the sites and hear the local legends about the Menehunes and their love of fresh island pork wrapped in Ti leaves and the haunted hotel which had been built on a burial ground without benefit of a Kahuna, but those are stories for another time.

Meanwhile, back at the Command Center, our tests were not going well, and it was the fault of the WLR-8 itself. We were able to establish clearly that the P-3 could pick up the submarine with its radar before the WLR-8 could hear it. That goes completely against the "radar equation,"[19] which states that the power received from a target varies with the fourth power of the distance to that target, but the power at a receiver which originated from a transmitter only varies at the square of the distance because the radar signal must be transmitted out to the target and bounce back to the receiver at the start point, whereas, the receiver only has to listen for the source since it doesn't transmit.

These results rendered the WLR-8 useless to an operational commander of any submarine, so we had no choice but to place the system back into deficiency status. My developer CDR was not happy with us, but the facts were irrefutable. When we got back to San Diego, we wrote up our findings and submitted them to the CNO (Chief of Naval Operations) for whom we worked. The project officer then retired, and one day, I was told that the Navy had started procurement of the WLR-8 for installation on the *Los Angeles* Class submarines. I was furious and asked my superiors how that could be possible since the system had failed OPEVAL every time we tested it. They answered that the Navy Staff took the results from our Barking Sands tests and changed the specs to reflect what we had measured, despite the fact that it showed the system to not be operationally effective. Once again, the Navy had broken another bubble for me.

About this time, all of our POWs had been returned from North Vietnam, at least so far as we could determine. So the River

---

19. $P_r = \dfrac{P_t G_t A_r \sigma F^4}{(4\pi)^2 R^4}$, where

   P_t = transmitter power
   G_t = gain of the transmitting antenna
   A_r = effective aperture (area) of the receiving antenna
   σ = radar cross section, or scattering coefficient, of the target
   F = pattern propagation factor
   R = distance from the transmitter/receiver to the target

Rats, who had had many "practice" reunions up to that time, decided it was time to schedule the First Real River Rat Reunion to welcome them all home. As luck would have it, the group decided it would be held in Las Vegas, so Peggy and I determined to go. It was a singular event in our lives, and I very much doubt that we will ever experience anything quite like it again.

The Dodds had to be reassigned after VA-165 to Nellis AFB, Nevada, right next to Las Vegas, and they invited us to stay with them—kids and all. So we packed up and headed out, arriving Friday afternoon. That night, there was a s———t hot flight suit party, where everyone wore their party flight suits. The booze was free! It was a time to be loud and rowdy, and we managed it quite well. Saturday night, however, was a formal supper to which we all wore mess dress. It was held in one of the biggest halls I've ever seen. The ladies were all dressed to the nines in their evening attire, and it was quite a contrast to the previous evening. We all stood behind our chairs until everyone had filed in, and the president of the River Rats commenced the proceedings—all quite formal, except for the gun camera video they had playing on giant screens behind the stage. Of course, they all came from the Air Force because none of the Navy planes carried any video equipment. After a wonderful supper, where everything was served hot despite the huge number of people present, every entertainer then playing in Las Vegas performed for us—one after the other. It was an evening never to be forgotten, and I hope our brothers, the former POWs, enjoyed themselves. It all was, after all, on their behalf.

Pretty soon, I had begun discussions with my detailer for my next duty assignment. I very badly wanted to go back to a Fleet A-6 squadron, especially since the new A-6E was beginning to hit the Fleet. He informed me, however, that the general rule in BUPERS (Bureau of Naval Personnel) was "two tours in type prior to screen," which meant the second tour had to be a department head because that was a necessary block to check in order to screen for command. Those jobs went to fairly senior LCDRs (Lieutenant Commanders). Therefore, I was looking at a ship's company job of some sort. That held no appeal for me at all, so we were at a standstill.

Meanwhile, I was given the project officer's job of conducting the Fleet Operational Appraisal of the AN/SPS-55 Radar. It was a fairly modern surface search radar in a higher frequency band than the old Fleet workhorse: the AN/SPS-10. So it should have greater resolution in addition to other qualities, and it should be easier to the Fleet technicians to maintain it. Unfortunately, it had no stealthy characteristics, and in 1974, we were finally starting to ask questions like: "Why not make our radios and radars harder to detect?" and "Why not build ships with smaller radar cross-sections?" There was some very interesting research going on at the time, not only in those areas, but also in the area of signal propagation through the atmosphere, an area of study inextricably tied to those other topics. We had discovered that the world's atmosphere was not isotropic, rather it was strongly anisotropic, and in some areas of the world, the effects of those non-uniform characteristics could be quite pronounced. I agreed with many of the researchers that the Navy not only needed to understand these things but had to procure equipment and develop tactics to take advantage of those in our favor while mitigating those which negatively affected our operations.

None of my arguments gained any traction. It seemed that those in the Pentagon knew better about everything, and my job boiled down to taking this available surface search radar system and seeing how best to use it. It wasn't the best we could do for the Fleet, but it was all we were allowed to do. Yes, another bubble burst.

My project ship was USS *Buchannan* (DDG-14), and I spent several months aboard her in all kinds of weather, taking dozens of photographs of the radar scope, with different settings, to determine the best ones for any given set of conditions. At the end of the testing period, I wrote my final report, and it sailed through our local "murder board" with very few changes. Then, I had to take it to our Headquarters in Norfolk, Virginia, to undergo their murder board. The Headquarters staff declared it was the best report they had seen in a long time and made no significant changes to it. I was quite pleased.

USS *Buchannan* (DDG-14)

Then, one day my detailer called to ask if I would mind going to VA-52 at Whidbey Island, the first West Coast A-6E squadron. It seems I had been requested by the perspective skipper, currently the XO, CDR Darryl Kerr. Of course, I jumped at the chance to fly the A-6E, and my family was eager to get back to Whidbey after three years in San Diego. So the decision was made, and we traveled up there to look for a place to live, determined that it not be in housing this time.

CHAPTER 6

VA-52

After much looking with an agent in Oak Harbor, we bought 2½ acres out in the Silver Lake District and chose a home design with one of the largest home builders in the area. Returning to San Diego, I started to wrap up my various projects with DEPCOMOPTEVFORPAC while construction got underway in Washington. By the time I detached, the house was still not quite finished, so the family moved into two adjoining rooms in the BOQ at Ault Field, where the kids started school, and Peggy and I worked on finishing our unfinished basement. We quickly became expert drywall installers and discovered just how hard that work was. We even found a pallet of old worm-eaten cedar shingles from one of the local lumber yards and put them up on the wall which would be behind our bar. The effect was quite stunning.

Later, when my parents and maternal grandfather (my grandmother had died earlier) came out to visit, my grandfather, my father, my son, and I finished up the downstairs fireplace with brick. I was very proud of our work and the four generations it represented. I spent one winter in front of it reading Tolkien's *The Hobbit* and his *Lord of the Rings* Trilogy to our kids. We never started until their homework was finished, and they watched very little TV that winter.

It was a great time for our family, and I will cherish those evenings for the rest of my life.

The A-6E was the definitive version of the Intruder with vastly upgraded navigation and attack systems, introduced in 1970 and first deployed on 9 December 1971. The earlier separate search and track (fire control) radars of the A-6A/B/C were replaced by a single Norden AN/APQ-148 multi-mode radar, and onboard computers with a more sophisticated (and generally more reliable) solid state-based system, as opposed to the A-6A's DIANE discrete transistor-based technology. A new AN/ASN-92 inertial navigation system was added, along with the CAINS (Carrier Aircraft Inertial Navigation System), for greater navigation accuracy. We did not yet have the characteristic chin turret which would hold the FLIR (Forward-Looking Infra-Red) and laser systems because they were still under development, but the aircraft was a Cadillac compared to the A-6A.

VA-52 Knightriders' History

VA-52 made two more deployments with the Skyraider to Vietnam before entering the jet age with the advanced A-6A Intruder on 10 November 1967. The Knightriders also made a squadron move to NAS Whidbey Island that same year. The Intruder's side-by-side seating enhanced its ability to fulfill its primary mission: a true medium-attack, all-weather capability. The Intruder utilized its advanced radar to navigate through mountain valleys at low levels in order to minimize the aircraft's risk from enemy radar-guided missiles. The Intruder could carry a large payload over long distances and deliver its weapons more accurately than ever possible before. On 7 September 1968, VA-52 made its first Vietnam combat deployment with the Intruder aboard the USS *Coral Sea* (CVA-43) with Carrier

Air Wing 15. The *Knightriders* again saw combat in Vietnam during their next two cruises with Carrier Air Wing 11 aboard USS *Kitty Hawk* (CVA-63). On their second *Kitty Hawk* cruise, the *Knightriders* flew the A-6B and were introduced to the KA-6D tanker.

In January 1972, the Knightriders left for a one-month deployment aboard USS *Kitty Hawk* that lasted for eleven months. North Vietnam had invaded South Vietnam and CVW-11, with the *Knightriders*, began the first sustained air operations over North Vietnam in over three years. The *Knightriders* participated in all of Operation Linebacker I. Among their tasking, they were responsible for mining many of North Vietnam's harbors and inlets, including Haiphong. Using the A-6B, the *Knightriders* shot 113 Standard ARMs at enemy radar defenses. As a result of their mini-cruise extension, VA-52 became the most decorated Intruder squadron and, for its sustained efforts, was awarded the Naval Air Force Pacific Fleet Battle Efficiency Pennant for 1973.

In November 1973, the *Knightriders*, aboard USS *Kitty Hawk*, began their first peacetime cruise in over ten years. In July 1974, they were the first West Coast squadron to transition to the A-6E. They deployed with their new A-6Es aboard *Kitty Hawk* in May 1975 and returned to Whidbey in December 1975 to transition to the advanced A-6E with the Carrier Aircraft Inertial Navigation System (CAINS). In October 1977, VA-52 began its third peacetime cruise with CVW-11 onboard *Kitty Hawk*, returned to NAS Whidbey in May 1978, and then joined CVW-15 that July. In May 1979, the *Knightriders* headed west again, onboard *Kitty Hawk*, and in November, under President Carter's orders, sailed into the Indian Ocean in response to the Iranian hostage crisis, where they remained until returning to Whidbey in February 1980.

The *Knightriders* saw combat again on 19 January 1993, as they struck targets deep in Iraq. Their performance was nothing less than superb, hitting all targets assigned to them with laser-guided bombs. On 24 June 1994, the *Knightriders* began their last cruise with CDR Rivers Cleveland at the helm. They no longer had the KA-6D aircraft, but the A-6E SWIP with Night Vision Goggle (NVG) capable aircrew and aircraft. These improvements made the *Knightriders* the most combat-capable squadron ever to fly the venerable Intruder. VA-52 was the first A-6 NVG squadron on the West Coast. The squadron was decommissioned in April 1995.

Joining Up with VA-52 Deployed

Viceroy 503 A-6E of the VA-52 *Knightriders*

Completing the RAG (VA-128) once again, I reported into VA-52 who was already deployed. I had to fly to Clark AB and take a bus south to NAS Cubi Point in the Philippines to meet USS *Kitty Hawk* (CV-63) there. Notice that the Navy had dropped the "A" for "Attack" after the CV because we now carried S-2 ASW (Anti-Submarine Warfare) aircraft with us. This was an experiment to try and make the aircraft carrier more versatile. We were to do a lot of experimenting that cruise—the only peacetime cruise I would ever make. The Pentagon had decided that we had over ten years' experience dropping bombs on land targets but didn't know how to attack the Soviet Fleet. That was certainly true. So a lot of emphasis was going to be put on trying to figure it out. Unlike the Japanese Imperial Navy of WWII, the Soviet Navy had a high degree of electronic sophistication, including their LRA (Long Range Aircraft) support. They could pick up and fix just about any sort of electronic emission and have a supersonic air assault called in on us in very little time.

War at Sea

We had to become adept at operating in EMCON Alpha (Emission Control Condition Alpha—no emissions at all) if we were going to be able to locate the Soviet Fleet units before they located us. To do that, we executed many operations in the Central Pacific under Blue Water Ops (no bingo fields: if you can't land, you swim) conditions against "Red" units played by our USN auxiliaries, using our E-2s to locate them. I think the tactic would have worked if we had ever had to fight the Soviet Navy, but we would have suffered significant losses. Their ships bristled with antiair weapons, both missiles and guns, and we didn't have any ship-killing weapons in our arsenal, like a torpedo.

Flying aircraft to and from aircraft carriers under these conditions was demanding. As the ship turned into the wind and prepared to launch aircraft, a crewman would drop a smoke flare over the side. We would launch off the bow, turn left to fly down the port side of the ship, and then cross abaft the stern to cross over the smoke on the pre-briefed outbound heading for rendezvous with the other elements of the strike package. We had to stay at very low altitude until we were a significant distance from the carrier, so as not to reveal its position from our radar returns. Of course, we had all of our emitters in standby, even our radar altimeters. Once we rendezvoused, the strike leader would head out toward the "enemy" surface action group to conduct the strike. Only when we were about to turn in to our target would we start transmitting our radars. After our runs, we would all head back independently with everything turned off once again to the pre-briefed location of the ship for recovery. Once we spotted the ship, we would simply fly up the starboard side of the ship at pattern altitude, break at the bow, turn downwind, dirty up, and land. The only communication with the ship was when the LSO would flash his "cut" lights on the optical landing system. That would be the visual response to our normal radio calls to him with fuel state and side number—Roger Ball. As difficult as these operations were with the A-6E, they were demanding in the extreme with the KA-6D, which had no navigation system at all. It was absolutely essential for the B/N to (a) keep a kneeboard pad record of all headings, airspeeds, and altitudes, with a rough plot of where they had flown in addition to all the tanker information because the tanker had to fly out to a distant rendezvous point with the F-14 *Tomcat*s to tank them before returning back to the ship. So there were turns, altitude changes, orbits, and other maneuvers which would occur during one of these missions. All of them had to be taken into account by the B/N if he had any chance of finding the ship again without electronic navigation support. I learned to read the wind on the waves very well. It proved to be a big help, and Al and I never got lost, always finding the ship and landing without incident. That was not true of all of the *Knightriders'* B/Ns. We had one guy who just couldn't do it, and the XO, CDR Kerr, blamed me as the squadron's B/N Training Officer. I worked with this guy for hours, telling him all the things that I did and that he had to if he wanted to get back to the ship without asking for them to turn on their TACAN for him (which he had done twice already). He did improve.

A KA-6D from VA-35, *Blue Blasters*, Tanking an
F-14 from VF-101, *Grim Reapers*.
This evolved into a major peacetime roll for the A-6
since the F-14s were essential for Fleet Defense.

Since I had a background with Navy Procurement from my last tour, I knew that many projects were initiated at the request of the Fleet, so I suggested to our Ops Officer and Skipper that we urge the Navy to develop an upgraded version of the torpedo, which the A-6 could carry on our centerline rack (I believe it was rated for 3,000 pounds), could be dropped at high speed and low altitude with some sort of retard device (e.g., a parachute or Snakeye retard fins) to slow it down so it wouldn't hit the water too hard and at too shallow an angle to prevent damage and resist a ricochet.

I was met with laughter and criticism from the Air Wing 11 staff and commander who asked me if I had forgotten about "Torpedo 8" at the Battle of Midway.[20] Of course, I knew all about them, but they were flying an obsolete aircraft at the time of the battle and carrying defective torpedoes. If they shot one at a fast Japanese ship, like their aircraft carriers, the Captain would turn away from it at flank speed and run away from it until it ran out of fuel and sank. The combined

---

20. VT-8 was decimated by Japanese Zero fighters on their approach to their carriers. All of them were shot down, and not one torpedo found its target. There was only one survivor, ENS George Gay.

speed of the *Devastator* torpedo bomber and the torpedo itself were insufficient to catch the ship before the fuel ran out. Our 500kt+ aircraft coupled with a modern, fast, reliable torpedo would overcome those shortcomings while allowing us the possibility of sinking the Soviet ship in order to avoid coming back for another strike and lose more aircraft. But once again, no one in "management" wanted to listen—bubbles bursting again.

This cruise dragged on and was characterized by a lot of alert standing and very little flying. Some of our pilots who had made the whole cruise couldn't even make Centurion (100 arrested landings) on *Kitty Hawk* that cruise. We were operating in the Northern Pacific and had to fly and stand alerts in wet suits because of the water temperature. They were miserable.

Intruder ASW

We also experimented with helping the S-2s, which were twin piston-engined aircraft, with their ASW mission. The ship modified some rocket pods to take sonobuoys, so the theory was that once a submarine had been found, we would launch immediately and fly out to the "datum" at high speed and drop the sonobuoys in a circular pattern around that point. Then, by the time we finished, the S-2 would be on station to actually prosecute the contact. It was a miserable failure. Most of the time, we couldn't get the sonobuoys out of the rocket pods, and when we did, the S-2s never seemed to be able to find the submarine. I guess our brothers beneath the waves got a good laugh out of our feeble attempts at finding them. I still believe to this day, that if you want to find a submarine, use another submarine—one that's faster and more quiet than its target.

One in-port period at Cubi Point, we were told to get a Marine A-6 squadron ready for carrier qualifications on board our own ship. It turned out to be VAM(AW)-533, Hawks, and most, if not all, of their pilots hadn't seen a flight deck since the Training Command. Our LSOs (Landing Signal Officers) worked with them for hours out on the runway at Cubi Point until they thought they might not kill themselves when they tried it "at the boat." When we finally did get underway, everyone was glued to the PLAT (Pilot's Landing Aide Television) monitors in the ready room to watch "the show"—and what a show it was. It was a thrill a minute—at least for us—but no planes were wrecked and nobody died, so I guess it was successful.

Kitty Hawk was in such bad shape during this cruise that she had to be towed into Guam during her initial transit to the Philippines. She dragged one screw because the bearings were shot, and that screw left an oil slick everywhere we went. After a while, we learned to follow it into the break during Case II recoveries. Real fires happened all the time, especially in the #1 Main Machinery Room, just under our ready room. Since aircrewmen's station during GQ (General Quarters) was in the ready room, we were always neatly assembled just above the fire ranging in the #1 Main because they were major enough to cause the ship to go to GQ. That really made no sense to me at all. But management knew better. It didn't matter that the fire was just beneath us, and you couldn't walk on the deck barefoot, aircrew belonged in their ready rooms during GQ, and that was that—period! More bubbles bursting.

We deployed up to the Sea of Japan in response to some unpleasantness that the North Koreans were staging once again and planned a lot of targets there in the event the president wanted to make a point. I had been told that there was always a large Soviet Navy presence there, but when I finally saw it, I thought all the stories didn't do the facts justice. Soviet surface ships were everywhere, and our fighters kept launching to intercept in-bound *Bear* reconnaissance aircraft. Manning up on the flight deck, we got a good look at their ships, and they were beautiful with their shining red decks. Not only that, they could really perform. I watched as *Kitty Hawk* turned sharply into the wind away from the current Soviet ship trailer we had with us, but despite our hard turn, I watched a "rooster tail" appear aft of the Soviet as he accelerated at an incredible speed to take up his position on our new heading. They weren't just pretty. Then, as we returned to the ship, we would watch the oil slick streaming out from behind our ship as she was being shadowed by these beautiful Soviet types. It was embarrassing.

In-Flight Emergency

One night, Al and I were awarded the recovery tanker mission for the last event of the night. I never liked night cat shots, and I never liked the KA-6D: the aircraft simply did not require a B/N in the right seat. Had we had enlisted aircrewmen, they could have easily handled the job of operating the tanker package and keeping track of who got our fuel. Nighttime on the flight deck was just all too surreal. The deck was dark, and all you could see were colored wands moving around wielded by various members of the flight deck crew. Taxiing was an act of faith. The pilot had to take his taxi directions from a pair of yellow wands without knowing where he was going and sometimes thinking he was headed off the flight deck. Once on the catapult, all you could see were the very small white deck edge lights up on the bow. On a dark night, there was no sea, no sky, and no ship—just darkness.

This night was no different, but we found ourselves on the #2 catapult (port bow cat) staring into the darkness with 26,000 pounds of JP-5 on board. Al received the run-up signal, and he went to 100 percent on both engines as we checked all the cockpit gauges, and he "wiped out the cockpit" with the controls (moving the stick and rudders to their full deflection). Everything looked fine, and I held up my gooseneck flashlight with a red lens aiming at the VSI (Vertical Situation Indicator, rate of climb). This was something Jay Grafton had taught me years ago. It was essential if the aircraft had a double generator failure on launch since all the instrument lights would be lost, and the VSI is the only instrument which tells the pilot where he will be not just where he is. Flying off the bow, where the carriers usually launched the A-6s, it was vital to know that the plane was actually climbing.

Now, Al turned the lights on, indicating we were ready to go. In the daytime, he would have saluted the catapult officer. In a second or two, we felt the holdback fitting break and the aircraft surged forward. Just then, that dark cockpit lit up like Times Square. The Master Caution light starting blinking and all the firelights (both engines and the wheel well temp light) came on as we left the ship and started flying into that dark night. Since Al was a nugget, I didn't think he would think about the Emergency Jettison button, although he did have the landing gear coming up, so I screamed at him to jettison everything. He hit the button, and all our five drop tanks with 2,000 pounds of fuel each dropped off the aircraft, making us over 10,000 pounds lighter instantly. Then I had him start the fuel dumps from our wings and fuselage tanks.

I then got on the radio and declared an emergency, explaining our multiple fire lights. Our XO, CDR Kerr, was in CATTC as our squadron rep for this event, and he got on the radio right away. As we talked, I was looking through the PCL (Pocket Checklist, a small version of the NATOPS Manual which can be carried on the kneeboard) and started trying to find a procedure to help us. The only thing in it was the procedure for a single engine fire, and of course, it concludes with: "In the event of positive indications of fire, eject." Well, here we were seconds ahead of *Kitty Hawk*'s bow contemplating ejection. Since my boots were burning yet, I rejected that out of hand. If we ejected, the ship would run us over. There were examples of A-6 crews ejecting off the bow, and the results were rarely good. So I never mentioned the "e" word to Al. I just kept thumbing through the checklist to find something that wasn't there. CDR Kerr didn't have anything to add really either, but I was glad he was on the radio.

Suddenly, I looked up from the PCL and noted we were clearing 32,000 feet with both engines still at 100 percent power. We were on the verge of exceeding the EGTs (Exhaust Gas Temperatures) on both of them, even if they weren't on fire. So I got Al to back off on the power while the ship gave us a heading to proceed downwind to get into the pattern for an emergency landing. At this time, all the fire lights were still on, but we had no other indications of fire, and the aircraft flew well, so we started down from our lofty perch to land this beast.

As we started down in the groove, once again, I was watching the landing area and the ball when Al told me he couldn't see the ball because the fire lights were blinding him. I took off my fire-resistant gloves and wrapped them over the fire lights. That seemed to work, and Al got us back aboard with no further problems. Then, as we taxied out of the wires, the flight deck crew started taxiing us around as though we had not declared an emergency for the aircraft being on fire. I never did learn why they had done that, but today, I believe they had never been told that we thought we were on fire. As we taxied into our final parking spot, and Al prepared to shut down the engines, out of habit, he hit the Fire/Oil Test button, so he could read our oil level (a procedure taught to all A-6 pilots which they did instinctively), and all the fire lights went out. Revelation!

Since we had declared an emergency, that KA-6D was down until Maintenance took action to find and fix the problem. As the Avionics/Armaments Division Officer, the electricians worked for me, so as it turned out, it was my responsibility to get the aircraft fixed. My electricians tested everything they could think of and failed to find any problem. Since some action had to be taken in order for the aircraft to be placed in the Op Ready status, they finally changed the Fire/Oil Test Box for no reason other than that; they had to do something if we were ever going to fly that aircraft again. After they did that, that KA-6D never showed any of those symptoms again.

Al and I talked about our experience, and we both told each other that ejection was definitely in our thoughts but that we had rejected the idea for similar reasons, never mentioning it to the other. And we both agreed that had one of us even mentioned the "e" word, we would have gone swimming in the Sea of Japan.

The next day, I was told to come to the ready room to meet with our Skipper. When I got there, he told me I had been cited with a Bead Window, a breach of security over the unencrypted radio. I thought back and couldn't think of anything I had said over the radio that could have been construed as a security violation and told him that. Then he advised me that the ships cryptologists had written me up for declaring an emergency. I was furious, and I threatened to go find them and explain the facts of life in Naval Aviation to that idiot who had filed the report. The Skipper calmed me down most by telling that he, himself, had rejected the "violation" as being groundless. That wasn't quite a burst bubble, but it came close.

LCDR Joe Mobley

The best thing to happen to me during this cruise was being assigned a room with an old classmate of mine from USNA, LCDR Joe Mobley. Joe had been a nugget B/N with VA-35 from NAS Oceana when he was shot down doing an armed reconnaissance mission over a road segment in North Vietnam. He had survived the injuries he had sustained in his ejection, seven and a half years in the Hanoi Hilton where he endured incredible torture and a nasty divorce. His wife, living in California when he was a POW, not only divorced him for "desertion" but also managed to take all the money he had in his "protected" DoD savings account. So instead of being a rich man when he finally was repatriated in 1973, he was penniless, except for his Navy pay. And who was there to meet him when he got off the plane in California? His sister-in-law, Mary, who had been married to his brother but herself was divorced. She had even named her only son, Joseph, in his honor. It wasn't too long before Mary became Mary Mobley, and we all liked her very much. They were a wonderful couple, and I am very glad that I had the opportunity to know them. Living with Joe on *Kitty Hawk* definitely made the cruise easier to deal with for me. Joe would go on to make Vice Admiral and retire as Commander Air Forces, Atlantic.

The crowning incident to this whole deployment was when we were ordered to leave our brand-new A-6Es in the Philippines for VMA(AW)-533 and take their A-6As back to CONUS. That meant our fly-off for Whidbey Island wouldn't even be in our own aircraft. So the Maintenance Department spent the whole trip back to CONUS working on these deplorable wrecks with technicians who had been trained to work on the A-6E, not the A-6A. Since the biggest differences were in the fire control and navigation systems, we tended to leave them alone and concentrate on safety of flight issues. It was important to get these aircraft off the ship and back to Whidbey where they could be transferred to NARF.

We departed the Philippines in December 1975 and began a PT (Physical Training) competition between the pilots and the b/ns. We had started earlier getting into shape to actually start this competition, and after one of my runs on the flight deck, I came back to my stateroom dying for a cigarette, when I realized that all the wheezing I was doing during the run was coming from the cigarettes. So I quit. Once *Kitty Hawk* left, I never smoked another one, and that's true to this day. After a long, tedious passage back to CONUS with little to do but play games, watch movies (I think I saw every episode of *Victory at Sea* at least twice), and work out, the pilots managed to beat us anyway.

Fly-Off for Home

When the fly-off day came, it was as bad as any of us had feared. As I recall, I think we left at least one aircraft on the ship. It might have been more. The flight of four that we (LT Al Lundy had been my pilot for the whole deployment) were in had no operating radios, except our own, so we had the lead, with the other three tucked in tight. When we penetrated the ADIZ (Air Defense Identification Zone), Seattle Air Traffic Control Center, normally very friendly toward us, was really upset because, as it turned out, almost no one else in the fly-off had radios either. But we worked through all that, and Al was able to get our wingmen down to the duty runway one at a time for safe landings despite the very cloudy conditions that day. Then, we finally came around and landed ourselves. As we were taxiing in, we could see our families assembled in front of the hangar with a podium in front manned by our Admiral, a fine sight. Unfortunately, I began to hear noises which sounded like a hydraulic pump scavenging fluid. I was beginning to fold the wings so we could park in line with our other aircraft; I told Al, "We'd better get the canopy open or we might not get out." So I popped it open, but it only moved about a foot before it stopped. Then I noticed the left wing was standing straight up, while the right wing was moving up and down near its stowed position, almost as if it were saluting the Admiral. We barely squeezed out of the cockpit but managed it somehow, with hydraulic fluid spraying out from under our aircraft. What a dismal fly-in, but the homecoming was great! Our wives and families didn't care about anything else other than our being back. I don't think the Admiral was impressed with us, though.

Since *Kitty Hawk* was going into the yards for a long-delayed and much-needed overhaul, CVW-11 was going to be without a ship for just about the rest of my tour with VA-52. So our new skipper, CDR Darryl Kerr, had to design innovative ways to keep our squadron sharp and stand out from the other A-6 squadrons, and he would prove to be up to the challenge. Our new XO was CDR Bill Galbraith, and he and I were to become good friends and still are today.

Refresher Training Begins

After our normal turnaround, with old personnel checking out and new ones checking in, we reshuffled flight crew assignments, and since the XO and I had started diving together and our families seemed to get along very well, we teamed up. He turned out to be the best pilot around the ship I ever flew with. Bill had already had an ejection in an A-6A, a result of a cold cat shot (too little steam pressure resulting in too low an end speed off the ship). So he knew what he was talking about when we discussed our procedures around the ship. But we were to spend many months flying in CONUS before we ever saw another ship.

The squadron now had brand-new A-6Es to replace the Marine A-6As we had brought back from our last cruise, and they were beautiful. It was like driving new cars. The paint hadn't even been scraped off the decks of the cockpits. So we started right out getting our bombing expertise honed up. One of the first things I discovered was how much better our AMTI capabilities were. During my time with this new model, I managed to set two moving targets (remotely operated dune buggies) on fire with hits from a Mk-76 25lb practice bomb. They had white smoke cartridges in the nose, and I suppose the flame from their ignition triggered gasoline fires. By the time I left the squadron, I had the best overall bombing average across all of our attack modes. I couldn't seem to beat the top runner in a single category, but in the aggregate, I came in first. I attribute 90 percent of that to this new model.

One of the most fun things we did during this long turnaround was to start participating in the Air Force's Red Flag exercises held periodically out of Nellis AFB. We deployed to NAF Fallon, Nevada, and flew our sorties from there as the People's Republic of Fallon when we were the bad guys. Otherwise, we utilized the Nellis ranges for practice against modern air defense threats. We learned a lot about how to defeat them mostly by making mistakes and getting shot down in simulation. It was great training.

The first time we deployed for CarQuals (Carrier Qualifications), I experienced Bill's amazing ability to land on the ship. I had flown with a lot of pilots both in real operations and during CarQuals, but I never flew with anyone who could make an approach like he did. The ball was always centered, and our lineup was flawless—every time! It seemed as if the ship had a "tractor beam" illuminating us which brought us right down the rails for an OK 3 Wire (the best landing a pilot can make) landing every time. We landed and launched in "hot mike" (if you talked, your crewmate would hear you without having to press the ICS button), and he would sit there staring at his approach indexers (A system which provides speed indications to the pilot, mounted on the dashboard, so he didn't have to look down at the airspeed indicator. It worked on angle of attack, so the aircraft would be in the correct nose up attitude in order for the tailhook to engage the wire.), the ball, and the centerline painted on the flight deck, talking to himself all the way down: "Work, work, work." I noticed that he never let the stick stay still; he made small movements with it all the way down the glide slope. It was uncanny, but he was the greatest carrier aviator I ever knew.

Cross-Country

One day, Bill decided he wanted to fly a cross-country to NAS Brunswick, Maine. I decided that I would exercise the A-6E's new computer in the practice of "great circle navigation."[21] Since we used a chart projection known as a Lambert Conformal, any straight line I draw on it would be a great circle because of the way they are made. If one used a Mercator projection, like the surface Navy does, a straight line would be a rhumb line and therefore would be a greater distance to any destination.

I got all the charts for the entire coast-to-coast trip in 1:1,000,000 scale—not very detailed, but when I fitted them together for our trip, they still stretched all the way across our living room at home. I snapped a chalk line pinned at one end on NAS Whidbey Island, Washington, and on the other at NAS Brunswick, Maine. After I snapped the chalk line, I inked in our route of flight. Previously, I had contacted the FAA at Seattle Center to ask about the legality of such a flight in their air space, and I was told it was fine. Normally, high altitude aircraft fly on FAA-established routes between radio aids to navigation. That would not be the case with our flight, so I had to make sure that there were radar features along the way that I could use to update the computer's navigation program in the event that our inertial navigation system might drift off. It took a lot of planning.

The day finally came for the launch, and it was interesting to note that our initial course out of Whidbey was north of east, taking us into Canadian Air Space. Our final course into NAS Brunswick would be south of east, a feature of great circle navigation. Our transition over to Vancouver Center was very smooth, and the controllers were very accommodating. I recall that along the way, one of the air

---

21. A great circle is the curve formed on the surface of the earth if one passes a plane through its center. It results in constantly changing compass courses throughout the trip as opposed to a rhumb line, which maintains the same course throughout. The former is much shorter than the latter, and they had been used by seamen since the days of sailing ships.

controllers called us and said, "I thought you might like to know that our computer shows your computer right on track." That was indeed good news.

As we passed the halfway point, we took a really close look at our fuel condition, and Bill wasn't happy with the amount of reserve we would have on our approach to NAS Brunswick, so we stopped for fuel at Selfridge AFB, Michigan. We took on fuel and continued our trip, although our great circle had been interrupted by the fueling detour. Bill was right, though, to get fuel because when we started down on our approach to Brunswick, the approach controller reported ground fog with the field below minima (Even for the A-6, which was now rated by the FAA as "dual piloted" even though there is only one set of controls. Duel rating allowed us to use the minimum published weather conditions for any field in feet of ceiling and miles of visibility. At Brunswick, that was 100 feet and a quarter of a mile.). So we had to report that we would be flying a "close approach." That gave us the ability to shoot the approach but not land, although we could take a look at the conditions on the approach end of the runway, go around with a PIREP (Pilot Report) that the weather was above minima and land on the next approach. Bill flew on the instruments while I stared out my side of the canopy. I was to call the runway the minute I saw it. Unfortunately, by the time I saw it, we were already over it, and Bill was executing a missed approach. We shot that landing about five times and just couldn't see the runway soon enough, so it was time to divert. With all the closer airfields in New England similarly below minima due to this fog, we had to go to Plattsburgh AFB, New York, on the banks of Lake Erie. It turns out that this was a SAC (Strategic Air Command) Base and was loaded with FB-111s—SACs version of TAC's (Tactical Air Command's) F-111s. That, of course, made security very tight.

We were able to land without incident only because Bill had made the decision to stop for fuel in Michigan. Without it, we couldn't have flown that far after our approach at Brunswick. We secured the aircraft on the transient line with many others who had had to divert that night from all over New England, checked into the BOQ, and went to sleep. We arose the next morning to go out and get our plane refueled and then proceed to Brunswick as originally planned.

The A-6 had a "single point refueling" system which allowed all the tanks on the aircraft to be refueled from a single fueling port. You could either select the tanks you wanted filled or you could let the system do it by itself. It was really quite a nice setup. There was no way to refuel the internal wing and fuselage tanks without electrical power. Of course, we needed that power to start our engines, too. There was no self-starter capability on the Intruder. Unfortunately, none of the power carts which the FMS (Field Maintenance Squadron) brought over to us worked with our aircraft, even though they were listed in our documentation as being compatible. This began a long series of phone calls back to our base at Whidbey with our maintenance personnel, since the Air Force ran checks on their power carts and determined them to be working within spec.

About dusk, as Bill and I were standing up on the left wing in a snowstorm, trying to remove a fuselage panel behind the cockpit, while I was holding a flashlight and he was working on the Dzus fasteners, a young Security Policeman stuck his head over the wing with his M-16 pointed our way to ask what we thought we were doing (remember: SAC). I was shocked, but Bill didn't miss a beat. He looked at the young man, and in his best Eastern Oregon drawl, he said, "Hey, partner. It's good to see ya. D'ya think you could shoot this thing off for us?"

I thought the young man was going to fall of the pilot's ladder when he started laughing. The tension was gone, and once we explained it was our airplane, he was satisfied. But we were no closer to solving our problem. The suggestion we were acting on from our maintenance guys didn't work. So it was back to the BOQ.

We went back to the aircraft the next day and met with the sergeant from the FMS and continued to troubleshoot both at the plane and on the phone. Finally, our sergeant, who had been with us from the beginning, decided to test our refueling panel, and lo and behold, he found a bad circuit breaker. Of course, it was the one which governed whether power would be accepted by the aircraft. We were now hopeful, as he returned to his shop. When he returned, he told us the bad news was he didn't have any spare circuit breakers of the type we needed, but the good news was, he had one anyway, and he enjoined us not to ask where it came from. We really didn't care. He replaced the breaker, the aircraft was refueled with enough to get us over the NAS Brunswick with a comfortable reserve. I went into the Tower and filed for an instrument flight over to Brunswick, and we launched—finally, after calling our home base to tell them we were up and running. It was a great feeling to be flying again.

Everything at Brunswick went according to plan, and I re-filed with the FAA for our return great circle route back to NAS Whidbey Island. We took off well before sunrise and very quickly flew into Canadian Air Space again. The Canadian controller was not at all busy (I think we were the only aircraft he had), and he decided to have a chat with us. He asked us all kinds of questions about the aircraft and was very friendly. Flying west in CONUS, one has to face the prevailing westerlies, winds predominately from the west all the time. That means, the Intruder did not have the range to fly nonstop from the East Coast to the West Coast, so a fuel stop heading that way was always necessary. We had chosen to stop at the ANGB (Air National Guard Base) at Fargo, North Dakota. As we descended and were handed off to the approach controller at Fargo, he said, "I hope y'all boys are wearing your long handles. It's 27° below zero down here." That was shocking news, but it was still dark since we were flying away from the sun and should have expected it.

As we landed and were taxiing in to the line, the ground controller told us to watch out for the jackrabbits on the taxiway. Of course, there was one right in front of us, and Bill, always irrepressible, answered up, "Them ain't jackrabbits. Them's more like gophers. If ya wanna see jackrabbits, come out to Oregon!" Once again, we were to have a warm welcome, thanks to Bill's incredible sense of humor and his way with people. One civilian came out to our aircraft as we went into the terminal to activate the continuation of our flight plan. He did everything. The man was amazing. He operated the power cart, dragged the fuel hose to the aircraft, had everything grounded in accordance with standard safety procedures, and got us ready to go in record time. I don't think we were on the ground for an hour.

We launched out of Fargo, climbing to our cruising altitude of 39,000 feet in the dark. As we were settling in for the last leg of our cross country, the sun, at least from our altitude, broke across the rim of the earth. What I sight! I will never forget it. The sky above was a very dark azure, the sun behind us was golden, and our contrails were billowy white. It's moments like those that make you want to keep flying forever. All too soon, though, we were home, and another mission was completed with a full-up aircraft.

Bomber Stream

Our Air Wing at NAS Whidbey, COMMATVAQWINGPAC (Commander Medium Attack and Electronic Warfare Wing, Pacific) sponsored a competitive bombing derby each year, known as the Bomber Stream. Each squadron present at NAS Whidbey was responsible to fly four airplanes, as I recall, around the course which would be laid out by the Wing Staff and kept secret until just a short time before the start to keep anyone from flying around it to familiarize themselves with it. So when a crew launched, it would be the first time they had ever flown the route.

This particular Bomber Stream incorporated mining at our range in Admiralty Bay, on the west side of the island, followed by a low level route to the east, radar bomb scoring on the Air Force range at Spokane, Washington, RSP (Radar Scope Photography) of each of the navigation turn points along the route, an initial straight path attack at our range in Boardman, Oregon, followed by two dive-bombing runs. Each plane would then fly back at high altitude under control by Seattle Center, switch to the tower at NAS Whidbey Island, be put into a marshal pattern where the crew would have to make their push time within three seconds, and make a carrier approach to the field where Wing LSOs would be grading each pass. You lost points for just about anything: miss distances with the bombs, too soon or too late with "smoke on target," not "bombs away," poor RSP techniques, early or late push times, and the pass itself. So each crewman had a lot of pressure on them to perform well, and our maintenance department was under a lot of pressure to have our aircraft and the bombing systems tweaked to perfection. It was a total squadron team effort.

Each squadron would pick its top crews and aircraft to participate, and each plane had to have a hot spare who would take the runway with the designated plane for that takeoff time (assigned sequentially by the Wing) and even run up his engines with the primary until the lead B/N gave him the "kiss off" hand signal, which meant that they would go and he should stand down. Bill and I were picked as one of our crews, and I planned the route with great detail, once the Wing provided us with the details of the mission. We carried two stopwatches in the cockpit, in addition to the two clocks which were part of the instruments on each side of the cockpit. None of those timepieces varied by more than a second throughout our entire mission, but we had to be sure.

We launched right on time and flew over to the mining range, where I dropped two high-drag practice bombs (to provide the scorers with the bearing of our mine line) to simulate mines (each smoke was scored). Then we started east across the state on our low-level route, and I took RSP of each of the designated turn points along it. As we got close, we reported in with the Air Force controllers at Spokane, who cleared us in on the Wing's designated "target" and "dropped" right on our assigned target time. The Air Force tracked us with old *Nike* missile trackers as we flew into the City of Spokane. We used the ballistics for the Mk-83 LDGP and selected "bomb tone" in the cockpit so that when the pilot pressed his "commit" trigger on the stick, the tone would start to transmit, and when the computer sent out the fire pulse to the bomb station (here, the Master Arm was in "Practice" so that pulse stayed inside the computer), the tone would cut off, and the graders would mark the position of the aircraft and calculate, based on the ballistics tables, where the bomb would have landed relative to our designated target: a building in the middle of all the other buildings in the City of Spokane. Radar bombing in a metropolitan area is very difficult and requires a lot of target study and a detailed knowledge of the radar to be used.

After Spokane, we took off onto the next leg of our low-level flight toward Boardman, Oregon, on the Columbia River, called in "really ready" to the target controllers, were cleared in hot, and I dropped a bit early on our straight path attack in order to get "smoke on target" at the designated time. Bill said he thought it looked like a good hit, as he broke left at around 4Gs and started to pull up to get ready for his first visual dive. We had determined that unlike in the A-6A because of its poor reliability, we would use the system to actually drop the bombs in these diving attacks, if the system looked good at that point in the flight. The time of the hit was not graded for these two dive-bombing runs, so I asked Bill to take it around once when he got up on his "perch" because I didn't like what I was seeing. The system seemed to be erratic at that time. It had been rock solid up until now, so maybe it was the 4G break and the climb that had it hiccoughing. I didn't know, but I didn't like it. It didn't matter, though, because Bill insisted on rolling in on the first pass anyway; and he did. After all, he had the stick. So we repeated the maneuver and then began to climb out of the range as I called Seattle Center to activate our IFR (Instrument Flight Rules) flight plan back to Whidbey.

Approaching Ault Field, we were assigned our marshal position, and Bill got us right to it and made his push exactly on our designated time. And of course, he made a perfect landing. As we taxied into the line, I felt exhausted. I'm sure he did also, but we really didn't know how we had done. Our maintenance guys had to remove my film and deliver it to the Wing for processing and scoring, and all of the other scores had to be collected. It was a nervous evening. When it was all over and the dust had settled, we were told that I had dropped bull's-eyes at Admiralty Bay, Spokane, and Boardman. My RSP was perfect, so we lost no points for it, but Bill's first dive drop was seventeen feet, as I recall. His second was a bull's-eye, and his landing was perfect. That seventeen-feet dive hit cost us the bomber stream. I think we came in third or fourth. I was very disappointed because I knew I would probably never again have the opportunity to fly in another, and that turned out to be correct. But each of VA-52's sorties had done so well that the squadron won the trophy. So that was something to be proud of.

Accident and Death

One of our new pilots had broken his arm during an intramural basketball match at the Air Station and had been grounded while it healed. Hence, he was far behind the other pilots in our turnaround training syllabus. Our operations officer, LCDR Joe Mobley now, set up a back-in-the-saddle syllabus for him to get back up to speed once the flight surgeon put him back in flight status, and he started flying some instrument round robins (airways flying at high altitude like airliners under the control of the FAA but landing at the place where the flight originated), which he would normally be assigned a KA-6D to fly because we needed our bombers for our other flight crews to continue their training. Of course, for a hot pilot, that type of flight is very boring, and we found out later that he had started to introduce some personal variables into these flights. For example, he began making "heavy approaches" or approaches with the aircraft way over its maximum gross landing weight. There was no such maneuver listed in the NATOPS manual. Since none of our B/Ns wanted to fly with him on these boring flights, he started taking one of the newly graduated ensigns from the Naval Academy who were stashed with us while they awaited the class convening dates in the Naval Aviation Training Command.

One Friday afternoon after work, Joe and I went to the Officers' Club and were drinking tequila shooters when the bartender announced he had a phone call for anyone from VA-52. Since Joe was the senior officer present, he took the call. I stood there listening but couldn't make anything out of the conversation from his responses, other than it was something bad. He hung up the phone and told me we had to get back to squadron ASAP because one of our planes had crashed. So we got in our cars and headed back to find out from the Duty Officer that our newly returned pilot had crashed off Runway 06 in the Strait of Juan de Fuca, and there apparently had been no survivors (the Naval Academy ensign had been in the right seat). About this time, the CO, XO, and the other department heads showed up, and we established an Aircraft Accident Investigation Board under our safety officer. He called our local EOD (Explosive Ordnance Disposal) Detachment to ask for assistance in surveying the crash site, and then he asked the XO, CDR Bill Galbraith, and I to go with them to investigate and photograph the cockpit before the EOD divers touched anything since he knew we were dive partners and obviously knew the cockpit.

Bill and I then went to the local dive shop in town to secure some supplies (e.g., underwater camera, underwater writing tablet, gas-filled buoys, etc.). The owner had already heard about the crash and offered us everything we needed at no charge. That was the relationship the Navy had with the Oak Harbor Community in those days. It was fantastic!

The next morning, Bill and I showed up at the EOD Det's pier at the Seaplane Base (over on the east side of Whidbey Island (Ault Field was on the west side) so we had to take their boat around the island and through Deception Pass on the north side to get to the crash site just to the south of the pass in the Strait. It took a good bit of time, but there are no harbors on the west side of the island. Once we arrived on the approximate site of the crash, the EOD divers went in first to locate the cockpit, which was #2 priority, just after finding the bodies. It didn't take long, and they put a buoy on it, and Bill and I went in to survey the cockpit. When we approached, it was immediately obvious that the canopy and the ejection seats were gone, so they had ejected. I took several pictures for the safety officer, but it was clear when we looked in the cockpit that the flap switch was in the "up" position. That would have been bad enough, but we later found out that the pilot had reported himself "heavy." It wasn't possible for the A-6 to fly at that weight at approach speeds with no flaps, so it seemed clear that this was a case of pilot error, and with no rated B/N in the right seat, no one was checking him on the landing checklist, or the flaps would never have been missed. It was truly a sad story altogether.

We continued working with EOD and debriefing with the safety officer for the next week to gather as much information as we could as well as search for the bodies. All we ever found were the seats themselves and one helmet. The currents in this part of the world are very severe, so we speculated that the bodies were sucked out into the

Strait and possibly all the way to the Pacific Ocean. No other trace was ever found of either of them.

Interviews by the Accident Board with various fishermen who were plying their hobby just off the runway and were eyewitnesses to the crash confirmed that the aircraft had stalled on the cross-wind part of his approach, causing both crewmen to eject, but the sink rate on the aircraft was by then so excessive that their parachutes did not fully deploy before they hit the water. In those days, we did not have auto-inflators in our life vests. Rather, you had to pull the toggles to fill them. If their impact with the water had knocked them out, they would have easily drowned without regaining consciousness.

Our EOD Det continued working on the site until all the debris had been recovered, loaded onto barges, and shipped out. It was the end to a tragedy for VA-52. We were all shocked but thought a lot harder about being vigilant in the use of our checklists.

Conventional Weapons Exam

During this extended turnaround period, VA-52 had to requalify with both nuclear and conventional weapons; and for some reason, I, a B/N who had never looked through the pilot's gunsight, was tasked with training our selected crews for the Wing's conventional weapons written examination, a big part of which was calculating the lead angle for visual dive attacks. I think we had to provide six crews for the test, and I spent several hours a day for about a week going over our Conventional Weapons NATOPS Supplement with them and answering their questions until they were fully satisfied, and I was confident that they would all do well. The day of the test came, and it didn't disappoint. It was quite long and complex and covered the entire scope of conventional weapons for the A-6 Intruder. I questioned everyone after they left the room, and all of them felt confident that they had done well.

That night, however, I received a phone call from an old VA-165 squadron mate who was now in the weapons department of the Wing Staff. I thought the call was a little strange, but he quickly explained that he called because he knew I had prepared our crews for his test and that we had done far worse than any squadron he had administered his test to. Of course, I was shocked, but I asked him if he could tell me if there was anything in particular that our crews had trouble with. He was happy to tell me that we had all gotten the same question wrong. It was a multiple part, one with each part affecting the next. So if one got the first part wrong, everything would be wrong, and that was the case with us. Then he reviewed the question with me, and I remembered it vividly, and I told him his answer was wrong and went on to explain why. He became very quiet for such a long time, I had to ask him if he was still there. He said he was and that he would get back to me. When he regraded our tests, we found that we had the highest scores ever achieved on that test, and the results went a long way in helping us win the Battle Efficiency "E" for Pacific A-6 Squadrons that year.

Promotion and Disaster

About this time, I was told that I was on the promotion list for LCDR (Lieutenant Commander, or O-4)—not only that but I had screened within the top 10 percent, which qualified me to attend Junior Officer Staff College. I was very pleased and proud, and it seemed as though all the sacrifices my family had made to support my decision to join the Navy again would earn significant benefits when I met senior rank.

I had been serving as the Maintenance Department's QAO (Quality Assurance Officer) for quite a while, so I was rotated to Personnel Officer in the Admin Department. Of course, being an engineer, I was infinitely more qualified for the former rather than the latter, but I took it as a chance to broaden my perspective and dove into the job with great enthusiasm, reading everything I could about the job and what the Navy expected of me. The senior man in my shop was a 1st class (E-6) personnelman who really didn't like "Airedales." I had noticed when I was the QAO that sailors from our department would be kept waiting at the office window for interminable periods, while the PNs (Personnelmen) ignored them. So the first thing I did after settling into my new position was close the window at the service desk and had a meeting with them. I told them that the most important job they had was taking care of our sailors. Nothing else they had to do was even close to that responsibility, and if one of them came to the window, I expected someone to greet him and find out what he needed from us. The message seemed to sink in because I noticed a great improvement with our customer service.

Then, one day, my ESO (Educational Services Officer) came to me to ask if he could speak with me in private. When we moved to a closed office, he told me that our Senior Chief (E-8) in Maintenance Control had a long-standing reservation with an Elk hunting guide over east of the Cascade Mountains, and the dates interfered with the Navy examination for Master Chief (E-9), the highest enlisted rate in the Navy. I knew, of course, that if he didn't take the exam, he would not be eligible for promotion that year, and while I didn't personally like the man, I thought the squadron owed it to him to help him out, if possible. So I instructed my ESO to investigate his case to see if he could find a way to help him out. Frankly, I put the issue out of my mind after that meeting, until several days later, I happened to run into my ESO in the passageway, and I asked him if he had found a way to help our E-8 Maintenance Control Chief out. He replied that he had, so I went on with whatever business I was conducting at the time and put the whole thing out of my mind.

A few days later, my PN1 (1st Class Personnelman) asked if I knew anything about our E-8 taking the E-9 exam early. I told him about the meeting with my ESO and explained my instructions to him, saying that I had assumed that he had found a way to help our senior chief out. That's the last I heard from him. Then, I was called at home by the XO, my pilot, to tell me that my PN1 had reported that I had broken a major Navy regulation in administering the test early to one of our men. So the story had come full circle at last, and I now knew that my ESO had broken the rules not just bent them; he had never told me that he intended to administer the test early. Of course, our E-8 was gone, out hunting in the wiles of Central Washington, but the whole incident began to take on a life of its own.

I was relieved as the Personnel Officer and sent back to QAO, and my ESO was transferred out of Admin to some other job. Then, apparently one of the admirals at AIRPAC (Air Forces Pacific in San Diego), if not the commander himself (I never did find out who it was specifically), had heard about it and decided that we had sold the test to our E-8 and were probably getting ready to engage in similar actions with other enlisted tests. Of course, that was all as far-fetched a theory as one could conjure, but senior officers will not tell admirals that they are fantasizing. So before you knew it, we were facing a full-blown court of inquiry convened by our admiral (COMMATVAQWINGPAC). My ESO and I got lawyers immediately and would talk to no one else about the incident until the court delivered its findings.

I guess the thing that I remember the most about that incident is how fast the Navy turned on us. There never seemed to be any presumption that our zeal for the squadron and our men, fueled by the severe "can do" attitude that our skipper poured into us, had been at the heart of the matter and not some nefarious purpose on our part. After all my service, exposure to near-death experiences in the air, and my overall outstanding performance in everything, the Navy considered me guilty of trying to "fix" the Navy's promotion exams. It was one of the most depressing periods of my life, and I found myself very glad to have a lawyer who not only believed me but intended to do all he could to have me exonerated. I never have liked lawyers, but I was very close to liking that one.

Well, the court convened, and of course, the President, COMMATVAQWINGPAC himself, could find no substantiation of the charges that we were attempting to "fix" the promotion exam, and his report went to COMAIRPAC. My skipper wrote a letter of reprimand, which I had to sign, and he put it into my service record maintained by the yeomen, not the personnelmen, at the squadron. He told me the letter would be removed when I departed the squadron.

About the same time, officer FITREPs (Fitness Reports) were due, and mine was a disaster. I was rated last out of all the O-3s in the squadron, and Skipper Kerr explained to me that I would still be promoted because I had already been selected but that I had no further future with Naval Aviation. Goodbye to senior rank. He recommended that I go into some other field. I had been an overachiever all my life and now found myself at the bottom of the class. About the same time, one of our Maintenance Control Officers, LT Rick Yount, asked me why I was wasting my time with the squadron anyway. He said I was way too smart for that. So when I heard that, despite everything that had happened, I was still selected to go to graduate school at the Postgraduate School the Navy operated at an old hotel in Monterey, California, I was elated—a chance to start working on a new career!

My remaining time in VA-52 was bad. The XO divorced me as his B/N, and since I had orders to depart the squadron in December 1977 (my class convening date at Monterey), and *Kitty Hawk* was scheduled to depart with CVW-11 in October, the Navy chose to have me leave the squadron before the ship left San Diego, and the squadron chose not to crew me up with another pilot. So while at sea on *Kitty Hawk* doing work ups, I did very little flying. I spent my time hanging around the ready room looking for a mission I could fly: sometimes it was a tanker and sometimes in was a maintenance test flight, but it was almost never a bombing mission. The XO demanded that, as the QAO, I provide him with a full report of every flight which was scheduled but did not launch due to a maintenance problem. I spent a lot of time talking with the shop supervisors and trying to piece together the string of events with each aircraft which was reported "down" by its crew prior to launch. Many times, my reports were not detailed enough for him, and I had to go back and repeat everything until I was able to satisfy the XO. It made for very long days and very little flight time or landings.

One day, the XO called me to the ready room to tell me that I was out of uniform. I couldn't understand what he meant. I was standing before him in the uniform of the day at sea for officers: working khakis—rank, wings, and no decorations. Then, he told me, I guess because I looked puzzled, that my promotion had come through, and he handed me a set of oak leaves. I immediately went to the Ship's Store and bought a box of cigars and went around distributing them to all the shops in the Maintenance Department. Our sailors seemed genuinely please that I had been promoted. I don't think it was an act. That happened in September 1977. I retired on 1 February 1988 and was never to be promoted again. I expect that I was blackballed by one of the Management at AIRPAC, but I'll never know for sure.

Several more weeks passed, and I was finally separated from the squadron, but not until the day before *Kitty Hawk* departed San Diego on cruise. I was elated to be gone. All my excitement for VA-52, our mission, our achievements, and our awards had soured completely with me. But I was excited about getting my Master of Science degree in Aeronautical Engineering and couldn't wait to get started.

After driving back up to Whidbey Island, I picked up the family and wrapped up our affairs. Selling the house we had built hurt a lot. Our eldest daughter, Jeannine, was just starting Junior High School, and she was doing very well. I didn't want to separate her from that, but we had no choice. So once again, we packed up and headed for Monterey, California.

The Rest of the Life of the Intruders

Beginning in 1979, all A-6Es were fitted with the AN/AAS-33 DRS (Detecting and Ranging Set), part of the "Target Recognition and Attack Multi-Sensor" (TRAM) system, a small gyroscopically stabilized turret, mounted under the nose of the aircraft, containing a FLIR boresighted with a laser spot-tracker/designator and IBM AN/ASQ-155 computer. TRAM was matched with a new Norden AN/APQ-156 radar. The B/N could use both TRAM imagery and radar data for extremely accurate attacks or use the TRAM sensors alone to attack without using the Intruder's radar (which might warn the target). TRAM also allowed the Intruder to autonomously designate and drop laser-guided bombs.

In the 1980s, the A-6E TRAM aircraft were converted to the A-6E WCSI (Weapons Control System Improvement) version to add additional weapons capability. This added the ability to carry and target some of the first generation precision guided weapons, like the AGM-84 Harpoon missile and AGM-123 Skipper. The WSCI aircraft was eventually modified to have a limited capability to use the AGM-84E SLAM (Standoff Land Attack Missile).

In the early 1990s, some surviving A-6Es were upgraded under SWIP (Systems/Weapons Improvement Program) to enable them to use the latest precision-guided munitions, including AGM-65 Mavericks, AGM-84E SLAMs, AGM-62 Walleyes, and the AGM-88 HARM anti-radiation missile as well as additional capability with the AGM-84 Harpoon. A co-processor was added to the AN/ASQ-155 computer system to implement the needed MIL-SPEC 1553 digital interfaces to the pylons, as well as an additional control panel. After a series of wing-fatigue problems, about 85 percent of the fleet was fitted with new graphite/epoxy/titanium/aluminum composite wings. The new wings proved to be a mixed blessing, as a composite wing is stiffer and transmits more force to the fuselage, accelerating fatigue in the fuselage. In 1990, the decision was made to terminate production of the A-6. Through the 1970s and 1980s, the A-6 had been in low-rate production of four or five new aircraft a year, enough to replace mostly accidental losses. The final production order was for twenty aircraft of the SWIP configuration with composite wings, delivered in 1993.

A-6E models totaled 445 aircraft, about 240 of which were converted from earlier A-6A/B/C models.

The following is a memorial for the A-6 Intruder which was written by my friend, Bruce Wood, the original Box Man:

An Extinct Species[22]
By CAPT Bruce Wood, USN (Ret)[23]

Within the past year, Naval Aviation's version of the evolutionary time clock clicked over and one of its most demanding jobs was placed into inactive status.

The handwriting was on the wall for the last three years or more in the Darwinian evolution of men and machines. When the last A-6 Intruder was chocked and shut down in the dry air of Davis Monthan AFB, it became final. There are no more bombardier/navigators in the world of dual-anchored Wings of Gold. For the past thirty-five years, B/Ns have been the premier subspecialty in the Naval Flight Officer world. They have been the seldom-disputed kings of the NFO trade.

No more will B/Ns sit alongside their pilot and play their electronic keyboards to find the target or select the switches that instruct the pilot and the machine to drop ordnance. No more will they look into the eyes of their pilot as they prepare to descend into twisting valleys on a night low level. No more will they run their ejection seats down and press their faces into the radar hood as the call for turns and altitude changes to dodge the rocks as they fly at two hundred feet altitude to the target. No more will they share cockpit responsibility so intimately with their pilot nor hold mission success in the palms of their hands and on their fingertips as they did in the past. They will now move into back seats or a crew with three or four others to share the mission and job skills.

---

22. Published in *The Hook*, Winter 1997.
23. Bruce committed suicide (I was told that, like me, he had suffered from PTSD) and was buried at sea from the USS *Ronald Reagan* (CVN-76) on 19 April 2008. Farewell, old friend.

Sharing Agony and Ecstasy

More than any other version of NFO, the B/N was closest to the teeth of the mission. He sat in his half of the cockpit and saw everything his pilot saw. From his position alongside the pilot, he was able to double-check fuel, hydraulics, rate of descent, airspeed, and angle of attack, and could hold an approach plate or cup of coffee for his pilot. He could hang on to his canopy bow handgrip, twisting in his seat to call a break turn in Air Combat Maneuvering (ACM) or to avoid a missile. He could pat his pilot's knee to congratulate him on a great hit, a great move, a great landing, or to reassure him that everything is looking good on a dark night. He was there to help "kill the snakes" in the cockpit after a night bolter or the third rim shot in the tanker circle.

The B/N had more control in the cockpit than any other NFO. He could look out through the windscreen and see clearly how the mission was unfolding. He was in the front row with hands-on access to all things required to get the job done. In the cockpit, he was like an organ player who uses his hands and feet to play his music. He could point to a chart or a photo to get his point across or reassure his pilot that all the circuit breakers are in or they are tuned to the right frequency.

He could back up his pilot with lineup calls at the boat, confirm the target is three miles ahead or call for a hard right turn to get below a ridge line. He could trade his oxygen mask or helmet with the pilot who needed to hear and talk to the Landing Signals Officer (LSO) as they pass "platform" on an approach to the ship. His vantage point let him cross-check and double cross-check every critical decision. He shared the agony and ecstasy in the cockpit as could no other NFO. He was inside the bubble of the pilot, and they both knew they were in it together. He could reach across the pilot's right knee and fly the aircraft, run the pilot's seat up after the break at the ship, or run it down after joining a close formation of three. He could reset the bug on the horizontal situation indicator while reading back missed-approach instructions. Side-by-side seating in the A-6 brought wide capabilities to the Intruder that other NFOs don't enjoy. The B/N regularly exercised his 50 percent voting rights.

It was not always so. Before the A-6, NFOs were often considered second-class citizens in Naval Aviation. Pilots controlled everything and didn't like to share responsibility. The demanding, complex mission of the A-6 developed B/Ns into positions of responsibility and leadership that won the respect of the single-anchor guys.

Before the A-6 B/N, NFOs had no opportunity to command a squadron, the exclusive territory of pilots. B/Ns won the respect of the power brokers and were given the first chances to wear the sheriff's badge of command. The Big Guys decided if a person could handle the job as a B/N, he could certainly handle the responsibilities as a commanding officer. Other NFO communities quickly followed. Some single-seat communities were late to accept NFOs as equals. It only took a few missions in the A-6 to change their minds.

CHAPTER 7

GRADUATE SCHOOL

We arrived in Monterey in October of 1977. We moved into housing right away since we couldn't afford to buy anything in the Monterey area (it's even worse now). I'll never forget my son's reaction when we walked into our new home: one side of a duplex with black tile floors the Navy had scavenged from some shipyard or another. He just started to cry, and he was a tough kid! On top of that, the entire area was in the throes of a severe drought, and a large area of Big Sur was on fire. The sky was full of smoke almost every day, and we were on water restrictions. We had reluctantly left the garden spot of Whidbey Island and moved to this. What a colossal disappointment for all of us! I sincerely started rethinking my decision to stay in the Navy, but the thoughts of getting a Master's degree convinced me to stay.

Since I checked in a whole quarter ahead of my class convening date, I was able to acquire a battery of at-home brush-up courses in engineering and mathematics. My calculus was very rough then, and the courses helped me prepare for the start of real classes in December. At the time I was in the Department of Aeronautical Engineering, we had two curricula: straight Aero and Aero Avionics. The former was 1½ years to an MS, and the latter was 2 years. I was enrolled in the latter.

The big difference between the two is the large number of electronic engineering courses we took in the EE Department. The other guys didn't. I had never had many courses in EE, and I found them very interesting and challenging. After the first year, we had to select a thesis topic, and I chose "Low Cycle Fatigue in Wing Panels," since I was familiar with LCF from my days at Pratt & Whitney Aircraft, and I was still a little unsure of my expertise in EE.

Change of Designator

About this time, I applied for a change in designator from a 1320 (NFO: Naval Flight Officer) to a 1510 (AEDO: Aeronautical Engineering Duty Officer), and to my surprise, given the problems I had had as the Personnel Officer in VA-52, I was selected as a LCDR. We were all told that if we had gotten selected for AEDO as an O-4, we were pretty much assured of making Commander (O-5). I was very pleased.

Our eldest daughter was in Junior High School, and our two other kids were still in Elementary School. All of them seemed to get settled very quickly. Our eldest enrolled in senior Girl Scouts (Mariners), our son in the local Boy Scout troop, and our youngest in a midget soccer league. As we got accustomed to our new lives, everyone seemed to start enjoying Monterey very much, especially when the Triple Cone fire was put out and the drought finally ended. After a while, our eldest daughter transferred over to the local Explorer Scout Post, which specialized in Indian Dancing. She made a gorgeous costume and enjoyed all the activities, especially the camping. She had to go with me as chaperone, but she never seemed to mind.

I had recruited all the bachelors in my class to join our troop as committee members, and they made most of the camping trips. Our troop, led by an Army Lieutenant Colonel in one of the other departments, was great, and our numerous committeemen were a big part of our success. They were actually excited about teaching the kids topics like cooking, camping, and land navigation. In fact, toward the end of our time in Monterey, our senior boys challenged the committee to an overland navigation contest. Believe me, those kids were diabolical in laying their course for us, but as they say, old age and treachery overcame youth and inexperience, but we were good losers.

As the end of my two years at the PG School got closer, I was given my own office (cubicle really), where I could do my homework and work on my thesis. Plus, I had my own lab space where I could prepare samples of aircraft aluminum for the tests I was planning to run in one of our tensile testing machines. I finished up my thesis and had it approved by my thesis advisor and submitted it to the faculty.

New Assignment

Then, one day, I was called to my curricular officer's office. He was an AEDO CDR. He told me that he had received a phone call from a Captain back in DC who had recently been the AEDO Career Officer; and he wanted to talk to me. I hadn't a clue what this was all about, but I called the Captain immediately. He told me that he wanted me to come to work for him in a project office he had in Washington, DC. I asked him what the job was, and he said he couldn't tell me. So I thanked him, hung up, and had a chat with my curricular officer. I asked him if he knew what it was, and he said he didn't but that if CAPT Tom Betterton said it was a good job and had handpicked me for it, I should take it. Well, I really didn't want to move back east, and neither did my family. I had been hoping to get a job at the NARF (Naval Air Rework Facility) at NAS Alameda, right across the Bay from San Francisco, because I might even be able to keep flying test hops. But the strong recommendation my Curricular Officer gave the job convinced me I should take it. So I called CAPT Betterton back the next day and accepted.

Unfortunately, we could not start our overland trek back to the East Coast until after the graduation ceremony on 19 December 1979, even though I was finished: my course work was done and my thesis had been accepted and printed. So once again, we packed up the house, moved to a motel for a few days while we struggled through our check-out inspection from the housing people, and then attended the ceremony. We were on the road before first light the next morning, hoping to make it to my parents' home in Baltimore before Christmas, but no pressure.

Peggy was driving the cantankerous Audi 100LS we had bought in San Diego because she couldn't bear to part with it (No, I don't why). I was driving the old International Harvester truck I had bought when we were still in Whidbey Island, hauling a motorcycle trailer with my Honda Gold Wing aboard. In the back of the truck rode my eldest daughter with her 120# Great Dane, and we kept in touch via CB radios. We had to spend long hours on the road in order to get to Baltimore before Christmas, but we took the southern route in order to avoid snow at that time of year in the northern mountains and plains. It was a tough trip. Our remaining cat managed to escape the car in a blinding rainstorm in Dallas, and we could not find her, despite searching for some hours. Then, in Arkansas, in another rainstorm, I almost jackknifed the trailer when a woman cut me off, but somehow I managed to save it. By the time we had gotten to Western Maryland (about dusk on Christmas Eve), Peggy had to stop every twenty miles or so, so I had to make engine repairs by the side of the road in the rain (It really seemed like it was raining throughout the entire trip once we got out of the Southwest Desert). I was wet, cold, and getting increasingly incensed at that Audi, the car I wanted to sell before we left California. By the time I70 ran out, and it did just like that, the Audi had quit altogether with steam pouring out from under the hood. So we parked it alongside a street in the Western part of Baltimore, unloaded the car into the truck, and continued to the East. We had a tough time because the City had changed so much, we didn't recognize very many landmarks, but we finally made it to my parents' home where they greeted us with all the warmth anyone could want. Their grandchildren would finally spend a Christmas with them.

We had arranged to rent a townhome in Burke, Virginia, remotely from California before we started back East. After the holidays, we headed down there from Baltimore to get our furniture delivered to the new house and begin to settle in.

CHAPTER 8

THE NAVY SPACE PROGRAM OFFICE

I started work in early January, but I had to get clearances I didn't previously have in order to work in that office, so I was engaged in "busy work" until I was approved.

Quality Assurance Officer

Then I began working in an entirely different field than any I had ever experienced before—or even knew existed! At this job, I actually was able to make a substantial contribution to ending the Cold War. The civilian that I worked for in the Operations Department was James E. Morgan, a man with considerable reputation in the Navy Cryptology Community.

He appointed me as the LNO (Liaison Officer) to the Army and Air Force who used our products. Since Europe was the focus at that time due to the continued existence of the "Evil Empire,"[24] I found myself making quarterly trips to visit customers all over Britain and the Continent. I would take down their problems and complaints and would take those back to my project office for resolution. It seemed to fit, so Mr. Morgan also appointed me the QAO. After that, I established the QUAB (Quality Assurance Board), which would meet monthly to review, work on, and try and resolve the problems our customers were having. I would then take the results of that work and go back to Europe to brief our customers on what we had fixed, what we were still working on, and how long we thought we would need to fix the things hadn't as yet managed to fix. If they had new problems, I would collect those, take them back, and the cycle would start over.

I learned a lot from Mr. Morgan, and it would definitely benefit me in the future.

Failure to Promote

While I was working in that project office, I came up for promotion for Commander (O-5) and I really thought I had a great chance of making it, but I didn't, and that was a terrible blow. I actually contemplated suicide, but my wonderful wife pulled me out of it—again. The next two years, the results were the same, despite the fact that my Admiral had listed me #1 LCDR out twelve in his command. You never know why you fail to select, but I think that Admiral at AIRPAC had blackballed me with his friends, and my career was over. It was some comfort to me when I realized that out of all the outstanding combat leaders I had flown with over North Vietnam, only one achieved high rank. Apparently, the Navy only wants combat leaders when there's a war on. After that, their selectees

---

24. NATO's (North Atlantic Treaty Organization's) big fear was that the Soviet 3rd Shock Army would come storming through the Fulda gap between East and West Germany, cut the Allied line, and storm into West Germany to roll up both wings with support from other units of the Warsaw Pact.

must be pristine in the politically correctness department. That was certainly never a description of me.

Mentor

After I had been in the office for almost a year, I made the acquaintance of one of our senior contractors, Dr. Robert Hess. His doctorate was in particle physics from UC Berkeley just outside Oakland, California, where he was born and raised. He also had the distinction of being a Captain (O-6) in the Naval Reserve. Originally, I was called in to work with him on some analyses he had been asked to conduct, and I found him not only brilliant, but quite innovative in his thinking. I learned a lot from him, and we became friends. We were together for over three years, and I never failed to marvel at his brain. Unfortunately, many of the suggestions he made, the Navy failed to act on (seems to be a pattern here; remember my ideas for a new torpedo and a stealthy radar?). While frustrated, he took it all in stride, almost as if he expected they wouldn't listen to him. I guess he had experienced that sort of thing frequently in his very long career. He was fond of telling me about his first assignment as an Ensign with a PhD on a destroyer. His CO didn't like people with advanced degrees, and he had a tough time.

Buying Another Home

Our oldest daughter had graduated from High School and was at Virginia Tech in Blacksburg, Virginia, our son was about to graduate and was planning on joining the Army, and our youngest daughter was about to enter High School. Peggy and I really didn't like living in Burke, Virginia, because it seemed very artificial. Everyone in the neighborhood either worked for the government or was a contractor working on government contracts. No one we knew seemed to be employed in anything else. We had gotten into sailing in a big way; had bought a boat slip across the Chesapeake Bay on Kent

Island, Maryland; and we found we liked it there. We were spending all of our weekends there anyway, so we decided to look for a home.

We found another three-bedroom, two-bath place on a 1+ acre lot, and it had a nice fireplace with a Heatilator. So we closed on that place just before our son graduated, and we arranged to have him board with some old friends from Peggy's college days who also happened to live in Burke until he graduated. We all came back for his graduation, of course. He had joined the Army by then and was to be inducted at the end of the summer, but until then, he had gotten a job at a YMCA Camp on the Eastern Shore teaching sailing. What a great way to spend his last "free" summer.

Once we finished moving in, my work commute started to Washington, DC, fifty-four miles each way. So I used my motorcycle when the weather wasn't icy. I was to perform that commute for the next twelve and a half years. Even though my old commute was only eighteen miles, the traffic had gotten steadily worse in the years we lived in Burke until it was taking up to an hour. My new commute was about the same time, but I usually wasn't sitting in traffic. Best of all, we liked the Eastern Shore. We were surrounded by real people: farmers, watermen, etc., who had nothing to do with federal government.

Final Orders

By this time, I had been in the project office so long that BUPERS was eager to move me on. Our office had to produce an officer for the DSPO, and they nominated me. At first, the Director didn't want me because I had been passed over for promotion, but my project manager told them I was the only officer he was going to get, so I moved over to the Pentagon in 1985.

CHAPTER 9

DEFENSE SUPPORT PROGRAM OFFICE

Obviously, I was starting my final tour of duty with the burden of not being promotable. My new staff chief, and Air Force Colonel, took a dim view of that. Nevertheless, I was assigned as the Navy and Marine Corps LNO and began to develop strong ties to both the Navy and Marine Corps TENCAP (Tactical Employment of National Capabilities) Offices.

I worked very hard at DSPO, trying to ensure that the Fleet had the right equipment and training to be able to receive and use the data that what being collected on the national level. Obviously, all of it was not of interest to every Fleet entity all the time. In fact, that would be a terrible burden of information for them to deal with, and most of it would be irrelevant to their current problem—whatever that might have been at the time. There were many battles which had to be fought in changing the imbedded thinking of many of the national intelligence people, but we made real progress and developed SATCOM (Satellite Communications) networks to give all of our military elements easy-to-use pathways to our data. We had to find the money to build these things, and we had to develop the equipment to make them work. At this time in my career, I worked with a lot of talented people; and I will be forever grateful for having had the opportunity to know them. Their very real contributions to ending the Cold War will never be known.

Retirement

As I neared retirement, which was scheduled for 1 February 1988, I began to seriously look for a job, which could sustain my family after my relationship with the Navy would be over. I really wanted something in engineering that had nothing to do with DoD, but despite my best efforts, I couldn't get an offer. Then one night, while I was getting ready to sit down to supper, my old mentor, Dr. Bob Hess, called to ask why I was looking for other work when I belonged doing what I had been doing when I was on active duty. In short, he wanted me to come to work for him. He couldn't offer me very much money, but he promised to get me in touch with Dr. Gary Federici, a common colleague we had both worked with extensively. Dr. Federici had a very senior position with CNA (Center for Naval Analyses), and he agreed to hire me to do part-time studies for him. So with both job offers in my pocket, I agreed to work with them both. I went on terminal leave (up to sixty days can be taken at the end of your career) and started working as a contractor with the two good doctors.

My actual retirement ceremony was held on the gun deck of the sloop of war *Constellation* moored in Baltimore Harbor. My retirement flag was flown from the mizzen gaff of that old sailing warship, and I was piped over the side with senior officers from every service acting as side boys. My old pilot, Bill Galbraith, who was now a Captain, serving in the Pentagon, managed to make it. I was very grateful for that. I received letters of commendation from both the Secretary of the Air Force, the Honorable Edward C. "Pete" Aldridge, and the Commandant of the Marine Corps, General A.M. Gray. Peggy and I had our reception for all attendees at the Naval Academy Officers' and Faculty Club in Annapolis, Maryland. It was quite a party; after all, I had worn the same rank for ten years! I was ready for another challenge.

CHAPTER 10

LIFE AS A CONTRACTOR

I started life again as a defense contractor, but at least I was working for people whom I both knew and respected. It wasn't all that different from what I had been doing on active duty.

The End of the Cold War

I found myself in Kaiserslautern, Germany, in November 1989, providing support to a new national simulator we had installed with the Warrior Prep Center in Einsiedlerhof. One evening after work, I was sitting in my hotel room watching the evening news when they announced the fall of the Berlin Wall. It was the nineteenth. The German people celebrated wildly. It was a wonderful time to have been able to be in Germany when that hated wall came down after President Reagan made that famous speech which started the cracks forming: "Mr. Gorbachev, tear down this wall." I remembered clearly that I had been in boot camp on 13 August 1961 when it went up.

The Cold War had started to fall apart, and I was personally very proud of the role I had played in it from the beginning.

The Operational Support Office

The Captain who had hired me had been promoted to Rear Admiral (Lower Half), and he was promoted to our Program Manager who, of course, had several projects under his direction. The project to which I was assigned specialized in trying to improve the interfaces between our collection and processing capabilities and the receipt and exploitation capabilities of the Services.

Desert Shield/Storm

The first war with Iraq, 2 August 1990–28 February 1991, started out as a deployment of forces to stop Saddam Hussein's further incursion into Saudi Arabia from the recently conquered country of Kuwait and was known as Operation Desert Shield. My Navy boss at OSO was Lieutenant Jeff Graham, who had been an ECMO (Electronic Counter Measures Officer) in EA-6B Prowlers. Jeff would go on to have a brilliant career, retiring as a Captain with a wonderful family. But at the time of Desert Shield, he was still a bachelor LT. But he had been raised in an Air Force family who had been stationed in Europe for many years, so Jeff certainly knew the territory well. Our management decided that it would be a good thing if we visited the EA-6B squadron stationed on USS *Independence* (CV-61) in the Red Sea, VAQ-136, since we had special receiver/processors on board their aircraft to enable them to receive and display selected data from our collection and processing systems. This equipment would enable the crew to have detailed awareness of the battlespace beyond their own line of sight, a powerful advantage in combat. It was serendipitous that LT Dan Graham had been an ECMO in that squadron during his previous Fleet tour of duty.

This trip would take us from COMNAVEUR (Commander Naval Forces Europe) in London, UK, to Naval Station Rota, Spain, to COMSIXTHFLT (Commander Sixth Fleet), and finally to USS *Independence* cruising in the Red Sea, where we would ensure the aircrews were fully up to speed on our equipment and had no further questions on how to operate it for maximum benefit. We then planned to fly off the ship to a base in Saudi Arabia and fly home from there. This trip was decided on with little time for preparation, so we could not get the Visas we needed from the Saudi Embassy in DC but would have to get them in London, while we were briefing the COMNAVEUR staff.

Of course, it was January when we arrived in London, so we had to have warm clothes with us for that portion of the trip, even though we would be in Southwestern Spain and the Middle East for the rest of the trip—that ensured we would be lugging around a lot of baggage. According to the instructions we had received from our State Department in DC, we reported to our embassy in London, introduced ourselves, and they arranged an appointment for us at the Saudi Arabian Embassy on the other side of town. They told us that it took weeks normally to gain a visa for that country, but that they had asked the Saudis to give us special treatment and process our applications immediately. While we didn't find a very welcoming atmosphere over at the Saudi embassy, they did, in fact, manage to give us our Visas in just over twenty-four hours, which was the speed of light for them. With our briefings and some refresher training, completed at NAVEUR, we departed for Jerez, Spain, via Madrid.

Our meetings at Rota went very well, and I was able to do some more training with the watch standers in their Intelligence Center before we had to catch a plane to Italy and COMSIXTHFLT (Commander Sixth Fleet), but the warm clothes were packed for the duration of our trip. We rented a car in Rome and drove down to Naples to meet with the rest of the COMNAVEUR staff (their staff was split between London and Naples). LT Graham briefed the staff on our visit and the new capabilities of VAQ-136's EA-6Bs, and once again, I did some refresher training with their watch standers, like I had done in London and Rota.

From there, we drove to the home port of the 6th Fleet at Gaeta, Italy. I hadn't been there before, and I found it to be a very beautiful place. The 6th Fleet's flagship at this time was the cruiser USS *Belknap* (CG-26). We found the ship to be very crowded with the 6th Fleet Staff aboard, but while LT Graham met with and briefed the senior staff officers on our visit and the new capabilities of VAQ-136's EA-6Bs, they requested that I do refresher training with their watch standers. That required us to return periodically to catch all of the watch standers while they were on watch. I found their operators to be well-trained, needing some more emphasis on certain points and a better understanding of how the data was collected, processed, and transmitted. At the conclusion of our visit, we were informed that their operators were so pleased with the training they had received that the staff decided we should brief their counterparts on USS *John F. Kennedy* (CV-67), which was anchored in Gaeta Bay at the time, awaiting a change of command for their Captain. We had originally planned to drive back to Rome and take a commercial flight into Saudi Arabia, so we could hook up with USS *Independence* (CV-61).

Now, 6th Fleet told us they wanted us to do the training when the JFK, or "Big John," got underway after the change of command, fly off on the COD (Carrier On-Board Delivery) C-2, and get a military airlift flight into Saudi Arabia from NAS Sigonella, Sicily. We had no choice but to change all of the rest of our travel arrangements to accommodate their request. The next day, after turning in our car, we waited around the docks for all the VIPs to be ferried back from the ship, and we were able to catch the Captain's gig returning to the ship (with all of our baggage in tow). When we off-loaded at JFK, I thought I was going to have a heart attack carrying all that stuff up the boarding ladder to the quarterdeck, but somehow, I made it without injury. We were assigned a stateroom, and we proceeded to meet with various entities on the ship. I trained both officers and enlisted personnel straight through our time aboard. It was very busy. Then, the time came to load all of our junk onto the C-2 and launch off the ship, but the COD, we found out, was not going to Sigonella but back to Naples. So when we got to Naples, we had to find another military flight over to Sicily, which we were able to do without too much trouble.

We went straight to the MAC (Military Airlift Command) Passenger Terminal at Sigonella to get seats for both of us on the first available MILAIR flight out to Saudi Arabia. The desk sergeant sort of sneered when we requested seats, but when LT Graham pulled out his orders and showed the priority to him, he paled a bit, but immediately put us on the next plane out. We loaded aboard that evening, and the C-141 Starlifter launched into the night sky for King Fahd Naval Air Facility, Jeddah, Saudi Arabia. We arrived early the next morning and were put into a tent full of cots and mosquito netting with cases of water bottles. While the other personnel who had arrived with us settled down to await events, LT Graham and I walked over to the Air Cargo Handler's Office, who happened to be a reserve CDR who had been called up to active duty for the duration of this crisis with Iraq. He was not only unhappy about being called up, but he was also a very harassed man. Many people accosted him throughout the day to have him get their stuff, whatever it was, out to wherever it was supposed to go. I would not have wanted his job. We did learn from him that *Independence* was well north in the Red Sea and out of COD range from King Fahd. That was not good news because at that time, we really didn't know when the *Desert Shield* part of this operation was going to end and the active combat part, *Desert Storm*, would begin, and we had to get to VAQ-136 before that happened.

He was understanding and offered us the chance to go on board the replenishment ship USS *Seattle* (AOE-3) which was currently in the port facility of Jeddah nearby loading fuel for the *Independence* Battle Group. Since that would keep us moving toward our final destination, we accepted happily. He was able to arrange ground transportation for us over to the ship. We arrived late in the afternoon and were billeted, with a few other vagabonds, in the ship's sick bay since they didn't currently have any patients there. The ship got underway the next morning and headed north into the Red Sea. Our rendezvous was scheduled for the next morning, and we were briefed on where to be and when so we could be loaded onto one of the ship's CH-46 helicopters and flown over to *Independence* while *Seattle* was alongside for an UNREP (Underway Replenishment). The next morning, we loaded onto one of the CH-46s which flew us the short distance over to *Independence* and deposited us and our junk onto the flight deck. At long last, we had arrived at the only place where the entire trip had been focused. All the other stops were made to keep the upper echelon staffs apprised of our mission. Theoretically, any of them could have forbidden us to continue our journey to *Independence*, but they hadn't and here we were—finally.

Following a pattern similar to that established at all of our other stops, LT Graham briefed both the squadron and ship's company officers, while I concentrated on training them, ensuring that they were ready to use their new equipment and skills to gain a superior edge in the combat they were facing in, we all thought, the very near future. We slept very little and got a lot done during our brief stay on the ship. I was able to catch up with my old friend and roommate, Joe Mobley, who was now a Captain and CO of *Independence*. We were able to spend a few minutes together on the port wing of the bridge one night as the ship ghosted along at bare rudder speed. It was quiet and quite beautiful, and we had a nice visit. It would be the last time I would see Joe until years later when he retired. The next morning, we launched off in the COD for King Fahd NB, now within range since we had moved further south.

Once back in Saudi Arabia, it was time to get our flights fixed since our schedule had changed drastically since we visited the 6th Fleet staff. After waiting around all day, we were able to catch a ride with a contractor, who was there supporting the P-3 Orion squadron which was temporarily stationed at King Fahd to the airport at Jeddah. Once there, we made a couple of false starts but were finally able to sit down with an Alitalia agent who was able to exchange our tickets for reservations on the next Alitalia flight to Rome with a follow-on connection to Washington Dulles Airport outside DC. Then it was time to work our way through customs and immigration, board, and start back on our way home. LT Graham went through with no problem with his passport and visa backed by his active duty ID card. It was a different story with me, however. When the Saudi border guard saw that I didn't have an entrance visa, he asked me how I had been able to get into the country without one. When I tried to explain about the MILAIR connection, he told me to follow him to another room. The alarm bells were ringing in my head at that point, and I had visions of getting an up front and personal understanding of the Saudi Arabian penal system. Then, LT Graham showed up, looking like a knight in shining armor on a white charger to me. He flashed his green ID card and emphatically told the border guard that I was with him, and the guard's attitude changed completely. His scowl became a smile, his attitude became friendly, and he almost kowtowed, I thought. I will be forever grateful to Jeff for his rescue. Had he not been there, my situation could have turned out to be very bad indeed.

The rest of our odyssey turned out to be "normal" travel, with no further glitches. It was good to finally get home. We had been gone about three weeks, and I felt good that we had completed our mission successfully.

The National Reconnaissance Office Revealed

In 1992, the NRO (National Reconnaissance Office) decided to "come out of the closet." Of course, I had been working for them ever since I took that first job after graduate school in Washington, DC, but Peggy never knew. She always thought I had been working for the Navy, and she was more than a little upset when I told her for whom I had really been working. But being a good Navy wife, she understood the need for security and got over it rather quickly.

The NRO was established by President Dwight D. Eisenhower in September 1961 as a result of the shoot down of the U-2 piloted by Francis Gary Powers, and the international pressure to end reconnaissance flights over the Soviet Union. It was probably the most embarrassing incident to which the US was ever publicly connected. The office would remain black (not acknowledged) for the next thirty-one years, but it produced an amazing family of reconnaissance satellites which helped keep the Cold War from going hot. It was a very engineering-heavy organization wherein innovation was rewarded. I am still proud today that I had an opportunity to be a part of it all.

Project Challenge Athena

These days, 1990–1991, I was doing a lot of thinking about all the data we collected every day that I would have given anything to have had access to when I was planning bombing missions in the Gulf of Tonkin, but we didn't have any way to get it from TFA then and the Navy still didn't. During Operation Desert Storm, the Navy learned, once again, that they did not have the communications aboard their carriers to handle the receipt of the very large files containing high resolution digital images along with the metadata (the metric data about the image which enabled one to make measurements and locate targets in three dimensions). Of course, they also needed the processing and display equipment to enable the level of mission planning required for precision bombing and that applied to the new precision-guided weapons which were used so extensively during that war.

I teamed up with Dr. Gary Federici, at CNA, again to try and get Navy backing to allow us to demonstrate the use of commercial SATCOM (Satellite Communications) to receive the necessary high volume data required to accomplish the mission planning required to execute precision attacks. I had also been working with Mr. Paul Coakley of the JCMPO (Joint Cruise Missile Program Office) because they had a requirement for the TLAM (Tomahawk Land Attack Cruise Missile) to be reprogrammed at sea in a minimum amount of time. They had determined that the only way to do that was to receive and process the necessary imagery they needed while underway at sea, but the Navy did not have the MILSATCOM (Military Satellite Communications) capacity to perform the mission they already had plus provide the digital metric imagery needed for TLAM reprogramming. So Paul funded me to go out and explore ways that we could do that.

Initially, I ran a very small demonstration aboard the 2nd Fleet's flagship, USS *Mount Whitney* (LCC-20), utilizing their weather satellite antenna and receiver system to receive, process, and display the kind of digital metric imagery which would be required to meet the TLAM's operational requirement. This project was interesting because rather than responding to a Naval Intelligence Requirement, which didn't exist at the time, we were responding to an Operational Requirement for targeting a precision long-range weapon. While we were able to prove that the concept was viable, our communications pipe was so small, we could only receive extremely small images and, even those, very slowly. But we did demonstrate that it could be done, and we now had to find the funding to establish a suitable satellite communications path to a ship at sea.

Dr. Federici and I had many strategy sessions on how to tell our story to the various senior entities on the Navy Staff in order to get initial funding to demonstrate this capability in an operational environment (i.e., an aircraft carrier at sea). We then met with a myriad of those senior officials over the course of six months or more and were basically thrown out of all their offices. No one wanted to take the step to deliver digital metric imagery to the carriers so they could do precision targeting aboard. It was one of the most frustrating periods of my life, and I recalled all bumbling we had done in Vietnam because these same people had no concept of what was needed then, and they wouldn't listen now.

We were approaching the end of the FY (Fiscal Year), and the NRO had announced that it would entertain requests for some of their leftover money for good projects. I put together a PowerPoint presentation, which told the story of the Navy's unrecognized need for precision metric digital imagery at sea, and attended the screening meeting with about a dozen others who had presentations for their projects. I admit that I didn't hold out much hope of being selected, but in a few days, I was notified that my project had been selected along with several others, so the money was very modest, and I would have to figure out how to demonstrate this capability at sea on a shoestring.

I started by going to one of my contacts on the Navy staff: CDR John Hearing, who had been one of the only vocal supporters of this whole idea. He smoothed over all the staff issues with the Navy hierarchy, for which I was and still am eternally grateful, and got a project ship nominated: USS *George Washington* (CVN-73). She was the newest aircraft carrier at that time and had not yet been commissioned, so she was still owned by the shipyard at Newport News,

Virginia. John and I traveled down to brief their IO (Intelligence Officer), EMO (Electronics Maintenance Officer), and Operations Officer on our proposed project. Because we had very little money and were only authorized to demonstrate this capability, we couldn't make any permanent alterations to the ship. So we were going to use a receive-only system (to avoid issues with using a transmitter on the flight deck) whose antenna would be strapped down to the flight deck away from the landing area. The only impact to the ship would be the loss of some aircraft parking space.

USS *George Washington* (CVN-73) Underway with her Battle Group

Here again, we had come up against strong opposition at the Fleet level in Norfolk. A key senior government official was adamantly opposed to our demonstration, saying, "It'll be a cold day in Hell before I let you send images out to the ships before my guys look at them first back here!" Normally, that would have ended the project before it had gotten started had it not been for the fact that it wasn't Navy money, and the requirement we were trying to satisfy was an operational one from the JCMPO not an Intel one. So we thanked him for his time and went ahead with our plans. Since he couldn't stop us, he arranged to have another demonstration provided next to ours on the same ship using different SATCOM technology. I don't want to make this a technical description, so suffice it to say that his system, while promising potentially greater bandwidth, required a beam from a communications satellite to aim at the ship and track it as it moved. Ours did not. And that made ours the winner in the end.

The demonstration was performed while the ship was operating in the Caribbean. Only part of the Air Wing was embarked, so the flight deck that we took up with our antennas did not impact their limited air operations. As we remained at sea, we continued to tweak our system, which included the processing, display, and exploitation equipment required for the metric digital imagery we were receiving. We were able to demonstrate what this would mean to flight crews in mission planning, and they were very enthusiastic about its potential. One night, while cruising off Grand Turk Island, we were actually able to achieve our goal throughput of 1.544 Mbps (Megabits per second, or 1,544,000 bits per second), known as T-1 in the communications world. It was the first time in the history of the Navy that such a data rate had ever been received aboard a ship at sea. We were very proud.

After we returned the ship returned to Norfolk, and we removed all of our equipment and went back to our offices, CDR John Hearing raised a lot of interest on the Navy Staff in the Pentagon about what our demonstration could potentially mean for both the JMPO and Naval Aviation. But budget cycles being what they are (five years), there simply was no money to proceed with a full-scale duplex (transmit as well as receive) demonstration aboard ship without cancelling someone's pet program, and that simply wasn't going to happen.

So I started working through OSO to identify the money we would need to install and support such a demonstration for an extended period (we envisioned supporting it at least through a competitive Fleet exercise) while John worked within the Navy Staff to get a ship assigned and work out the installation details. It was a perfect partnership! I was, once again, able to identify the funding through my channels while John persuaded the Senior Navy Staff to assign us *George Washington* again and allow us to install a 3m (10ft) diameter antenna on a platform the shipyard had installed for another Navy SATCOM program. This time, our radio equipment would all be installed in the existing racks in *George Washington*'s Radio Room. So this next phase of our demonstration was going to look a lot more like an operational system than our first efforts did. My team of engineers picked a commercial maritime SATCOM company (SeaTel) to do the installation because they had just about every Commercial SATCOM installation on the world's cruise ships. We had neither time nor money to change their designs, so we had to live with a cable wrap system they used on their antennas.[25] This time, the JCMPO actually installed their processing and mission planning equipment in a space adjacent to the Intelligence Center on the ship (the imagery carried additional security that many on the ship did not have, so it had to be kept separate from the general spaces). Knowing that this was going to be an all-out effort to show the Fleet what they could get and how they could use it, I moved down to Norfolk in February 1994 and established that room as a permanent administrative center, where our personnel could always meet up with the team and messages could be passed (cell phones were still relatively rare, although we had several team members who used them extensively). The day finally came when our antenna (the biggest component of the entire system) arrived at the pier and was craned aboard. The below picture was taken of me that day. I think you could say I was very happy to have come so far on my quest to fix the problems I had back in the early '70s—twenty years earlier!

---

25. Since cruise ships basically travel in a straight line from port to port, connecting the antenna to the receiver equipment was accomplished via a cable, which was long enough to wrap around the antenna pedestal twice. After that, satellite tracking would be lost while the antenna unwrapped itself. Since aircraft carriers generally operate with their Air Wings in racetrack patterns, oriented with the actual wind, this was going to be a problem, but we had no choice in order to keep within our budget and schedule.

Now the Navy began to realize that we would be bringing tremendous bandwidth to the GW and wouldn't need it for downloading imagery all the time. So they decided to also use it as a back-up to all their MILSATCOM systems. This, of course, would require that we develop interfaces for each one, so they could be managed from the Radio Room.

Ed Engle on the Flight Deck of USS *George Washington* (CVN-73) During Antenna Installation in 1994

The team spent several weeks getting everything installed, but we were slowed down by having to remove and reinstall the cable which connected the antenna pedestal with the Radio Room. We discovered it was the wrong specification and was not sufficiently shielded to carry our signal without a lot of noise interference (an aircraft carrier is a deadly environment for radio frequency equipment). That was a huge setback and took almost half a week to swap out cables (the Radio Room is almost half a ship away from the antenna, about 500 feet). It should have been caught before the initial installation, but we used one of the Navy's cable pulling contractors, and they simply didn't check the specs on the cable before installing it.

During this period, the ship would get underway for various phases of their work-up training, and we would be at sea for several days to a week at a time. While they trained, we worked. My lead engineer, who had been a Master Chief Radioman (E-9) when he had been in the Navy, wrote an SOP (Standard Operating Procedures) manual for the GW's radio crew to use, and he very cleverly designed a wheel on a card, which would show how much cable had been wound up on the pedestal and suggest which way the ship should turn in order to unwind it rather than wind it further. They were to actually use that thing for the duration of their upcoming cruise.

Our SeaTel team came up with the idea of installing telephones on the ship for the use of the crew, using the small amount of bandwidth we had been using on the satellite for an "order wire" (a reachback link to talk with the people at the transmitter in New Jersey). The ship wouldn't need that order wire any longer after we finished with the system checks, and they figured out that they could use it to provide several telephones (a half dozen as I recall) for the use of the crew. Since we already leased the satellite transponder for our main signal, this portion came with no additional cost. They briefed the GW's senior officers and were given approval to go ahead with the plan. These phones could only be used with a prepaid phone card (also provided by SeaTel), which would be sold through the Ship's various stores, and the money would go to their recreation fund. Further, the phones did not ring. No one could call in. The system eventually became known as sailor phone. "Cut-over" started while we were in port because it was necessary to be talking to each transmitter site while we were bringing their signal on line. My team worked around the clock for several days, stopping only for meals and head breaks. It was a brutal work environment, but no one complained. They just kept at it until the job was done. One of our most difficult problems was dealing with the ship's telephone system. They were using a new switchboard for the first time in the Fleet, and they were really not all that familiar with it. I remember that we got underway for one of our short at sea periods with AT&T's expert on the system, and he worked at it for the entire period, setting everything up so that it worked optimally. Then, when we got back into port again, it stopped working after a few days, and we were to find out that one of the crew reset the switches based on what he thought they should be set to. The expert's work was totally wasted, and now AIRLANT sent down their EMO to straighten everything out. He had a hard time, but eventually, he managed it, and our phones worked again and continued to do so (this included all the official Navy phones, not the sailor phones).

Toward the end of all this chaos, the Admiral in command of the GW Battle Group told me that if our system didn't work to his expectations during their upcoming competitive fleet exercise, he would throw it off the ship and replace it with the INMARSAT (International Marine Satellite) system that we replaced. So the pressure was on—like it wasn't already!

Since moving down to Norfolk in February, I had not been home once, so I took Easter Weekend off to spend with Peggy at our home on Kent Island. I really needed that break, and I came back refreshed and ready to go.

The day finally came in late spring when we got under way for FLEETEX. As some of us were standing on the flight deck prior to getting underway, my lead engineer remarked, while looking at the antennas on all the other carriers then in port, that GW had ten times the bandwidth that any of the rest of them had, just with our system alone. It was a sobering observation. The stakes for our performance couldn't have been higher. As part of this exercise, the Army flew out several helicopters with soldiers to the GW, and a few of them, led by a SFC (Sergeant First Class - E-7), were assigned to the Intel Division. As it turned out, the SFC was a very experienced imagery interpreter, and when he found out what he had in the "back room," he jumped on our equipment like a rabid dog! He started training both his soldiers and our sailors right away. The two groups got so close, the sailors all got "high and tight" haircuts and started doing pull-ups on the overhead piping in our space just like the soldiers. It was remarkable to watch how well they got along and worked together. If you have fine young men to start with, I suppose things like this should be expected.

Our system had outages during this period, but we were always able to recover within a very short time, and we trained the Navy operators on how to do what we did, so they could keep doing it after we left. There were some notable events which occurred during this exercise:

1. I was up in Radio one day when I noticed some lights come on our equipment which I had not typically seen, so I turned to my lead engineer and asked him what was going on. After he investigated, he found out GW's DSCS (Defense Satellite Communications System) had failed, but our equipment instantly switched all those circuits over to our Challenge Athena system, and the Radio Room sailors hadn't even noticed. Within a few hours, the Captain called me to the bridge, as he had done many times before to ask about different things concerning our system, so I expected to have to defend it again. But when I got to the bridge, he told me how impressed he was with how our system had picked up the DSCS services without the crew even noticing. Then, he ended with telling me if our system attempted to take over the bridge, like HAL from *2001: A Space Odyssey*, he was going to pull

the plug. I was very pleased and shared his comments with our team.
2. LANTCOM (Atlantic Command) had built a replica of the Scud missiles used by Saddam Hussein in the first desert war and had it towed up and down the coast in our OPAREA to see if we could locate it, since that had proven to be a huge challenge in that war. Our newly arrived SFC put his years of imagery interpretation skills to work on finding it, and he finally did. It was a huge success for our system, but it pointed out that the Navy was going to have to face some serious personnel issues in the future, if they were going to adopt such a system in the future.

FLEETEX ended, and the Battle Group Commander was very pleased with our performance and insisted that I stay on board for their transit to England to start their first operational deployment. He wanted me to stay on board for the duration of their first deployment, but I appealed to my boss, CDR Gunggoll, who satisfied the Admiral's request with a reserve LCDR. My division superintendent at OSO, MSgt (Master Sergeant) "Buzz" Roberts, was to accompany me to train up the enlisted Intel analysts on the ship on national imagery interpretation. Interestingly, the ship was to be the host ship for President Clinton in the celebration of the Fiftieth Anniversary of the Invasion of Normandy (D-Day in Europe). I then learned that Secret Service and WHCA (White House Communications Agency) personnel would also be aboard in addition to several veterans who had actually made the landing on 6 June 1944 (the year I was born). My team wrapped everything up, installed the sailor phones, provided the phone cards to the GW's Supply Officer, and left. I was able to keep a couple of engineers aboard to help WHCA cut over their circuits to our system. (The White House would take our entire T-1 bandwidth during the President's visit, but the sailor phones were not a part of that envelope and so would remain operational for the crew.)

The transit across the Atlantic was routine, but it was certainly different from anything I had ever experienced at sea when I was able to regularly check in with my office back in DC. When I was in Southeast Asia, snail mail was the only communication we ever had with CONUS until we got into port and could get to a pay phone. We were certainly making history. The Secret Service conducted a lot of interviews with the crew and inspected all of the spaces the President and his staff were going to be in while WHCA worked with us in the Radio Room and the Presidential and Press Staff spaces to ensure all the phones and computers were hooked up and working. Half the entire "dirty shirt" wardroom, regularly used by pilots and NFOs who could eat there in flight suits, was going to be devoted to the Press. It became filled with telephones and computers. By the time we reached Southampton, England, our entire T-1 SATCOM connection had been taken over by WHCA. It was a very smooth transition.

Buzz was able to do quite a bit of training during the transit, but since we had to turn over our bandwidth to WHCA, we could no longer receive current imagery, so he decided he needed to stay on board to continue his training efforts. In addition, the IO (Intelligence Officer, a Navy CDR) had tasked him with writing a training syllabus, so they would have it to work from after he had departed. I was able to work extensively with our reserve LCDR, who was a lawyer in civilian life, and I felt very confident in his ability to handle any problems or issues which might arise with our system during their deployment.

I departed the ship for a few days in England on one of our liberty boats. It turned out that was a good thing because all the other boats were ordered to secure due to very rough seas outside Southampton Harbor. When the weather calmed down, I was able to get a boat back to GW. The Queen had already visited in her yacht *Britannia* and things had calmed down while the ship prepared to get underway for Normandy.

Our Air Wing had painted the Invasion Stripes (alternating white and black stripes around each wing) on the aircraft that were going to participate in the festivities, and they were flown off.

Early the next morning, we weighed anchor and headed across the Channel for Omaha Beach in Normandy. I was on the flight deck in the predawn hours of our arrival, and I overheard one of the veterans saying that it looked just like it did on that morning fifty years earlier, except for the gunfire, of course. It was a scene I will never forget and one that stirred very strong feelings in me. Off on the distant horizon was a low coastline, shrouded in morning fog, and it didn't take too much imagination to picture gun muzzle flashes sprinkled across the scene. The President and his staff flew off to the festivities in Normandy along with the veterans we had brought across the Ocean, and things aboard ship started to return to normal. That evening, GW weighed anchor again for a night transit of the Channel to the French port of Brest. It was a hair-raising trip. I don't think any of the Bridge personnel were prepared for how many surface contacts they would encounter. Among them were yachts and small fishing boats which have very little radar return. Then, we encountered fog. About that time, I decided to turn in and find out what happened when I woke up the next morning.

We made Brest after a very tough night of piloting in all that traffic, and I was able to be up high on the Island to see our approach since I had never been there before. It is an impressive old fortress town, and it was easy to see why the Nelson's Royal Navy never tried to sail in and take it during the many wars between England and France. We dropped anchor in the outer harbor. I was already packed and said my goodbyes to Buzz and the ship's personnel I had worked with for so long, asked our reserve officer if he had any last questions, and went below and got my seabag (the very same one I had been issued in 1961), and moved to join the line at the stern of the Hangar Bay awaiting the liberty boats. A couple of the Senior and Master Chiefs (E-8s and 9s) standing in the line with me started ribbing me about my seabag because throughout their already long Navy careers, none of them had ever seen a white seabag. The Navy had changed to olive drab many years before. I guess they were saying I was old even by their standards, and I was beginning to believe them.

Once I left the liberty boat, I had to walk up a very steep grade in the town beyond the fortress until I found a place to stay. Then I made a reservation on a west-bound flight the next morning, arranged for a ride to the airport, had a good seafood supper, and turned in.

The next day started before dawn, but I got to the airport in good time, got on the plane, and crossed the Atlantic again, a lot faster than I did the last time. The *Challenge Athena* system had many hiccoughs during that first deployment, mainly due to issues concerning switchover from one satellite to another as the ship sailed out from under the footprint of the satellite they had been using and blockage of the antenna due to aircraft parking errors by the Aircraft Handler, etc. None of it was really serious, and the system gave remarkably good service during an operational deployment—not bad for a system designed for "The Love Boat" in a civilian cruising environment. In fact, when the Admiral got back and made his summary presentation at the Pentagon (a normal event for battle group deployments), he ended with a slide which said: "*Challenge Athena*—Don't Leave Home Without It." For the first time, I knew that the Navy Management would no longer be able to keep their heads in the sand and insist that they didn't need the kind of SATCOM throughput with which we had presented them—a real victory, and I felt very proud to have been an integral part of the effort.

The following years would see the Navy develop a replacement antenna, which used "slip rings" instead of a cable wrap system, but retained the same sponson we used on the port quarter, adjacent to the LSO (Landing Signal Officer's Platform), and the basic radio gear we had originally installed. So the entire project, after so many years and so much effort and rejection by the Navy, was fully transitioned to an operational system and continues to be deployed on all capital ships today. As a postscript, though, during the months after the Admiral had made his presentation at the Pentagon, Navy people were popping up all over who claimed that *Challenge Athena* was their idea—even that civilian Intel guy who said he would never allow imagery aboard ship until his people ashore had looked at it first. Sadly, if you ask anyone in the Fleet today who was responsible for getting a wideband commercial SATCOM system and the imagery processing equipment for enhance mission planning to our carriers, my name would never come up. That's life, I guess.

Support to the War in Bosnia

Since I had been at sea and away from home working in Norfolk, my boss, CDR Mike Gunggoll, asked me to take over as his executive assistant. I would be responsible for ensuring that his division was focused on his goals and our projects were progressing in accordance with our established schedules. I was also responsible for monitoring our budget and writing any documents he needed for justification of our budget requests. This job would keep me home, and after *Challenge Athena*, I was ready for that.

One of our great successes was building a network of wideband receivers in the Balkans for our peacekeepers deployed there supporting NATO's air campaign in Bosnia. DARPA (Defense Advanced Projects Administration) got involved and called the project BC2A (Balkans Command and Control Augmentation). We found an antenna lying around in a storage lot at the Naval Research Laboratory in Washington, DC, mounted it onto our roof, hooked it up to a suitable transmitter, got the funding to build a TV studio, secured the help of personnel from all the services' reservists to man the station, trained them all, provided them with housing and cars, built suitable receivers for the troops ourselves in our offices, deployed everything, and made it all work. So for the first time, those folks out in the boondocks of the Balkans were getting live TV, which in this case included large intelligence files in near-real-time. We even provided them with a narrow-band reach-back transmitter where they could order products as well as the ability to choose which channel they wanted to watch. It was very much like Direct TV, but it was all encrypted. USEUCOM (United States European Command) named our network JBS (Joint Broadcast Service) and asked us to expand it to include units throughout Europe and the UK.

We then transitioned the entire program, with the equipment and training, to DoD. Our engineers even moved the entire TV studio to the Pentagon for them. Transitioning such a "bootstrap" program to a sustainable operational system is rare, but this project could be considered the poster child for that transition. The network continued to function at least until the year 2000 when I left EUCOM but more of that below.

The engineers that worked on this project were the finest I ever met. Several worked straight through for days with no sleep and very few breaks. They were brilliant, and they were dedicated. It was a great place to be! While we changed names several times, we eventually became the OSO (Operational Support Office). Our mission was just what the name implied: supporting our military operators. Later, we moved into other areas like supporting the forestry service in fighting forest fires.

James E. Morgan Award

In 1997, OSO announced the establishment of the James E. Morgan Award to be awarded to that individual who had contributed the most to helping the Armed Services receive and use NRO data operationally. I was selected as the first recipient. The letter of commendation reads:

> 5 September 1997
>
> Memorandum for Mr. Edward C. Engle
> Subject: Recipient of the James E. Morgan Award
>
> It is a sincere pleasure to present to you this James E. Morgan Award. You have been selected as a recipient of this award for several unique contributions to the National Reconnaissance Office over the course of almost 20 years.
> Jim Morgan personally selected you for duty as the Liaison Officer to the Air Force and Army in 1980. Your knowledge of the tactical needs of air, amphibious, and land warfare led to numerous changes in the way national systems data is collected and disseminated. Your zeal in getting vital information collected from the high ground of space to the warrior is unparalleled.

I am pleased to have such an outstanding performer on the OSO team. Thank you, and keep up the great work!

> Daniel W. Wells, III
> Colonel, US Army
> Director,
> Operational Support Office

US European Command

By now, OSO had developed a reputation throughout DoD and many federal agencies for being a "can do" sort of outfit that got things done. I was now working with one of my senior colleagues, Dr. Bob Hanlon, as sort of senior advisors to all the project leaders within the Engineering Division. One of our big areas of effort was to try and get the receive and display equipment we had used with VAQ-136 for Operation *Desert Storm* installed in and integrated with many other aircraft types, including Air Force units. In addition, we were expanding the JBS system within the European Theater. While it was a busy time, I personally started looking for another challenge.

Some years before, OSO's Operations Division had started to assign military O-5s and contractors to each Combatant Commander as a LNO and a TSR (Theater Support Representative), respectively. It was a mature program which was fully supported by the Combatant Commanders. One day, while I was working on my computer, I noticed that our Ops Division was advertising for a replacement for our current EUCOM TSR, who was returning to CONUS because of his kids' entering High School. I immediately applied for the job, and after a lot of resistance by the prime contractor on the OSO Ops Support Contract (My Company, Delfin Systems, was the prime for the Engineering Support Contract but were a subcontractor for this one.) and intervention by OSO's government leaders, I got the job.

The kids were long gone by now, and Peggy and I were living on our boat, which was tied up in downtown Washington, DC. We had gotten rid of all of our furniture and sold our home on Kent Island in order to move aboard, so we really had nothing with which we could set up house in Germany. We knew this was going to be a challenge, but Peggy and I had both wanted to live overseas all our lives, and this was our chance, so we weren't going to pass it up. I had travelled to Germany many times when I worked for Jim Morgan, and Peggy had accompanied me on one or two of those trips, so we were both pretty familiar with the country and were eager to move there.

I started talking via secure phone every morning to the guy I would be relieving over there to get a feel for the environment and the day-to-day activities in which he was engaged. Unfortunately, my brother was taken very ill and was in critical condition in a hospital outside Baltimore, Maryland. So Peggy and I drove up there to see him and his family and found out from the doctors that there really was no hope of his recovery. His wife decided that it was best to pull his life support so he didn't lay there interminably awaiting death. I was able to meet with him before they removed his life support, but he was not coherent. It was a very sad day and what made it worse was that I had to be in Germany to start the transition process with the incumbent in the European TSR position, so I couldn't attend his funeral. Sadly, we both had to fly over before the funeral to find a place to live and for me to go around with the incumbent at work to learn my way around the US European Command Staff at Patch Barracks in Stuttgart, Germany.

There are two NRO support people at the Combatant Commanders' Headquarters Staffs: one military O-5 and the other a contractor. At that time at EUCOM, the arrangement was that the Air Force LtCol (O-5), the LNO, worked for the Operations Division and had his office in their spaces (J-3), while the contractor TSR worked for the Intelligence Division and had his office in their spaces (J-2). It was an arrangement that worked well, and it was used at all the other Combatant Commanders' Headquarters.

So while I was with my counterpart during the day, Peggy was spending time looking around the area with his wife and talking with the *Imobilien* (German term for a real estate agent) we had selected. (There are neither For Sale or Rent signs nor multiple listings in

Germany. Properties are listed in the newspaper, and unless you have very good German language skills, you really have to have an agent.) He found us a great place quite close to Patch Barracks in the Stuttgart suburb of Ruhr. My commute would be via secondary streets—no autobahns. It was a three-story end unit of a triplex with a nice backyard, and best of all, we became friends with the owners, Oswald and Erika Bach. We had to open a bank account with a local bank in order to pay our bills: rental deposit, power, water, garbage removal, etc. In Germany, your bank removes money from your account to pay all these things, and you get a statement from them. It was now April, and we had to return to CONUS to get packed up, buy furniture, and put our boat into long-term storage—a lot to do household-wise, and I still had to get fully indoctrinated into the Operations Division back at OSO.

So we flew back to DC and began our check-out process. Work was a lot smoother than our household pack-out. The furniture we had bought was delivered to the packers, so that was easy. However, we had two storage units: one close to where we had kept our boat in DC for winter/summer clothes swap-outs and other smaller items, the other a climate-controlled one for the art we had kept. In addition, the rest of our household items were aboard our boat, which we had moved to Oxford Boatyard on the Eastern Shore of Maryland. Our moving team had a long day, but they persevered and finished up in Oxford well after dark. I don't know about them, but we were exhausted.

The next day, we turned our boat over to the yard for long-term storage, and we drove back to DC where we delivered our new van (we had bought it after we moved aboard in order to deal with hauling things like sails and large batteries, etc., so it was fairly new) for shipment to Germany. It was really a pleasure to finally get checked in and sit down in our seats on the airplane for our trip back across the Atlantic to the "Old World" and the start of the next phase of our lives.

Not long after we received our shipment and moved into our new home, I bought a used old (175,000 km) Mercedes Benz 250D (No, that's not a typo. It was a five cylinder naturally aspirated diesel engine with everything manual: windows, sunroof, transmission, etc.). It was still a solid car I could use for work, while Peggy had the van to go wherever she felt the need to go while I was away. When I sold that car to an Air Force family in 2000 just before we departed Germany, it still had no squeaks in the body and burned no oil, and by then, it had over 250,000 km on it. Actually, Peggy preferred to drive that car on the autobahn instead of the van. She said she felt safer in it.

After I checked in at the EUCOM Staff, I moved into my predecessor's old office, a cubicle in a low-level security area. It was not ideal, but it was a start. I went through all of his files and holdings and wound up filling up over a hundred burn bags in cleaning them out. Apparently, his emphasis had been down at the unit level throughout the theater, doing hands-on training with unit analysts. Since I was the NRO's TSR at the EUCOM Staff, with a four-star officer as the Deputy Commander and a three-star as his Chief of Staff,[26] it didn't seem to me that the TSR should be down in the weeds but should represent the NRO to the senior staff. So I began to think along those lines and looked for ways to engineer that transition because everyone on the staff thought of the TSR as a local unit trainer at that point.

I found out that it was customary for the J-2 to invite the national agency reps who, like me, were assigned to the Staff in a liaison capacity, so I was able to get myself invited to these meetings. I found them very interesting because various briefers presented the current Intel picture to the General from all the various parts of the command's area of responsibility, which in those days included not only Europe but Central to West Africa as well. Showing my face at these meetings meant that the General now recognized me as

---

26. US EUCOM is unique among Combatant Commanders due to the US commitment to NATO (North Atlantic Treaty Organization), the Commander of EUCOM actually lives in Mons, Belgium, as the Supreme Commander, Europe, with the NATO Staff. He has a four-star deputy who lives in Stuttgart, Germany, and handles all the US-related activities from there. So only in EUCOM will you find two four-star officers.

his NRO rep, and he started to occasionally direct questions to me. Since I was able to answer them succinctly and clearly, he began to ask me more. Before much longer, I became a permanent fixture at these briefings, and he began to have a much better understanding of the NRO and the things we could do to support him.

The other part of my job was to support our component commanders, which included USAFE (United States Air Forces Europe) at Ramstein Air Base, Germany; USAREUR (US Army Europe) at Campbell Barracks in Heidelberg, Germany; USNAVEUR (United States Navy Europe) in both London, UK, and Naples, Italy; and USMARFOREUR (United States Marines Europe) at Panzer Kaserne in Stuttgart, Germany. Of course, their component commands are even more widely spread. It was a lot of territory for one man to cover and still provide the kind of support demanded by the Senior Staff at EUCOM HQ in Stuttgart, Germany. Later, the NRO would provide an additional TSR to cover USAFE and USAREUR, but he did not get into place until just before I departed the theater in 2000.

Overshadowing all my efforts at work was my status with the German government. They had recently started to crack down on American contractors who were being brought into their country to do jobs that their citizens could do, and they didn't pay taxes, even though some of them had been there for decades and had their kids educated in German schools. It was easy to understand their annoyance at this situation, but it created an instant confrontational relationship between them and me. I had already started filling out the large volume of paperwork to qualify as a "technical expert," the status a contactor required to avoid paying German taxes, which at my income level was about 62 percent! Of course, for the German citizens who paid that enormous amount, they received pretty much all services from cradle to grave—including a university education, if one qualified. So it was absolutely essential that I convince the German government to anoint me with that magical title. Unfortunately, at this time, the US government had started to debate the issue with the German government, and I found the latter unwilling to make any quick decisions since they didn't know what might come out of the negotiations. So while I awaited their decision, I was technically a tax evader since I had never registered with my local post office in order to make my presence known, and I didn't intend to. It was an anxious period—especially since the German government had started to arrest people.

My case was pretty clear-cut since I had to have clearances that German nationals could not get in order to do my job. In addition, I had accumulated over a decade of experience with our national sensors, which no German national could ever do, and that knowledge was key to my success on the EUCOM Staff. But still, I had to wait for months, making several trips up to Heidelberg and Darmstadt where USAREUR adjudicated these applications. It seemed that they always needed "one more thing." But after sweating it out for months, my approval finally came through, and I was granted status as a technical expert and, therefore, not subject to German income taxes. That was a great day!

The big focus at EUCOM HQ in the spring of '98 was the Balkans in general and Bosnia-Herzegovina and Kosovo in particular. As a student of European history, which most of us were not, would understand, this region has a long history of conflict—much of it ethnically based. The occupation of this region by the Ottoman Empire for so long left a strong Muslim presence right beside the Orthodox Christians, and they often came into conflict. Sorting all of it out was a difficult pastime. The ultimate goal, of course, was to restore order, allow the citizens to decide their national boundaries, and find a way to live in peace with their neighbors. US EUCOM also had a major operation underway from Incirlik, Turkey—Operation Northern Watch—the enforcement of the no-fly zone in northern Iraq, to keep Saddam Hussein from killing his Kurds—at least from the air.

The NRO provided unprecedented support to all the Balkan operations, and when NATO went to war in Kosovo, my LtCol LNO and I shifted to a 24/7 operation. He chose to work nights and gave me days. For more than a month, we kept that schedule, and it was exhausting. And no, I did not get overtime pay. Eventually, our home office started sending over augmentees, and we were able to get back to our other support duties to the EUCOM Staff and their components.

Another operation in which the NRO was very active was *Northern Watch*, NATO's patrol of the skies over Northern Iraq from the Turkish Air Base at Incirlik, Turkey. We provided support for their CSAR (Combat Search and Rescue) mission, tools for their Intelligence Center personnel, and training to both aircrews and Intel personnel. This mission continued for a long time and required constant attention.

By now, our J-2, an Air Force Brigadier General (O-7), recognizing the contributions we had made to his operations, provided us with the space for our own office on the top floor of the same building he was in. It was a long time in coming, but I really felt that I had been able to put us in a much stronger position on his staff than we had ever been. I attended all of his staff meetings and provided him with detailed status reports of any satellite failures we were experiencing and how those issues would affect him operationally.

Periodically, we would visit our Mediterranean-based components to see how they operated, what products they used, and what they needed that they weren't getting. These trips were difficult to schedule due to the distances between them and the lack of direct, convenient commercial transportation links. So we were able to get the Air Force to provide a small executive jet for our use. It gave us the opportunity to visit every site and return in just a few days rather than a few weeks.

All too soon, our tour was over, and it was time to head back to CONUS once again. This time, my old boss from OSO, now a Navy Captain, had asked me to come back to work for him on the Director of Naval Intelligence's Staff in the Pentagon (N-20), and I agreed. At my farewell ceremony, the J-2 awarded me one of his personal coins for my dedication to the Directorate during my time at EUCOM. I was deeply moved by his consideration of me.

We flew back to CONUS, got our boat out of storage, put it back into commission, and sailed up the Potomac to DC, where we set up housekeeping once again. Now, I was able to take the Metro subway to work in the Pentagon, so we didn't even need two cars. Our old van was fine for everything we had to do.

N20 and the Pentagon

Anyone who has worked in the Pentagon will tell you that life there is like one continuous study. You go from one to another and often change direction and focus before you even finish one. It is demanding work, and results are hard to see. One of the favorite posters sold in the Pentagon Bookstore is a picture of the Pentagon taken in the rearview mirror of a car. If you've ever worked there, you can understand the popularity.

My wife and eldest daughter were with me on a sailing vacation of the lower Chesapeake Bay in September 2001. On the morning of the eleventh, we were tied up at the Norfolk Harbor Pier on the Elizabeth River in Virginia, when we found out about the attacks on the World Trade Center and Pentagon. I tried all day to get in touch with my assistant on our support contract to N20 by cell phone with no luck. All the cell towers were jammed with people trying to do the same thing. Finally, in the evening, I was able to get through to him and found out that all of our guys were OK, but N20 would have to evacuate their space due to smoke and water damage.

We left Norfolk the next day and started back north on the rest of our vacation since I was told there wasn't any reason to return early since the office had to be moved. As we were pulling abeam of the carrier piers at NOB, Norfolk, we were hailed by one of the Coast Guard patrols in the Elizabeth River. He obviously had read the "Washington, DC," on our stern indicating our home port, and he said we couldn't get home. When I asked him why, he explained that the entire Potomac River had been closed, but he gave me a number to call in a few days as things settled down to see if the river had been reopened. We were very grateful to him.

I called that number from the last stop on our itinerary and spoke with a Coast Guard Ensign who told me the river was again opened but that procedures with the Wilson Bridge (through which we had to pass due to our mast height) had changed and explained what we had to do. I felt a lot better about our ability to get home, and we started back the same day. We did have to stop below the Wilson Bridge while we were boarded and searched by the Coast Guard, but then they actually had the bridge open for us in the middle of the day (normally, one cannot get the bridge open except by appointment and then only between midnight and 0400). That amazed us all!

Our staff had moved into offices in Crystal City, adjacent to the Pentagon, and I worked there for the rest of my time with N20. The Navy wanted to compete the support contract, so we did against a pretty tough incumbent. I led the effort, and we won. I had lost most of my summer in 2002 due to having to work on the proposal at night and on the weekends in addition to working fifty to sixty hours a week at N20. No, we didn't get overtime. This contract was worth over $340M, but my company gave me a pittance for a bonus. If it were about the money, I would have quit, but it never was. It was all about trying to help the Navy make the right decisions on investments, never about what it could do for me.

However, life in the never-ending and underappreciated study environment began to wear on me, and I began to look around for employment with the NRO again. Finally, a job did open up as a subcontractor on a support contract with the Advanced Systems and Technology Directorate, and I elected to take it. My loyal second in command would take over the N20 contract.

The NRO's Advanced Systems and Technology Directorate

Once I was able to get badged up and moved into my new office within AS&T, I discovered that my real job was to provide adult supervision to an Air Force major who didn't want to take it. While I was not pleased about the real job, I determined, once again, to do it the best I could. While I worked there for a year, he never really listened to me or acted on anything I suggested. Further, I discovered a very hostile contractor atmosphere with the incumbent, who eventually starting sending around poison e-mails within the office network. It really became intolerable, and I quickly starting looking for a better situation.

I discovered, through a former colleague from my N20 days, that the Navy was standing up a new command, NETWARCOM (the Navy Network Warfare Command), at the Amphibious Base at Little Creek, just northeast of Norfolk—ideal for us, since we had subsequently bought another home in Gloucester, Virginia. That would enable me to live on the boat during the work week and live in our home on the weekends. After a lot of negotiating, I got the job, and of course, then they wanted me yesterday. AS&T was not very happy, but then, I wasn't while I was there either.

NETWARCOM

I was assigned to the Intelligence Systems Branch of the Requirements Division, which was run by a Navy Captain. We worked in a much reduced security environment to that which I had become accustomed since 1979, and this was now August 2003, but one just has to shift one's mind to keep that clear so security violations are not committed. Work here turned out to be a lot like what I had left at N20 earlier—a lot of studies in addition to a lot of staff work. I worked very hard at this job, and as the months began to turn into years, the staff grew exponentially. After a while, we had to put in new trailers (yes, my office was in a trailer in the parking lot, but it was a really nice trailer), and there was no room left to park anywhere. That's when the new Deputy Commander, a government civilian, decided he didn't need any more senior contractors and let the funding on our contracts expire. Readers should take note, unlike government civilians who are nearly impossible to fire regardless of how poorly they perform, contractors can be eliminated simply by not funding their contracts. It's not even considered a breach of contract.

So after almost three years in helping to stand the command up and creating structures within it to improve the Navy's warfighting networks, I found myself out on the street. My boss, another government civilian, asked me where I wanted to have my farewell luncheon, and I told him that I really didn't want one because this was the first place where I felt like I hadn't made a difference. Everything I had tried to put into place died due to lack of interest on the part of our command's Navy leadership—including a job I did for him, which he told me was *the* most important thing in his division. I did everything he had asked, creating Memoranda of Agreements outlining our responsibilities and the Navy staff's in the Pentagon with all the technical support documents to back them up, but he allowed them to slow-roll the whole thing, which was his idea, until it simply died. I never worked for anyone that had ever done such a thing. After all, nothing I had done in my life would have ever been successful if it weren't for senior government people fighting to give it life.

I was very disappointed with that experience but left to start looking for new work. After almost a year and thousands of resumes, I finally concluded that I must be retired. Although I had never made that decision, I was no longer working, and I was getting Social Security. What an end to my professional life! But Peggy was right: no one would hire me at my age of sixty-six years at that time. Of course, no Human Resources officer would never say that because it would be discrimination—and it is. So ended my professional life.

AFTERWORD

I mentioned in the Preface that the Navy in which I flew "took no prisoners" when it came to demanding performance from its personnel. If you failed in your duty, you would be dealt with by your leaders—and it was rarely pretty. Today, however, the Navy would be unrecognizable to me according to reports I get from those I know still on active duty. Being "politically correct" is the most important principle under which the leadership operates. If a sailor doesn't do his duty, his supervisors say, "Well, that's OK. He/she tried." That's a very strange leadership approach to have when you are in a war-fighting service. In wartime, there is no second place: you either win or lose, you either live or die. Trying doesn't count for much. I hope the day never comes when our current ships and their crews are introduced to war at sea like our ancestors were through World War II because I don't think that type of training will prepare the sailors to do their duty even when the ship is afire and blood is running out of the scuppers, like US sailors experienced in the sea battles around Guadalcanal in 1942.

My own experience on USS *George Washington* (CVN-73) while doing the *Challenge Athena* project and more recently, from conversations I've had with Navy active-duty people, indicate that Naval Aviation has also changed in some very fundamental ways. While I was never a big fan of the rowdiness and lewd behavior exhibited at the old Tailhook Reunions, even when I was there, I think the Navy has gone too far in reigning in that camaraderie which had been so prevalent in Navy squadrons since World War II. It simply isn't there any longer, and I think it would hurt their performance if they had to fly into heavily defended targets and had to put their lives in the hands of their squadron mates. Of course, today's aviators don't have too much call to do that since they launch stand-off precision weapons from miles away—far outside the target's defense rings. Then, I suppose, none of it will really matter much longer because I see in the not-too-distant future an air wing composed mainly of unmanned aircraft, whose loss will only be mourned by the budget keepers.

Since I have accepted my old-age fate of being retired, Peggy and I live a quiet life in Gloucester Courthouse, Virginia, just above the York River and Yorktown, where British General Cornwallis surrendered to General George Washington on 19 October 1781. But as any local will tell you, the last surrender of major English troops didn't occur until the next day, the twentieth of October, at Gloucester Point, not Yorktown. Of course, Williamsburg, the colonial capital of Virginia, is only a bit farther away, and the original English settlement, the first permanent one in the New World (1607, more than a decade before the Pilgrims in Massachusetts), of Jamestown is nearby as well. It is an area rich in US history, and we love it. A friend of mine from my DC days drove down for a visit one weekend, and I walked out to greet him in our driveway. He had gotten out of the car but was just standing there. I asked him what he was doing, and he said with a sense of wonder: "It's so quiet!" Keep in mind that he doesn't even live in DC but Vienna, Virginia, a suburb.

So life goes on, and we grow older, but we have a lovely home which is visited frequently by wild turkeys and deer. I work out at the local gym every morning and continue to be active in various groups and enjoy writing. So retirement has really been a good transition for us.

I hope the reader will find the sort of serenity that we have after all those tumultuous years around the world when he retires because sooner or later, that day will come.

www.ingramcontent.com/pod-product-compliance
Lightning Source LLC
Chambersburg PA
CBHW030108100526
44591CB00009B/324